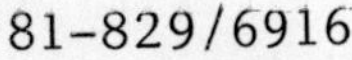

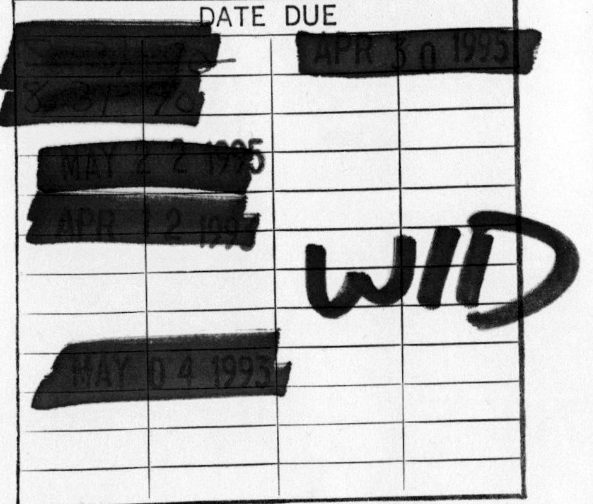

Style and Variables in English

TIMOTHY SHOPEN
Australian National University

JOSEPH M. WILLIAMS
University of Chicago

under the auspices of the
Center for Applied Linguistics

Style and Variables in English

Winthrop Publishers, Inc.
Cambridge, Massachusetts

Library of Congress Cataloging in Publication Data

Main entry under title:

Style and variables in English.

Companion volume to Standards and dialects in English.
Includes bibliographies.
1. English language—Variation—Addresses, essays, lectures. 2. English language—Style—Addresses, essays, lectures. 3. Sociolinguistics—Addresses, essays, lectures. I. Shopen, Timothy. II. Williams, Joseph M. III. Center for Applied Linguistics.
PE1072.S89 420 80-23211
ISBN 0-87626-866-1

Design by Amato Prudente

Credits

Page 1: Burk Uzzle/Magnum Photos, Inc.
Page 61: Martin Sandler
Page 115: F. B. Grunzweig/Photo Researchers, Inc.
Page 217: Dennis the Menace by Hank Ketcham
© 1980 Field Enterprises, Inc.

Printed in the United States of America

10 9 8 7 6 5 4 3 2 1

Contents

ments. We may speak and write within a general system of norms, but we have individual intentions that can be realized only by a unique shaping of a phrase, or a sentence, or a whole discourse, in a way that will let us achieve our intention. Perhaps we want to be elegant, perhaps moving, perhaps exact, perhaps abstract, aloof, impersonal. Perhaps we want to be all these things within the space of a single sentence, clear and simple at the beginning, aloof and impersonal in the middle, elegant and lofty at the end. Those individual moments require individual choices that seem independent of community norms—more "free," more creative.

And it is true. Despite the multitude of rules that our language and our speech community impose on us, rules that let us maneuver our way through the conventional situations we can expect to encounter from day to day, we must also be free to choose in order to create a special effect for a special moment. We can choose to write long elegant sentences or short simple ones. We can choose to use ordinary words or more rarified ones. We can choose to express an idea directly: *You're fired,* or indirectly: *A necessity has arisen in regard to the termination of your services.*

And yet, even these variables must exist within some sort of system; otherwise we could not, tacitly or overtly, recognize and respond in the way a speaker or writer intends us to. The choices are not entirely unconstrained, idiosyncratic or unpredictable, either in the inventory of choices that are available or in the way they are deployed. They are much more contingent upon a local environment infused with a particular intention.

So even within this set of constraints, the ways in which we can manipulate our choices still testifies to a freedom that a speaker or writer must have to achieve particular ends. William Wordsworth wrote a sonnet beginning, "Nuns fret not at their convent's narrow room," and he states in it that the rigid form of the sonnet itself—fourteen lines, ten syllables to a line, a certain meter, a certain rhyme pattern, and so on—did not confine him, was not a prison to his creativity. The more we study the ways we use language, the more predictable patterns that we find, the more constraints we realize we must acknowledge. Yet paradoxically, the more constraints we discover, the more we appreciate the local freedom to shape an utterance to achieve an end. The more rigid the rules of the game, the greater the inventiveness and originality we have to exercise within the freedom the game allows.

This book explores the rules of the game of English, and the freedom the game allows.

The Chapters

First, we have two chapters in a section entitled *Grammar and Usage*. In Chapter 1, Timothy Shopen presents the notion of a grammar, those conventions for the structure of utterances that are independent from functions and usage. By holding these conventions in common, members of a speech community can communicate in an evolving, changing and not fully predictable series of new situations. Just so, language can be a part of action, a part of the way people shape their existence as well as being shaped by it. Without agreed grammatical conventions, there could be no language culture, no customary language usage, and no commonly understood creativity in either the meaning or the form of utterances.

Joseph Williams, in Chapter 2, develops a model for a speech event, and shows how there is much, much more to knowing a language than a mastery of its grammar. Like any language, English is a living thing, intimately connected with the uses to which its speakers put it. The author takes the part of a mechanical android that people are trying to program as a native speaker of English. Through its resulting shortcomings, the android gives us a glimpse of the vast expanse of social and situational principles that have to be fused with the grammatical ones in order for a person to become a competent speaker of the English language.

Next comes a section entitled *Style,* and in Chapter 3 Ann Zwicky gives an introduction to the notion of style, with a wide range of examples in vocabulary, pronunciation and syntax. She demonstrates how much the shape of our speech events depends on who and where we are, who we are communicating with, and what about. Then she demonstrates how variables in vocabulary, pronunciation and syntax are coordinated on stylistic levels. For a given utterance there are a large number of choices possible for any of these aspects of structure; choices that may vary markedly in their stylistic value. But speakers ordinarily make these choices within harmonious limits, with stylistic fine-tuning.

In Chapter 4, Charlotte Linde presents the notion of a discourse unit. She shows that we communicate in such units and that they have a structure we can discover in the form of the utterances of which they are comprised. This structure links directly to the way we think and feel, and to the way in which we hope to evoke thoughts and feelings in our listeners; furthermore, it relates directly to what we assume to be our universe of shared knowledge and attitudes, our culture. She shows us this with material from menus, jokes, narratives, and finally descriptions that people have given of their apartments.

Chapter 5 stands by itself as the section *Literary Style*. Here Joseph Williams further develops his model of a speech event, and applies it to literary material. He shows how a governing sense of intended outcome for the literary composition shapes and is shaped by the social situation and the content matter, and how this in turn leads to decisions on genre, form and the actual words of the piece. Grammatical features especially characteristic of modern English turn out to be crucial parameters for stylistic choices. After taking us on a tour of stylistic options, the author gives a demonstration of his model with an analysis of Lincoln's second inaugural address.

The final section of the book is *Sociolinguistic Variables,* and it is devoted especially to phonological ones. Phonological variables occur more frequently than any, and most phonological variables permeate any speech event. In that way they are the most accessible to investigation—except that the study of speech sounds often requires advanced training in phonetics. But the two chapters of this section present research projects feasible for beginning students, and appropriate for virtually any English-speaking community.

In Chapter 6, Benji Wald and Timothy Shopen give a general introduction to sociolinguistic variables, and then describe research in Canberra (Australia) and Los Angeles on the (ING) variable. The results indicate a striking difference in the status and behavior of women, as opposed to men. The authors discuss the history of the variable and suggest that its remarkable longevity stems from the fact that such differences fulfill an essential need of our culture, allowing speakers to use a variety of devices to put out signals along a continuum of intimacy and respect.

In Chapter 7, Benji Wald investigates the notion of a speech community and presents evidence that Los Angeles is a developing speech community. He stresses that it is agreement on standards for speech behavior more than the behavior itself that makes a speech community. Using self reports on vowel targets by members of different ethnic groups, he shows growing homogeneity in Los Angeles, and not just towards some undifferentiated statistical mean, but towards the norms of one ethnic group, the most well-established and presumably the one with the most prestige.

The Sounds of English

In this book we use symbols for the sounds of English which include the following. For consonant phonemes see Table 1.

Table 1. ***The consonant phonemes of English, except [h]***

Manner of Articulation	*Bilabial*	*Labio-dental*	*Inter-dental*	*Alveolar*	*Palato-alveolar*	*Palatal*	*Velar*
	Place of Articulation						
Stops	p b			t d			k g
Affricates					č ǰ		
Fricatives		f v	θ ð	s z	š ž		
Nasals	m			n			ŋ
Central Approximants	(w)			r		y	w
Lateral Approximant				l			

Pairs of sounds appearing together in this table contrast just for voicing. For example, the place and manner of [f] and [v] are identical, but the vocal cords vibrate for [v] and not for [f]. Readers can feel and hear the difference by saying a prolonged [fffffffff], then [vvvvvvvvv], while touching their Adam's apple.

Not present in this table is the phoneme [h], a chameleon-like sound that takes the shape of whatever sound follows it and gives its voiceless counterpart, thus a voiceless [ī] in *heat* [hīyt], a voiceless [æ] in *hat* [hæt], and a voiceless [w] in *which* when it is pronounced [hwič]. We use some additional symbols at several points, but explain as we present them.

It might be well to single out some of the consonant symbols for exemplification. See Table 2.

These are symbols for *sounds,* and the correspondence to spelling is not one-to-one. Thus, although the letter *y* is not used, the sound [y] occurs in the word *cute,* and it is this sound that distinguishes *cute* from *coot,* [kyūwt] vs. [kūwt]. The sound [š] is represented by *sh* in *shoe,* but *ti* in *nation, ssi* in *mission, si* in *compulsion, se* in *nausea, sci* in *conscience, shi* in *fashion, ci* in *special, ce* in *ocean, ch* in *machine*

Table 2. ***Some of the consonant phonemes exemplified***

Symbols	*Examples*	*Symbols*	*Examples*
θ	*th*ink	č	*ch*ur*ch*
ð	*th*en	ǰ	*j*u*dg*e
š	*sh*oe	y	*y*ou
ž	gara*g*e	ŋ	si*ng*

and *Chicago, sch* in *Schlitz* and *Schweizer,* and when it combines in the sequence [kš] there is *x* in *luxury* and *xi* in *anxious*!

And these sounds are phonemes, distinctive sound units that produce contrasts in meaning. Their phonetic realization varies from one speaker to another and from one utterance to another. Some of this variation can be predicted from linguistic context. Just substituting [l] for [r] produces a different meaning both in *fear* and *feel* and in *reef* and *leaf*. The same phoneme [l] contrasts with [r] in each pair but its physical realization is different. An [l] at the beginning of a syllable in English is always 'clear,' and at the end always 'dark.' An [l] at the beginning of a syllable is formed with just the tip of the tongue raised to make contact at the top of the mouth; an [l] at the end of a syllable has the back of the tongue involved as well, humped up to 'color' the sound. If you record *feel* on tape and then play the tape backwards you will hear a peculiar-sounding *leaf* with a dark [l] at the wrong end of the syllable. You can hear these sounds distinctly in *holy* and *wholly*. *Ho-ly* has a clear [l] at the beginning of its second syllable, *whol-ly* has a dark [l] at the end of its first syllable. The two [l] sounds are *allophones* of the same phoneme in that although there is a difference in what the tongue does to articulate them, they are similar sounds and they do not contrast. One cannot substitute one for another in the same position and produce a change in meaning. Some languages have several [l] phonemes, English has just one.

For vowel phonemes we use the system of transcription shown in Figure 1, one suited particularly for American English. The phonetic norms specified there are reference points in terms of which we can describe variation. Speakers always have most of the 'contrasts' of this system, whatever their phonetic norms.

The vowel sounds written with two symbols are all glided: the major syllabic thrust comes at the beginning of the sound and then tapers off as the tongue glides up to a higher position. We have represented a common pronunciation where all glided vowels are tensed, with tenseness indicated by a bar over a vowel symbol, but there is considerable variation here as with other aspects of pronunciation. There is a pronunciation widespread in Canada, where the sound [āy] is tense in words like *why, wide,* and *wives,* but not tense and therefore

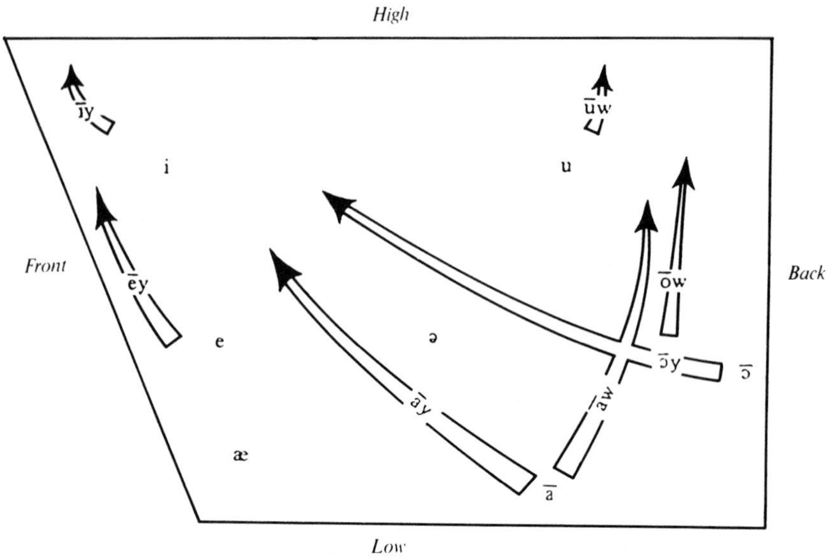

Figure 1. ***The vowel phonemes of American English in their approximate articulatory and acoustic positions.***

Tense vowels have a bar over them, lax vowels do not. Vowel sounds including one of the semi-vowels [y] and [w] are glided as shown by the arrows. For many speakers of American English the glides for the high vowels [īy] and [ūw] are minimal; for others they are more noticeable. The orientation of the vowel symbols and arrows refers to acoustic correlates for the gesture made by the tongue in the mouth, especially the position of the highest point of the tongue. Thus for [īy] the highest point on the tongue is as high and as far forward as it ever gets for a vowel sound, for [ā] as low as it ever gets. Some speakers have additional vowel contrasts. Many speakers lack one or more of the contrasts here. For example, before [r] speakers may merge tense and lax vowels into a single lax pronunciation: they *[ðēy] combines with* are *to give* they're *[ðer] with a lax vowel, sounding exactly as* there *[ðer]. Many speakers have neutralized the contrast between [ɔ̄] and [ā] in all positions, saying* cot *and* caught, hock *and* hawk *all with [ā].*

shorter in duration in words like *white* and *wife,* where the syllable ends with a voiceless consonant.

All vowels with a bar are tense. Vowels that are not tense are called lax. A consistent difference between tense and lax vowels is that the tense vowels are longer in duration. Thus tense [ā] is notably longer in *rod* than the lax [e] in *red.* Only tense vowels can occur in stressed final open syllables (open syllables have no consonant after the vowel). Examples are shown in Table 3.

Table 3. ***The tense and lax vowels of English, in closed and open syllables***

	Vowel Sound	*In Closed Syllables*	*In Open Syllables*
Tense	īy	beet	bee
	ēy	bait	bay
	ā	pot	spa
	āy	bite	buy
	āw	bout	now
	ūw	boot	new
	ōw	boat	no
	ɔ̄	bought	saw
	ɔ̄y	void	boy
Lax	i	bit	
	e	bet	
	æ	bat	
	ə	but	
	u	put	

Acknowledgements

We want to acknowledge the generous support of the National Endowment for the Humanities, the Center for Applied Linguistics and the Australian National University. At Winthrop Publishers, Paul O'Connell has provided important direction, and Clive Martin and Pat Torelli have done thoughtful and skillful production work.

At the Center for Applied Linguistics, our gratitude goes to Begay Atkinson, Peggy Good, John Hammer, Diana Riehl, Roger Shuy, and especially—a person who has been a help in this series from the beginning, and the one most helpful to us in editing this volume—Peg Griffin.

Valuable contributions to the work at various stages have come from Michael Cook, Bob Dixon, Bill Foley, John Haviland, Shirley Brice Heath, Agnes Huhn, George Lombard, Peter Peterson, Phil Rose, Gavin Seagrim, Joel Sherzer, Pablo Shopen, Carmen Silva-Corvalan, and Anna Wierzbicka. Our greatest thanks to all.

TIMOTHY SHOPEN
Canberra, Australia

JOSEPH M. WILLIAMS
Chicago, U.S.A.

Table 3. ***The tense and lax vowels of English, in closed and open syllables***

	Vowel Sound	*In Closed Syllables*	*In Open Syllables*
Tense	īy	beet	bee
	ēy	bait	bay
	ā	pot	spa
	āy	bite	buy
	āw	bout	now
	ūw	boot	new
	ōw	boat	no
	ɔ̄	bought	saw
	ɔ̄y	void	boy
Lax	i	bit	
	e	bet	
	æ	bat	
	ə	but	
	u	put	

Acknowledgements

We want to acknowledge the generous support of the National Endowment for the Humanities, the Center for Applied Linguistics and the Australian National University. At Winthrop Publishers, Paul O'Connell has provided important direction, and Clive Martin and Pat Torelli have done thoughtful and skillful production work.

At the Center for Applied Linguistics, our gratitude goes to Begay Atkinson, Peggy Good, John Hammer, Diana Riehl, Roger Shuy, and especially—a person who has been a help in this series from the beginning, and the one most helpful to us in editing this volume—Peg Griffin.

Valuable contributions to the work at various stages have come from Michael Cook, Bob Dixon, Bill Foley, John Haviland, Shirley Brice Heath, Agnes Huhn, George Lombard, Peter Peterson, Phil Rose, Gavin Seagrim, Joel Sherzer, Pablo Shopen, Carmen Silva-Corvalan, and Anna Wierzbicka. Our greatest thanks to all.

TIMOTHY SHOPEN
Canberra, Australia

JOSEPH M. WILLIAMS
Chicago, U.S.A.

Grammar and Usage

Chapter 1

The English Language as Rule-Governed Behavior: Grammatical Structure

Timothy Shopen

***Timothy Shopen teaches linguistics at the Australian National University. He became interested in linguistics while a language teacher, teaching French in a high school near Chicago, then English in Mali, West Africa. These experiences made him think about what it means to know a language. While teaching English he greatly valued Otto Jespersen's* Essentials of English Grammar.**

1. The Creativity of Ordinary Language Behavior

Like those who speak other languages, English speakers need not have heard or read a sentence before in order to produce it or understand it. Consider the following news item:

> *Kansas City, Mo.*—Construction workers here uncovered a small hoard of *silver coins* buried in a bucket.

If you haven't chanced to have read or heard of an event just like this one before, then you have probably never encountered this particular sentence. And if the event were unfamiliar to the writer, the sentence was probably new for him too. No doubt he was familiar with all the words, including *uncovered, here, a, in, small, hoard,* and *bucket,* and even some of the phrases like *construction workers* and *silver coins;* what was genuinely new was the overall way these elements were combined. But if you had never experienced this sentence, how did you understand it, and how did the newspaper writer write it so you could understand it? You and the writer must share certain rules for combining the parts of sentences into wholes.

A great challenge in describing English is to discover how we have learned to construct and interpret new utterances. A learning demonstration devised by the psychologist Jerome Bruner provides insight into the problem.

2. Bruner's Demonstration

You are going to be given a number to memorize. To feel motivated to learn the number, imagine that some time during the next month, someone will offer you fifty dollars to repeat the number correctly. Spend a moment seriously attempting to learn this number before reading further. Here it is:

2 5 9 1 2 1 6 1 9 2 3 2 6 3 0 3 3 3 7 4 0

The important question is *how* you went about learning the number. You could have chosen to learn each digit one by one: *two, five, nine, one, two, one, six* . . . etc. This is probably the hardest and most time-consuming method. A second method you might have used is to break the number into groups, treating the series of twenty-one digits as three telephone numbers of seven digits each. The telephone numbers can be further analyzed into an "exchange" of three digits, and a "number," with four digits:

259-1216 192-3263 033-3740

This method is easier for most people, probably because there is a hierarchical structure that helps them keep track of where they are in the series, rather than losing themselves in a string of disconnected units. The hierarchical structure can be represented by a "tree" diagram:

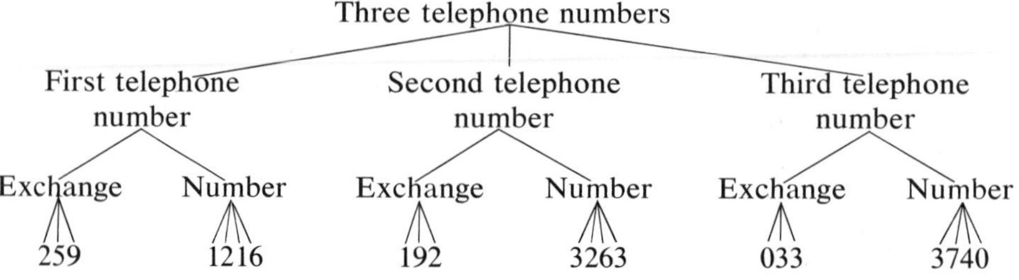

But no doubt some of you have hit on still another way to remember the number. This includes a regular progression where you do the sequence "add three, then four, then three, then four . . . ," and you continue until the number is completed (with this number you end with "add three"). This procedure will *generate* the number. To remember our number this way you need to retain three things: the progression "add three, then four . . . ," the starting expression (2), and the stopping expression (40). This amounts to a rule which can be represented in rough notation form as follows:

$$[2 \; \overset{\curvearrowright}{+3 \; +4} \quad 40].$$

Each operation produces a number that is added to the string. Thus, start with 2 and add 3, which yields 5, and 5 is joined to the string so that we have 25; then add 4 to the last number in the string (5) producing a new number to lengthen the string to 259, then add 3 again to the last number $(9 + 3 = 12)$ to give 25912, and so on. When we finish we have: 2 5 9 12 16 19 23 26 30 33 37 40.

Which seems to be the easiest way of remembering? Breaking the number down into parts is easier than trying to remember twenty-one individual, disconnected digits. But for most people the easiest way by far is to remember the three-part rule that generates the number. Note that if you choose this third method, *you set out to remember the rule but not the number itself.* In fact, you would probably want to avoid cluttering your mind with the long number and instead retain only the rule.

A child must acquire knowledge of his or her language in this way: rather than memorizing all the utterances that might be needed during the course of a lifetime, an impossible task under any circumstances, the child learns rules for generating utterances, which he or she applies as the need arises. While we may know many things we say by heart, we also have the ability to create utterances as they are needed. We may remember many chunks of sentences, frequently used combinations of words that we can produce as wholes when we speak and write (expressions such as *hasn't been feeling well lately* and *one of our neighbors*), but we cannot account for our ability to use those chunks in combination with each other or other expressions without saying that at the same time we know rules for recreating those chunks out of smaller parts.

There is a corollary to Bruner's learning demonstration that is particularly appropriate for language: you can create an unlimited series of new numbers by the same procedure of "add three, then four, then three, then four . . ." only by changing the starting and stopping expressions, for example making them 1 and 8 or 25 and 74. In this sense we can make the rule a "productive" one, in the same way rules of language can be productive. We know rules for the major sentence patterns in our language, and those sentence patterns can be varied on endlessly with new combinations of words within them.

Still another corollary goes as follows: you can retain very long numbers by rule. Instead of retaining the formula [2 +3 +4   40] with 40 as the stop number, you could have in that position the number 100,000. The resulting formula would be only a little longer and not much harder to remember, but the number the formula would generate would take a number of hours to say or write. Indeed, you can retain strings of numbers of *infinite* length by a rule, for example, divide any integer from 1 to 8 by 9; for 8, .8888 . . . , for 7, .7777 . . . , etc. That is, you already know how to construct numbers that you could never actually produce: you already know the principle by which to generate them but not the numbers themselves. Language is like this because there is no longest utterance. Most sentences can be made longer by simply adding *and* and then saying something more. The new longer sentence can itself be made longer by adding another *and* and saying still more, and so on. By knowing the grammatical rules of a language, we have the capacity to produce sentences longer than any we will ever actually say. We know the rules but not the sentences. We cannot hope to describe a language by recording all our possible utterances, but it is possible to discover rules that characterize the way in which we know a language.

3. The Sentence Expansion Demonstration

Here is another demonstration (one of Charles Bird's), that you have to do for yourself, but which once done can tell you something important. This demonstration can be done most effectively by a group of people working together. In the middle of a blackboard or a blank sheet of paper write a short declarative sentence then find ways to expand the sentence, making it longer and longer and longer, taking care only to create an overall sentence that is coherent and grammatical. You might start with:

The woman gave the man a package.

The best ways to expand a sentence are the recursive devices of *subordination* and *coordination,* the two principal means of combining sentence structures to form longer sentences. Recursion is the inclusion of constituents such as sentences inside instances of themselves, sentences which are subparts of larger sentences, which in turn can be subparts of still larger ones. This is how sentences escape any limit on their *potential* length. In subordination, additional sentence structures, call them subordinate *clauses,* will contribute secondary information that modifies or gives background information to the original sentence (the main clause). For example, the following are relative clauses that modify the nouns of the original sentence, *woman, man,* and *package.*

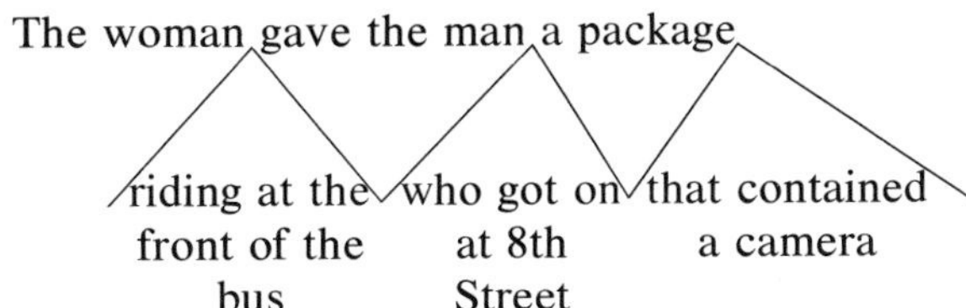

Note that expanding the sentence this way does not alter the meaning of the original sentence, which was that a certain woman gave a certain man a certain package. These are restrictive relative clauses that specify which woman, man, and package it was. You can also modify the sentence as a whole with adverbial clauses. There are all kinds of adverbial clauses, and you might use more than one (see Figure 1.1).

Most of these could go at the beginning of the sentence as well as at the end, for example, "Even though she didn't recognize him, the woman gave the man a package." Each time you expand the sentence, you create opportunities for still further expansions. You can put subordinate clauses *within* other subordinate clauses (see Figure 1.2).

The woman gave the man a package

before he moved to a rear seat
after he said something to her while the detective was looking the other way
even though she didn't recognize him
because she thought he was the special agent
in order to satisfy his curiosity
by passing it back to him over her shoulder
instead of telling him what time it was
so that he had one more thing to carry

Figure 1.1. ***Adverbial Clauses.***

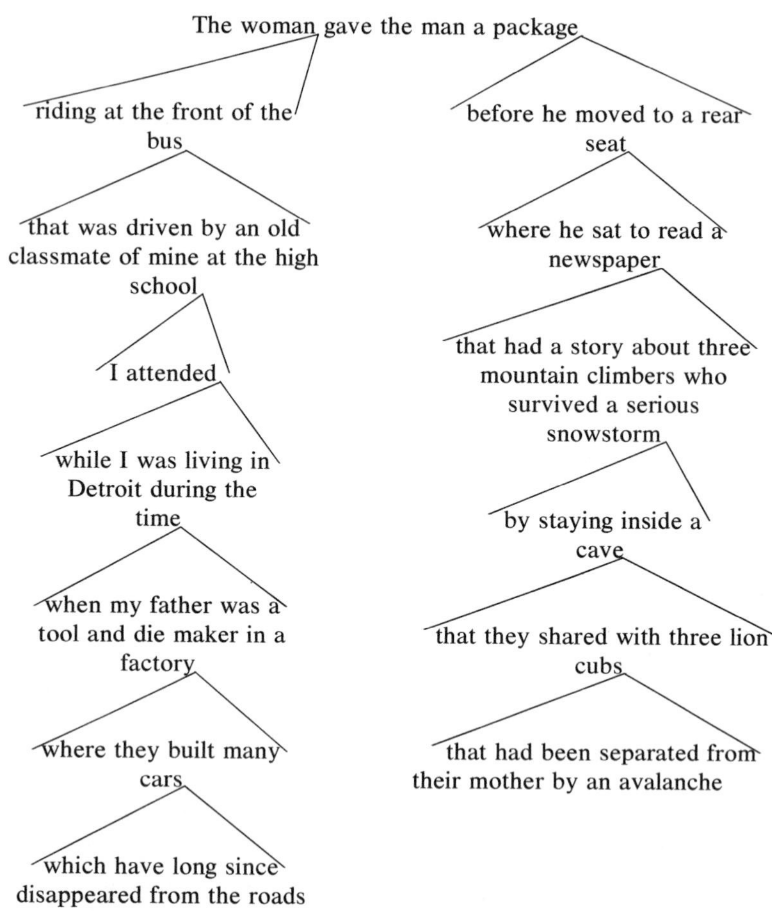

Figure 1.2. ***Subordinate Clauses within Subordinate Clauses.***

The other efficient way to expand a sentence is by coordination. You can expand the original sentence with one of the coordinating conjunctions *and, but,* or *or,* and an additional clause, for example:

> [The woman gave the man a package] and [the man handed the woman an envelope].

Now the two main clauses and the information in the sentence are parallel. Neither clause is subordinate to the other. You can use coordination inside your subordinate clauses, and subordination inside your coordinate clauses (for example, in Figure 1.3).

Besides coordinating clauses you can coordinate smaller ex-

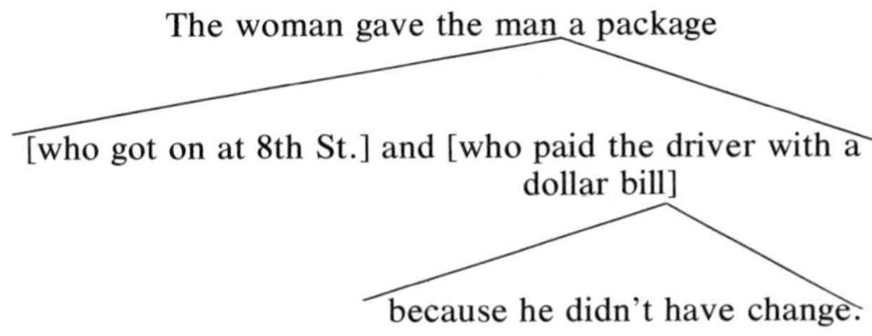

Figure 1.3. ***Coordination within Subordination, and Subordination within Coordination.***

pressions, for example, ". . . a package that contained [a camera] and [a notebook] . . ." And there are shorter modifying expressions that can be inserted, such as adjectives like *slender, middle-aged, old,* and *small* to modify nouns, and adverbs like *quietly* and *carefully* to modify verbs:

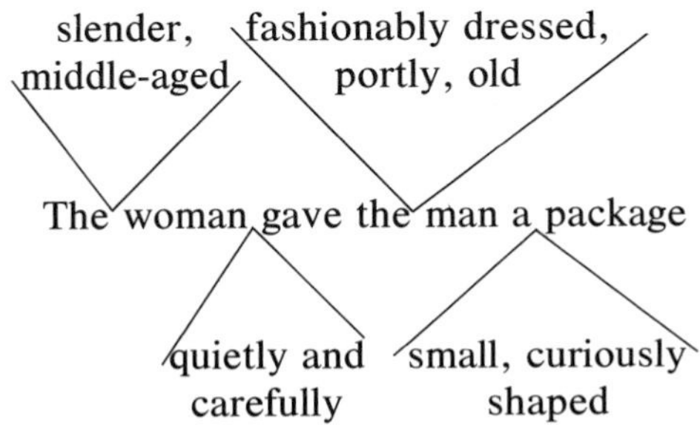

You can make original expansions of this sort, because whether or not you know terminology such as "subordination, coordination, relative clause, adverbial clause, adjective, and adverb," you are a speaker of English and you know how to use all these devices. You might start with, "The woman gave the man a package." or "The man telephoned the plumber." Use arrows or carets to make as many inserts and additions as you can. Do not worry about how beautiful the sentence is (it will be very cumbersome); take care only that each addition remains consistent with what is already in the sentence and that you do not violate your intuitions about what combinations of words are possible in English.

When you have created a very long sentence, read it aloud.

Now ask yourself if this sentence could be made longer. People hardly ever say or write sentences as long as the one you have probably created, but the important thing is that recursive devices make possible sentences of unlimited length. Given this potential, it is interesting to explore just how long and complicated the sentences are that people actually do use in various situations. To use a convenient, if not altogether accurate analogy, the grammar of a language is like having a 500 horsepower engine when only a 10 or 25 horsepower engine is generally needed. This reveals something about how we think: we tend to think best, it appears, by placing thoughts in some kind of linear order (only one at a time) and in chunks of only moderate size.

This fact about the *potential* power of grammars is evidence to support the claim that people learn the rules that generate utterances. It is a mathematical argument. Because all languages have a potentially infinite number of utterances, but no one person has an infinite brain capacity, no one could know all of the utterances. We can prove the first step in this argument as follows: we assume a systematic method to collect all the utterances in a language (in this case English but any natural language works in the same way). Start with the shortest utterances, those one word long:

Yes.

No.

Help!

Wait!

Sugar?

Cream?

.

.

.

There will be only a finite number of these, because at any given moment, people know only a finite number of words. There can be only as many one-word utterances as there are words. Next list all two-word utterances:

Come in.

Stand still!

The mailman.

No smoking.

Over here.

Nice dress!

.

.

.

There will be a finite number of these, too. We go on and list all the utterances three, four, five, six words long, etc., each time some finite number, but we never stop because we never get to the longest sentence in English. This holds true even if we limit ourselves to single sentences (where we would put a period if writing). When we have counted all the sentences one hundred words long, we can always create another that has one hundred and one words. No matter how many words in the last sentence we have created, we can always create a new one that is longer. The number of utterances is unlimited.

The most important question to ask yourself is the following: *Have you ever before heard or seen the sentence you created?* If the answer to this question is no, then how could you construct and understand it? We come to the same conclusion. If you didn't know the sentence, you must know rules that you used to generate it.

4. Implicit Knowledge

People know their languages implicitly. They express ideas without analyzing how they do it—unless they happen to take an interest in the structure of their language. They acquire their languages with little or no teaching, ordinarily before they reach school age. If they go to school, they are taught to read and write. But aside from the rules of the writing system, they seldom discuss the structure of language. The only exception is when teachers attempt to teach 'prescriptive' grammar, to teach students to construct sentences in what they consider a correct form: "Don't use double negatives." "Don't say *ain't*." "Don't say *Who did you see?* say *Whom did you see?*" "Don't say *Who should I speak to?* say *To whom should I speak?*" For the most part, however, the standard is presented piecemeal and not in terms of general rules. When children do modify their speech to make it more like that of their teachers, they do it in a largely unconscious fashion.

Linguistic analysis makes implicit knowledge explicit. Here is an aspect of the structure of English that you may be familiar with as a spelling rule, but chances are you are probably not aware of how you really use it. It concerns those little words in English, the indefinite articles *a* and *an*. How do we use them? We say:

a banana

but:

an apple

First hypothesis: "Use *an* when the noun following it begins with a vowel letter (*a, e, i, o, u*). Use *a* elsewhere." Additional examples would appear to give confirmation:

a cat	an owl
a dog	an elk
a fast horse	an orange ant

But if this principle is to be of much value, it ought to account for a general class of examples. The important work is to find counterexamples—instances in which the rule does not apply. If you have made a thorough search for counterexamples and have not found any, you have an interesting hypothesis. If on the other hand you can find counterexamples easily, your hypothesis is of little value. There often are exceptions to rules of grammar, ones that we simply memorize, but if we find too many of them, we should ask whether or not we have the right rule. And indeed, it is easy to find counterexamples:

An old banana. A big apple.

Now even though noun *banana* doesn't begin with a vowel letter, we use *an,* and even though *apple* does begin with a vowel letter, we use *a*. It is evident that these examples are not some special class of exceptions, but perfectly regular word combinations because we can easily find similar examples:

An early bus.	A huge ocean.
An itchy sweater.	A young alligator.
An open door.	A thrifty uncle.

Finding an error in one hypothesis is useful because it can help us formulate a better one. A revised hypothesis: "Use *an* when the word immediately following begins with a vowel letter (*a, e, i, o, u*). Use *a* elsewhere."

Now if we go back over the data we have considered so far, we find that there are no exceptions. But again, we must test against new data. Fill in *a* or *an:*

______ ear	______ eel	______ urn
______ year	______ heel	______ turn
______ owl	______ itch	______ utter failure
______ yowl	______ hitch	______ butter knife

So far, so good. But compare:

______ umbrella	______ hotel
______ union	______ honor
______ university	______ hour
______ utensil	______ honest man

H is not a vowel letter, but there are cases where you use *an* before it. *U* is a vowel letter, but there are cases in which you use *a* before it. Is there a better way to state the rule, *or* do we just have to remember these as exceptions? Make two lists, one with more examples like *an umbrella,* and one with more examples like *a union* (you can think them up, or you can look in the dictionary at words beginning with the letter *u*). Do the words like *union* differ from those like *umbrella?* What difference would account for why we say "*a* union" but "*an* umbrella"? If you can discover a principle that explains words beginning with *u,* you may also be able to explain what happens with words beginning with *h.*

It should be emphasized that what you are doing here is not a game. You are attempting to discover how English speakers know their language. If you can find no better generalization than the revised hypothesis stated above, you are conceding the possibility that people have to remember words like *union* and *honor* on an individual basis. You are allowing the possibility that what people know is a rule something like this:

> Use *an* when the word following it begins with a vowel letter (*a, e, i, o, u*); and use *a* elsewhere, except for *union, university,* and

utensil, which take *a,* and *honor, hour,* and *honest,* which take *an.*

What do you suppose people do when they have to say *a* or *an* before a word that is new to them?

Speaker A: That's John's quiffle.
Speaker B: What's a quiffle?

Speaker A: That's John's ope.
Speaker B: What's an ope?

For someone who has never before heard of a *quiffle* or an *ope* to be able to ask without hesitation, "What's *a* quiffle?" or "What's *an* ope?" indicates that at least for those words the speaker is applying a rule. The evidence would be all the more impressive if English speakers who heard *quiffle* and *ope* for the first time agreed on which one took *a* and which one took *an.* Supposing someone had never heard *utensil* before. If *utensil* were just an exception that had to be remembered by rote, you might expect the following dialogue:

Speaker A: That's John's utensil.
Speaker B: What's an utensil?

Does that seem likely? Or do you think it would go like this:

Speaker A: That's John's utensil.
Speaker B: What's a utensil?

We can in fact demonstrate that young children use *a* and *an* quite systematically. We can ask them the names of familiar objects:

You: What's this? (pointing to a toy)
Child: A bear.

You: What's that? (pointing to another toy)
Child: An elephant.

If young children who do not know how to read and write can do this consistently, there must be something wrong with our generalization because it is stated in terms of spelling: it refers to vowel *letters.* If the children do not know what letters the words *bear* and *elephant* begin with, it suggests that the appropriate generalization concerns not how the words are spelled, but how they sound. Sound out words like *urn* and *umbrella* and then words like *union* and *university* to see if you can hear a difference in the sounds associated with the letter *u*. Then do the same for the sounds associated with *h* in *horse* and *hotel* as opposed to *honor* and *hour*. This should lead to a better generalization.

5. A Word-Formation Experiment

Consider these English verbs which we now introduce into the language: *to royce* means "to make an unusual display of conspicuous consumption among one's peers"; *to snud* someone means "to disdain a person's taste in clothing"; *to week* means "to try to slip away without being noticed"; *to glarm* means "to walk backwards with smooth even steps." For the following sentences, write the proper ending (suffix) for each verb and then pronounce the word that you have created.

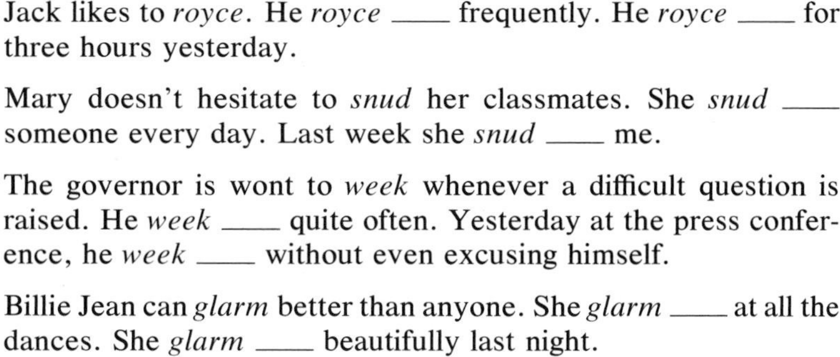

Jack likes to *royce*. He *royce* ____ frequently. He *royce* ____ for three hours yesterday.

Mary doesn't hesitate to *snud* her classmates. She *snud* ____ someone every day. Last week she *snud* ____ me.

The governor is wont to *week* whenever a difficult question is raised. He *week* ____ quite often. Yesterday at the press conference, he *week* ____ without even excusing himself.

Billie Jean can *glarm* better than anyone. She *glarm* ____ at all the dances. She *glarm* ____ beautifully last night.

Here are the words you have created:

The "s" ending:	royces	snuds	weeks	glarms
The "ed" ending:	royced	snudded	weeked	glarmed

Note the pronunciation of the "s" ending in each case. It is spelled the same way but is pronounced differently. What do we add to the pronunciation of *royce* to give *royces?* Is it the same thing to add to the pronunciation of *snud* to give *snuds,* or to that of *week* to give *weeks?* In how many different ways do we pronounce this ending?

Now the same questions for the "ed" ending. What do we add to the pronunciation of *royce* to produce *royced?* Is it the same ending that we add to *snud* to give *snudded?* In how many ways do we pronounce the "ed" ending?

If you compare your pronunciation of these words with that of other speakers of English, you will find that you all agree, even though these are new words that you have never heard before. This shows that you use a rule to pronounce these endings. You may not have been conscious that you pronounced these endings more than one way, much less that you did so by rule. The pronunciation of these endings follows a very general rule, and you can discover it.

Note that the third-person singular "s" ending on verbs has the same pronunciations as the plural suffix on nouns:

leach*es* dog*s* cat*s*

The same goes for the possessive suffix on nouns or noun phrases:

I saw Mitch'*s* house.

I saw Sue'*s* house.

I saw last week'*s* newspaper.

and even for the 'contracted' forms of the verb form *is:*

The church'*s* open.	(identical to church*es*)
The barn'*s* open.	(identical to barn*s*)
The tent'*s* open	(identical to tent*s*)

Here are three regular pronunciations of the *-s* endings:

I		*II*		*III*	
judge	judges	wade	wades	wait	waits
reach	reaches	love	loves	laugh	laughs
buzz	buzzes	robe	robes	rope	ropes
bus	busses	bag	bags	back	backs
Mitch	Mitch's	Sue	Sue's	Dick	Dick's

There is an important point here. If you are a speaker of English, you will notice that going down columns I, II, and III, the "s" suffix sounds the same, but reading across columns it sounds different; moreover, you can arrange new data in the appropriate categories. For example, you can add the following words to the appropriate columns: *teach, teaches; cop, cops; cob, cobs; bathe, bathes; bath, baths;* and *miss, misses*. That is, you can tell whether *teach, teaches* patterns like *judge, judges; wade, wades;* or *wait, waits;* etc. Most important, you can find more examples on your own. Categorize several more English words that take the "s" suffix according to whether they take pronunciation I, II, or III. When you categorize the new data in a systematic way, then you are doing one of the important steps in scientific analysis. Where the study of your language is concerned, you do not have to content yourself with *only* reading or listening to specialists talk about their science (though that is of course helpful); you can also get down to doing some of it yourself.

Here are the three regular pronunciations of the *-ed* ending:

I		*II*		*III*	
wade	waded	judge	judged	reach	reached
wait	waited	buzz	buzzed	bus	bussed
need	needed	love	loved	laugh	laughed
lift	lifted	robe	robed	rope	roped
trade	traded	bag	bagged	back	backed

Categorize the following examples yourself: *seize, seized; cease, ceased; sight, sighted; weld, welded; lunch, lunched; lunge, lunged.* Find several more examples for each of the three columns exemplifying the "ed" suffix.

Both the "s" and the "ed" suffixes are pronounced as an extra syllable, as [əz] or [əd], in column I (*judge -es, wade -ed*) but as part of the preceding syllable in the other two columns (wade*s*, wait*s*, judg*ed*, reach*ed*). In column II the endings are pronounced as 'voiced' sounds, as [z] or [d], and in III as 'voiceless' sounds, as [s] or [t].

Sounds usually represented by the letters *z, v, j, b, d, g, l, r, m, n, y, a, e, i, o,* and *u* are 'voiced'—pronounced with vocal cords vibrating. Sounds usually represented by the letters *s, f, ch, sh, p, t,* and *k* are 'voiceless'—when they are pronounced the vocal cords do not vibrate. In ordinary English only consonant sounds can be voiceless (unless you are whispering!). With a thumb and a forefinger over your larynx (Adam's apple), say a long vowel sound like *ahhhh* or *ohhhh,* and you will feel the vibration. Say a prolonged *zzzzzz* sound, then change to an *sssss* sound, then back to a *zzzzz,* and so forth several times: you will feel the vocal cord vibrations turning on and off. The sounds, rather than the spellings of these endings, can be represented as follows:

		Same Syllable			
I. Extra Syllable		**II. Voiced**		**III. Voiceless**	
Sound	*Example*	*Sound*	*Example*	*Sound*	*Example*
[əz]	kiss*es*	[z]	love*s*	[s]	laugh*s*
[əd]	need*ed*	[d]	bagg*ed*	[t]	back*ed*

This chart shows what every speaker of English does when pronouncing these endings. You do it without hesitation, even with words you have never heard before. You gave pronunciation I of the "s" ending in *royces,* pronunciation II in *snuds* and *glarms,* and III in *weeks.* You gave pronunciation I of the "ed" ending in *snudded,* II in *glarmed,* and III in *royced* and *weeked.* All the words where you give pronunciation I to these endings are the same in some important respect. This is also the case for pronunciations II and III. First, see if you can find a rule that describes where pronunciation I of the "ed" ending occurs. The appropriate hypothesis will have the following form:

> The "ed" suffix is pronounced as an extra syllable [əd] in the context ____
>
> ____

> One way of completing this is:
> The "ed" suffix is pronounced as an extra syllable [əd] in the context of words like *wade, wait, need, lift, trade,* etc.

This is all very well, but it doesn't explain anything yet. What does it mean for certain words to be like *wade, wait,* etc. and not like words that take pronunciations II or III? How do you and other speakers of English know that *snud* requires a suffix pronounced [əd] and that *royce, week,* and *glarm* do not? The hypothesis has to be like this:

> The "ed" suffix is pronounced as an extra syllable [əd] in the context of words that have characteristic X.

Try to find that distinctive characteristic X. If you cannot think of a hypothesis right away, find more relevant data, more words where the "ed" ending is an extra syllable and more where it isn't. Ask yourself, "How do the two groups differ?" When you find a hypothesis, check all the data to make sure you have no counterexamples. Ideally, your hypothesis should account for *all and only* the cases where "ed" is pronounced as an extra syllable. *All* the words with property X should get it and *only* those. In fact, rules often have exceptions, but you do not want to admit any until you are convinced you have the best generalization.

Proceed in similar fashion for each of the two remaining pronunciations of "ed." Pronunciation II [d] is voiced and III [t] is voiceless, you will recall, and you will need to refer to the voiced-voiceless distinction again to explain the alternation between pronunciations II and III. The hypothesis will have the form:

The "ed" suffix is pronounced [d] in the context ____________

____

The "ed" suffix is pronounced [t] in the context ____________

____

Again, in looking for a hypothesis you might collect more data, more words where the "ed" ending is pronounced as in *buzzed* [d] and *bussed* [t]. Ask what there is about words such as *buzz* that needs [d] and about words such as *bus* that needs [t]. When you have a hypothesis, check it against all the data you can.

Finally, look for the rules that govern the pronunciation of the "s" ending. Altogether, you are looking here for six hypotheses.

1. The "ed" suffix is pronounced [əd] in the context ____________
   ____.
2. The "ed" suffix is pronounced [d] in the context ____________
   ____.
3. The "ed" suffix is pronounced [t] in the context ____________
   ____.
4. The "s" suffix is pronounced [əz] in the context ____________
   ____.
5. The "s" suffix is pronounced [z] in the context ____________
   ____.
6. The "s" suffix is pronounced [s] in the context ____________
   ____.

It is possible to describe what English speakers do here with not six, but only two generalizations. The "s" and "ed" endings are pronounced as extra syllables when they follow a sound of the same type (as in the case of "s" [s, z, š, ž, č, ǰ] and in the case of "ed" [t] or [d]). In all other instances they are voiceless if the preceding sound is voiceless, otherwise they are voiced. Further training in linguistics would make it possible for you to articulate this more precisely, particularly the notion "sound of the same type," but this is the essence of what goes on, and all speakers of English "know" these generalizations implicitly.

The results of this experiment have shown that speakers of English know an important aspect of pronunciation not by remembering individual words, but by rule, and that nonspecialists or beginning linguists can do linguistic analysis; for in an important respect as speakers of a language they have as much access to the truth as experienced specialists. Language is a good area of study for beginners who want to get an idea of what it is like to do scientific research. The central aspect of science, which is so difficult to experience in most introductory courses, is inventing and testing hypotheses. In the study of language you can do this quickly because the data for testing hypotheses is so accessible. Anyone who speaks and understands a language can be his own informant, and most people are fairly perceptive about "sames" and "differences" in the speech behavior of others.

6. Some Syntax, and an Illustration of How Some Rules Are Harder to Find Than Others

Language has a double level of structure: phonology, the arrangement of distinctive sounds that gives meaningful elements audible form, and syntax and morphology, the combination of meaningful elements to express larger meanings. The word-formation experiment explored some rules governing the way sounds come together to form words. Here we will explore a few rules that govern the way smaller units of meaning combine to make larger units of meaning. Again, as a native speaker with direct access to the data, you can form and test hypotheses yourself. Consider:

John gave a book to Bill.

The verb *give* is among those that can take two objects, a direct object DO (a book), and an indirect object IO (Bill). Notice that the two objects can occur in different order:

John gave *a book* to *Bill*.
DO IO

John gave *Bill a book*.
IO DO

Not all double-object verbs allow both these orders. Consider the following examples. If one seems ill-formed to you—not possible as an English sentence—put an asterisk in front of it:

	Give	*Donate*
DO to IO:	John gave five dollars to the Red Cross.	John donated five dollars to the Red Cross.
IO DO:	John gave the Red Cross five dollars.	John donated the Red Cross five dollars.

You probably asterisked the last of these four examples, "*John donated the Red Cross five dollars." Speakers of English generally agree on which verbs allow both the *DO to IO* pattern and the *IO DO* pattern, and which ones do not. Classify the following list of verbs accordingly: *announce, bring, explain, introduce, lend, reiterate, sell,* and *teach.*

	DO to IO	*IO DO*
announce:	Al announced the news to Joe.	*Al announced Joe the news.
bring:	Sue brought a pickle to Ed.	Sue brought Ed a pickle.
explain:	Noah explained the accident to Jim.	
introduce:	Mary introduced Ruth to Paula.	
lend:	Andrea lent her raincoat to Phillip.	
reiterate	Carl reiterated the terms to Vic.	
sell:	Lois sold the platter to Tony.	
teach:	Olga taught French to George.	

Now find several more verbs that allow the *DO to IO* pattern and test them to see whether they also allow the *IO DO* pattern. After that make parallel lists of the two groups.

DO to IO and IO DO	*DO to IO but not IO DO*
give	donate
bring	announce
.	.
.	.
.	.

One of the first questions to ask is how we learn which verbs allow the *IO DO* pattern and which do not. You can find a rule that will define at least a tendency of one group of verbs to make them (or most of them) distinct from the others. A good way to think about it is to consider what would happen if a new double-object verb, such as *to glarf,* came into the language. Let's say that you become familiar with it in sentences such as the following:

Harry glarfed the letter to Norman.

How would you know whether or not you could say:

Harry glarfed Norman the letter.

It is always possible that people learn this pattern for each individual verb, which is to say that you would have no way of knowing whether "Harry glarfed Norman the letter" is possible unless you heard someone else say it first. But if you didn't hear it, you would not be sure. Your intuition probably tells you that you don't learn to speak this way. It is unlikely that you have heard anyone use the verb *explain* in the *IO DO* pattern, but if someone did say something like "Noah explained Jim the game," your reaction would probably be an instant "what?" You would be quite sure that the person had made a mistake.

How do we learn *not* to use a certain construction? No one ever told you "Don't use *explain* in the *IO DO* pattern." Yet you certainly have been made very familiar with the *IO DO* pattern with other verbs. If you learned these patterns by rote for each verb, you would think that someone would say something like "Noah explained Jim the game" if only by analogy with verbs like *show* "Noah showed Jim the game," and that the custom would very quickly spread. But it hasn't happened. Since the two groups of verbs have remained relatively stable for long periods of time, people probably know certain generalizations that assign at least most of these verbs to one group or another. But pinning down the rule is not so easy.

The more examples you can find, the more regularities will become apparent. One interesting generalization is that most verbs like *give* are only one syllable, while most verbs like *donate* have more than one syllable. Another generalization is that almost all the verbs like *give* are of Germanic origin, while almost all those like *donate* are of Romance origin (from French or Latin). Of course, successive generations learning English have no way of knowing the history of their language (unless they learn it in school, long after they have learned to speak English); however, many Romance verbs have a shape different from that of Germanic words, a shape that could be recognized by new generations learning the language. Romance verbs have prefixes like *re-, in-, pro-,* etc., while Anglo-Saxon verbs tend to have no prefixes—the immediate reason why the verbs like *give* tend to be shorter. A counterexample to this general trend is *promise* from Latin and French: it has the prefix *pro-,* and is therefore longer than one syllable. But even so, it patterns like *give;* however, there aren't many other examples of this kind.

Perhaps a hypothesis might be based on the meaning of the verbs. The meaning of *give* is close to that of *donate,* but *donate* has a more formal (less colloquial), specialized meaning, which is reasonable enough when one recalls the genteel origins of Romance vocabulary. Compare *tell* and *announce:*

Al told the news to Joe.	Al announced the news to Joe.
Al told Joe the news.	*Al announced Joe the news.

Again, *tell* and *announce* are similar in meaning, but *tell* is more colloquial, less specialized, and has only one syllable and no prefix. *Announce* has a less colloquial, more specialized meaning, two syllables, and a prefix (*an-*, from *ad-* where the *d* has been assimilated to the following *n*). Although a child learning English would have no way of knowing this (so it doesn't count), it is interesting to note that *tell* comes from Anglo-Saxon and *announce* from French.

Our apparent counterexample *promise* has a general meaning and is completely colloquial, so in this respect we would expect it to pattern like *tell* and *give*. Compare *promise* with *pledge*. We use *pledge* to say something high-flown like "They pledged their loyalty to King Richard" but not "They pledged a tricycle to Jodie"—in that context we would rather use *promise*. On the other hand, *pledge* is more like an Anglo-Saxon verb in being of one syllable (even though of Romance origin). We should ask whether *pledge* allows indirect objects in the same positions as *promise*. The answer is sometimes yes and sometimes no. One can perhaps say "They pledged *King Richard* their loyalty" parallel to "They promised *Jodie* a tricycle," but whereas one can say "They promised *King Richard* that they would be loyal always," one must use the preposition *to* and say "They pledged *to King Richard* that they would be loyal always," making the relationship to King Richard less immediate and less intimate. Note that colloquial words are the ones we choose to show sympathy for people we are talking about. It is just these verbs with colloquial meanings that most easily allow indirect objects to stand right next to them, without the preposition *to* intervening, and so allow us to foreground the role of a person whom we might want to treat as particularly important. We have a choice between "Give a nice gift to Ed" and "Give Ed a nice gift," the latter revealing far more sympathy for Ed. With the more formal verb *present,* one can say "Present a nice gift to Ed," not "Present Ed a nice gift," although it is possible to say "Present Ed *with* a nice gift." Such are the intricacies of a natural language.

In sum, we have the following *tendencies* with verbs such as *bring, lend, sell,* and *teach* patterning in one way; and those such as *announce, explain, introduce,* and *reiterate* patterning in another:

Verbs Allowing Both the DO to IO Pattern and the IO DO Pattern	*Verbs Allowing the DO to IO Pattern But Not the IO DO Pattern*
1. One syllable	1. More than one syllable

2. No prefixes	2. Prefixes *ad-, pro-, re-,* etc.
3. Colloquial meanings	3. Slightly more formal, specialized meanings

We can now say something a little more intelligent about what would happen if we introduce into the language some new double-object verbs. A new verb *glarf* would be likely to pattern like *give,* and a new verb *recontabulate* would be likely to pattern like *explain.* Our best conclusion is that people know a rule such as the one just summarized, but that some verbs are exceptions to that rule and are remembered individually.

Some rules are easier to discover than others. Even with verbs that pattern like *give,* it is not the case that the *IO DO* pattern can be used with just any combination of words. What generalization can you make about the following data? (Star the examples you find unacceptable.)

John sent the box to Al. John sent Al the box.	John sent the box to California. John sent California the box.
Ed brought a six-pack to his uncle. Ed brought his uncle a six-pack.	Ed brought a six-pack to our house. Ed brought our house a six-pack.

If you can form a hypothesis, try to test it with the verbs *take* and *carry* and perhaps several other appropriate verbs.

Another constraint is illustrated by the following data. Again, form a hypothesis, and test it against some of your own examples. (Star the unacceptable.)

Viola gave the message to Sue. Viola gave Sue the message.	Viola gave it to Sue. Viola gave Sue it.
Ernie lent his cuff links to Ed. Ernie lent Ed his cuff links.	Ernie lent them to Ed. Ernie lent Ed them.

7. Conclusion

So it is that English speakers know the grammatical structure of their language, the core of their expressive system; to this we will see added other principles important for the productive use of language as a part of our thought and our culture. Younger generations acquire a language not by imitation so much as by recreation, and so it changes from one generation, geographical area, or social stratum to another. New minds make new generalizations. The central notion to understanding the structure, use, change, or variation of the English language is that of creativity by rule. Human beings never behave in any mechanical or strictly deterministic way but with imagination and inspiration, as well as irrationality and perversity. We cannot make sense of the way we survive and do what we do, with our failures and our successes, our sanity and our madness, without understanding our ability to devise rules and apply them to new situations. As much as with any aspect of our behavior, we can see this in our language.

Suggestions for Further Reading

For an excellent reference work on the grammatical structure of English, see R. Quirk, S. Greenbaum, G. Leech, and J. Svartvik, *A Grammar of Contemporary English,* not a book one is likely to read from cover to cover, but one to consult when interested about specific aspects of English grammar. By contrast, Otto Jespersen's *Essentials of English Grammar,* an excellent book, is less of a reference grammar and more of an extended essay. Once you become familiar with Jespersen's theory and terminology, you will appreciate the cogency and insights of his work, and will probably want to go on to his other books.

For a theoretical orientation more recent than Jespersen's and one which has led to important insights in English as well as language in general, one should become acquainted with the work of Noam Chomsky and the theory of transformational grammar. A good place to start is in D. A. Reibel and S. A. Schane, eds., *Modern Studies in English.* This book has a useful introductory section and then readings of considerable interest on various topics in English syntax. For a good introduction to the philosophical thrust of Noam Chomsky's work on language, see his *Language and Mind.*

One of the best books ever written for a general audience on the nature of language, important for understanding English as much as any language is Edward Sapir's *Language,* 1921, available in paperback.

An excellent introduction to linguistics can be found in Dwight Bolinger's *Aspects of Language,* the companion volume by M. Alyeshmerni and P. Taubr *Working with Aspects of Language,* and Peter Ladefoged's *A Course in Phonetics.* Each of these books gives a good deal of information about English and an introduction to what languages are like all over the world, a perspective necessary for the best understanding of English.

Alyeshmerni, M. and P. Taubr. *Working with Aspects of Language.* New York: Harcourt Brace Jovanovich, 1975.

Bolinger, D. *Aspects of Language.* 4th ed. New York: Harcourt Brace Jovanovich, 1975.

Chomsky, N. *Language and Mind.* Enlarged edition. New York: Harcourt Brace Jovanovich, 1972.

Jespersen, O. *Essentials of English Grammar.* University, Alabama: University of Alabama Press, 1933.

Ladefoged, P. *A Course in Phonetics.* New York: Harcourt Brace Jovanovich, 1975.

Quirk, R.; Greenbaum, S.; Leech, G.; and Svartvik, J. *A Grammar of Contemporary English.* New York and London: Seminar Press, a division of Harcourt Brace Jovanovich, 1972.

Reibel, D. A., and Schane, S. A., eds., *Modern Studies in English.* Englewood Cliffs, N.J.: Prentice-Hall, 1969.

Sapir, E. *Language.* New York: Harcourt Brace Jovanovich, Harvest Book, 1921.

Chapter 2

The English Language as Use-Governed Behavior

Joseph M. Williams

Joe Williams is a Professor of English and Linguistics at the University of Chicago. He teaches writing, linguistics, and stylistics and practices what he preaches by consulting about these matters with the federal government and midwest corporations.

1. Building Hal

Each of us has experienced moments such as these:

- Someone asks us to call him by his first name. Or not to.
- An editor tells us that we shouldn't end a sentence with a preposition.
- We stare uncomprehendingly at someone who has just said *The door is open!* until we realize he wants us to close it.
- Someone giggles that he or she has to go to the little boy's room or to the powder room.
- We rewrite the sentence *He knew that the dog was dead without looking* to *He knew without looking that the dog was dead.*
- Instead of saying to someone *I can not trust you,* we say *You do not have my trust.*

In each of these cases, it is not just the information being communicated that is significant but how that information is expressed; what is important is not just the content but its form. In some sense, of course, form is content, for in these examples, the speaker/writer is communicating something beyond the strictly logical content of the sentence. The difference between *Get out* and *An order in regard to your immediate exit from this location is hereby extended to you* is less in the sum of the words than in the fact that one is direct and concise, the other indirect and impersonal. In one way, the two sentences "say the same thing." But in an equally important way, they say quite different things—about the speakers, about their audiences, about the situations in which they are uttered, and about the intentions that shaped them.

The acquisition of language is an astonishing accomplishment. Children not yet old enough to control their bladders utter sequences of words that are recognizable attempts at sentences. But no less astonishing is the ability they quickly develop along with productive speech—the ability to describe the same event in different ways. Every normal five-year-old can utter both *I spilled the milk* and *The milk spilled,* but few are so insensitive to their different effects as to choose the first.

For a child to acquire this ability, the ability to vary the way he describes the same event, he must first master the ways his language lets him formulate a sentence. If only cake crumbs are left on the plate, for example, he cannot say in explanation something like *The cake ate.* But as he matures, as he learns there are linguistic options, he must learn not only the options but which options best fit the particular requirements of a particular moment.

But more than that, he must learn that his options extend even to choosing what to refer to. To accomplish his goal of getting an ice cream cone, what child does not eventually learn to say *I'm hungry!* instead of *I want an ice cream cone!?*

So knowing how to use a language means more than producing grammatical sentences in that language, even more than learning to express the same ideas in different ways. It means selecting the words, manipulating sentence structure, modulating the sounds of a language, and even selecting what to talk about in order to achieve particular goals.

1.1 The Variables

A familiar figure in science fiction is the android so ingeniously constructed that, at least linguistically, it cannot be distinguished from the human it simulates. Like Hal in *2001,* it not only answers questions but asks its own and even makes its own observations without being asked. If such a device also looked like a human, we would have no way of knowing—short of disassembling it—that we were not speaking to an intelligent, thinking creature that qualified for personhood. Even if we were told it was an android, we would still have to grant that it certainly "knew" the language it spoke, just as we assume that a child "knows" how to talk when it responds to talk from others and initiates its own, when it both answers and asks questions, follows and gives orders.

If we set out to construct such a device, we would immediately face two kinds of problems. One is merely technological. The "merely" is ironic, of course, but not too much so. We probably think first of how difficult it would be to pack into the space the volume of a skull enough memory circuits to store whatever knowledge and behavior patterns we decide should be stored. But it is actually the second problem that is more difficult and which justifies the "merely" of the first. It is that prior problem of understanding just what knowledge and patterns of behavior we want to program into the machine in the first place. It is the problem of creating the ghost in the machine, the competence not found in the material of the hardware, the competence that directs its behavior.

Let us assume that we have solved the problems of skin texture, voice, movement, and so on. Let us assume that we are able to pack into a very small space all the information found in all the libraries and laboratories of the world. Let us assume that the only problem we have is that of understanding and programming into the android the linguistic behavior we want the android to exhibit—behavior that will not reveal it to be anything but a fully normal human speaker.

PROBLEM 1. (a) What would be wrong with merely storing in the android's memory cells all the sentences that have ever been uttered or written since, say, 1850? (Assume that somehow we have all those sentences available to us.) (b) Would storing every grammar book on the English language written since 1800 help?

Try to answer each question at least in your own mind before you go on.

Our android would at the very least, then, have to know how to produce completely new sentences, because we constantly create them. And needless to say, the sentences that the android produced would also have to be grammatical and would have to sound like normal English sentences.

PROBLEM 2. The android, of course, would also have to respond to sentences. Why we want it respond to both grammatical ungrammatical sentence? What kind grammatical mistake people ordinarily make? What kinds of grammatical mistakes should the android make if it is to sound like a human speaker making human mistakes? Listen to the grammatical structure of the sentences others use in casual conversation. Are they always . . . well that it is to say are they usually—at least as we respond to them—Look, what I mean is does it sound odd if a sentence doesn't always . . . never mind.

PROBLEM 3. Here are some sentences that contain "errors" of different kinds. One kind of error is like those you were drilled on in high school. Don't end sentences with a preposition: *who* vs. *whom, shall* vs. *will,* and so on. The very existence of such rules testifies to the fact that many people are speaking in ways they are being told not to. Otherwise, we wouldn't have to learn the rules. The other kind of error would reveal that we had botched the job of programming the android to sound like a competent speaker of English. Which kind of error is which in these next sentences? How does the age of a speaker relate to this problem?

1. He ain't got no money. And he don't know nothin' either.
2. Just between you and I, I'm broke.
3. He finally made a decidement.
4. Man the walked street the down.
5. My father, he been sick for a long time.
6. I know the boy who and a girl were there yesterday. (i.e., I know the boy. The boy and a girl were there yesterday.)
7. Fortunately, where are you going?
8. Who because left you stayed? (i.e., because someone left, you stayed. Who is that someone?)
9. The food sickened me. The milk illed me too.
10. My friend's appearance of the man surprised me.
11. Me and him don't be friends no more.
12. The poet gave a read of the poem.
13. My friend may be done gone now.
14. He spends most of his time resembling.
15. Hopefully, the problem will be solved by then.

Assuming that first, we can teach the android not to make mistakes like those in sentences 3, 4, 6, 7, 8, 9, 10, 12, and 14, we must then decide whether we also want it to produce sentences like 1, 2, 5, 11, 13, and 15, because they are sentences that perfectly normal, competent speakers of English utter. Shall we make the android sound like a Bostonian, a Yorkshireman, an Australian, or a New Yorker? Within any of these geographical dialects, shall we make him sound like a lower-class speaker with little formal education, an educated middle-class speaker, or an upper-class speaker? All these social variables will influence the way the android should choose from among the words we make available to it, the way it pronounces them and puts together sentences with particular kinds of grammatical constructions.

PROBLEM 4. Would we also want to build into its language sex characteristics? That is, in addition to programming it to say things like *Us men . . .* or *You men . . . ,* would we want to distinguish its speech as male or female in any other way? If you were given a written transcription of a conversation between a man and a woman, do you think you could distinguish who was speaking to whom? What other variables would influence how it spoke?

In short, there are features of every language that inescapably identify a speaker in regard to his geographical origin; often his social class; and possibly even his sex, age, occupation, intelligence, personality, and so on. And if our android is to be a believable speaker, it will have to be consistent, for all these variables fall within relatively fixed boundaries. Though many speakers have the ability to switch from one dialect to another, we would not be seriously embarrassed if our android could not. There are a good many normal speakers who also cannot, who speak only one social dialect within one geographical dialect. But each speaker must speak in some social and geographical dialect, in some way that makes him sound like others of his social class and geographical origin.

1.2 Making Sense

Let us assume that we are able to program our android to speak consistently upper-middle-class educated sentences in a dialect spoken, say, around the Great Lakes. We also assume that we have taught it not merely to repeat sentences from a very large inventory of stored sentences, but to create new sentences never uttered before, a sentence such as this one, which none of you has ever read until this moment: *A small wombat is chewing on your kneecap.*

PROBLEM 5. To the next person you meet, utter in all apparent seriousness, *A small wombat is chewing on your kneecap.* Since we have no reason to assume that our android might not utter such a sentence at any given moment, what problem still remains in making it a convincing speaker of a human language?

Obviously, the android is still merely a sentence-producing device, unable to match sentences to appropriate topics in the shared physical or cognitive situation, present or potential. If it uttered *A small wombat is chewing on your kneecap* when one was not, if it were not a wombat but a camel, if it were not chewing on your kneecap but kissing your ear, we would know that the program was still flawed. And conversely, if a small wombat were in fact chewing on your kneecap and you said to the android, *A small wombat is chewing on my kneecap,* and it responded with *The population of Waco, Texas, is not as large as that of Calcutta,* we might wonder what was going on inside such a creature's head.

So our android must "know" from two points of view what it is to speak English. First, it must be able to construct grammatical (and plausibly ungrammatical) sentences in English. But it must also demonstrate its ability to utter and respond to sentences in a way that appropriately associates the sentences with a shared cognitive framework. The topic mutually referred to need not be concretely there in front of us. But a sentence must be pertinent to something we can potentially share. If the android begins talking about the population of Waco, Texas, it ought to have some reason that an audience can understand.

PROBLEM 6. A characteristic of human languages is that they are open, allowing their speakers to construct an indefinite number of new sentences never before uttered. The utterance of a sentence may also be displaced from its topic, allowing us to talk about referents that are not physically present. We can talk about China even if China is not here in the room. In what other ways can "things" that we may refer to be absent from our immediate perceptual experience? To what extent are animal languages open and displaceable?

1.3 Being Coherent

Let us assume that we have solved the problems mentioned so far: the android produces grammatical sentences that refer to the world in a seemingly rational way. Moreover, it can produce sentences never before uttered pertinent to a variety of topics that need not objectively exist in its immediate perceptual space. It can talk about the past, the future, about hopes and dreams; it can lie; it can fantasize about things that could never be: *I have a triangular circle etched in this vacuum.* It can even produce wildly ungrammatical sentences, but appropriately so: *It is ungrammatical to say "The man down which in the go with for."* It can at least seem to appreciate the poetry of:

anyone lived in a pretty how town
(with up so floating many bells down)

e. e. cummings

PROBLEM 7. There is another capacity which we would have to build into our android. I just wrote that sentence on an electric typewriter. I bought my first portable typewriter in New York. I don't like New York very much. *Much* has four letters in it. Mailmen deliver letters. The other day I wrote a letter to New York. I bought my first portable typewriter in New York. I don't like New York very much. *Much* has four letters in it. The other day I wrote . . .

Our android must now be able to do at least the following:

1. Pronounce the sounds of English to make English words (and to know which sounds are not English sounds).
2. Know a minimum number of words and pieces of words that those sounds constitute and know how to add the pieces to the words and combine the pieces to make new words.
3. String those words and pieces together into phrases, clauses, and sentences in ways that appear to be grammatically correct (in the special way we are using "correct").
4. Make its sentences appear to be relevant to something within the shared cognitive experience of the speaker and listener.
5. String sentences together into longer stretches that constitute not strings of randomly associated utterances but coherent discourse.

PROBLEM 8. We want to consider one more human linguistic capacity. What follows is a dialogue among the Three Stooges. One is a faulty android. Which one? How do you know?

Larry: Hi ya, Mo. Hi ya, Curly. How are ya?
Mo and Curly: Hi ya, Larry. What's new?
Larry: I gotta go see an optometrist.
Curly: You got problems with your feet?
Mo: (to Curly) You dope! An optometrist is a guy who always looks on the bright side of things.
Larry: No. It's my eyes. I gotta go see him about my eyes.
Curly: I didn't hear ya. About what?

Mo: He says it's his eyes that he's gotta go see the optometrist about, dummy.
Larry: No I didn't. I said I gotta go see him about my eyes.
Curly: Oh. What y'gotta see him about is your eyes.
Larry: Are you deaf? I said I gotta go see him about my eyes.
Mo: (poking Larry in the eye) You numbskull. That's what Curly said. Your eyes are what you gotta go see the optometrist about.
Larry: (punching Mo in the stomach) No! What I said was (pulling his nose) I gotta go see him about my eyes!
Curly: Oh! What you gotta do is go see him about your eyes!
Larry: (twisting his ears) You jerk! I said I gotta go see him about my eyes!

We must build into our android one more capacity. It must not only be able to organize sentences relating to a shared cognitive universe into a coherent discourse, but it must also be able to understand how the meaning of one sentence relates to the meaning of another. It must understand that some sentences mean either exactly or at least very much the same thing. It must also know that some sentences can imply other sentences:

A: George is still a bachelor!
B: You mean he never got married?

or contradict other sentences:

A: George got married.
B: No. He's still a bachelor.

PROBLEM 9. Why is it not a revelation of androidhood not to know that *gorse* and *furze* are synonymous, but it is tantamount to such a revelation if it does not know that *That he left is fortunate* and *It is fortunate that he left* are in some sense synonymous?

1.4 Linguistic Units

What we have been exploring here are merely the preliminaries to describing a language in a way that integrates two perspectives in answering the question, "What is it to be a speaker of a language?" Everything we know, from the universe to the quark, can be, must be described in terms of (1) its internal structure, and (2) its external relationships. A city has an internal structure of blocks, streets, and buildings. It is externally related to the land about it, to other cities, and so on. A person has an internal structure—bones, nerves, muscles, and organs—and is related externally to family, employment, and society at large. The number 4 has an internal structure and is related externally to all the other numbers.

Neither description alone can completely account for anything. In the same way, a language can be viewed as how, at a moment in its history, its sentences are constructed. Such a description would account for the phonological, grammatical, and lexical features of sentences—for their internal structure. This knowledge is, in some sense, controlled by a speaker of English. Were it not, he could not speak English. The knowledge need not be consciously available to him in the form of a complex grammatical explanation. Indeed, most of our linguistic knowledge is tacit. In some nonconscious sense we simply "know" the grammatical structure of English well enough to produce new grammatical sentences.

But a language must also be understood as the ways that sentences, the largest linguistic structures from an internal perspective, function as constitutive parts of a larger system of linguistic behavior—as parts of a larger social whole. (We should immediately point out that the sentence is not the smallest unit from an external perspective, unless we count as sentences *hmmmmm, Oh, ahhhh,* and *huh*. For that matter, in the larger context of conversations and other linguistic events, even silence can be a linguistic unit.)

This is analogous to studying the internal structure of an automobile engine and then shifting perspective to study how the engine functions within its larger system, how it participates in the system called *automobile*. For it is, after all, only to the degree that the engine fits into the larger structure that an engine has any function or significance. The internal structure of an engine is partly a consequence of what the structure must be if it is an internal combustion engine. But its *particular* internal structure is to a large degree determined by how that specific engine fits into a specific automobile. We can define many of the characteristics that an engine must have if it is to fit into a particular automobile. And we can deduce from a particular engine the nature of the automobile it is designed to fit.

So if sentences have internal structures of grammar, sound, and meaning, sentences and their structures also function in a variety of larger systems. They fit into sequences of sentences constituting a discourse. They relate to the outside world of matter and form and the inside world of the mind. They link speakers and audiences, intentions and consequences.

The problem is to integrate, even theoretically, these two perspectives. A good deal more is known about the internal structure of sentences than was known a decade ago. And in recent years, some indications of structure have been found in those larger units of discourse in which sentences function. But in the current state of the art in linguistics, the two perspectives have no simple or obvious fit. The way grammarians have been describing sentences for over two thousand years has not provided us with any deep insights into the way sentences function in those larger structures, the largest of which we shall call *speech events*. And the as yet little-understood nature of speech events has not persuaded linguists to abandon the way they have been describing the internal structure of sentences. This simply means that when we turn from one perspective to another, we require different theories of language to account for what we perceive to be the structure of a sentence.

Be that as it may, we shall attempt here to explore some of the ways in which these two perspectives must be joined before anyone—adult, child, or android—can be considered a speaker of a language. This requires a linguist to be at times as mundanely specific as pointing out how often lower-middle-class speakers in New York City do not pronounce *r*-sounds in words like *card, four,* and *shower* as they excitedly recount an incident when they thought their lives were threatened; at times the linguist must be so abstract as to speak of teleological immanence, a topic once the preserve of medieval theologians of an Aristotelian bias. But "knowing a language" means knowing how both to select, shape, and arrange parts in anticipation of a whole and its effect and to apprehend such a whole from its parts, an ability that ultimately depends on postulating, sometimes consciously, but usually unconsciously, the end toward which language is directed. Teleology, the study of aims and of ends, is a topic we cannot avoid.

1.5 The External Context

Returning to our android, we find that it has not forgotten how to produce novel grammatical sentences appropriate to a shared frame of reference. We have even found a way to make it string sentences together into a coherent discourse. (*Cautionary note:* That last sentence slides over what is unquestionably one of our most profoundly human capacities, a capacity so complex, so difficult to understand—much less describe—that our easy assumption of it is tantamount to admitting that at this point we are unable to describe it concisely. It is a much more astonishing ability than the "mere" competence to construct sentences.)

PROBLEM 10. The android still seems to have something not quite right about it. Here are two snatches of its conversation. What is wrong?

1. To a good friend of the android upon its meeting him in the elevator, "Hi, Bill. Nice day today, isn't it? Nice tie. New? Sorry to hear about you having the flu. How's the job? Let's get together for a drink sometime. Bye."
2. To the Pope as it assists him to his place in St. Peter's for Easter Mass before an audience of the assembled Princes of the Church, "Hi, Gino. Hot day today, huh? Nice phylactery you have there. Old? Sorry to hear about your hay fever. How's the job? Let's have lunch sometime soon. Bye."

The android seems to talk in the same way in all circumstances to everybody it meets: to men, women, and children; to presidents, popes, queens, bandits; at weddings, funerals, chance meetings, ceremonial and intimate occasions; in bedrooms, ballrooms, boardrooms, public toilets, on buses, and in church. Clearly we cannot expect our android to deceive people into thinking it is a perfectly ordinary creature. It does not yet have all the ordinary social linguistic competencies we expect of anyone who knows how to adapt the internal structure of English sentences to fit the context and intention of their use.

PROBLEM 11. Here are some greetings and leave-takings. How must the android be able to match them with one another? Of course, speakers can shift their levels of style from the beginning of a conversation to the end, but if the stylistic level remained the same throughout, could the android be allowed to pair any greeting with any leave-taking? What factors in the conversation and its context would influence which expressions it should choose? Under what circumstances would a speaker plausibly switch the style of his leave-taking? How would we have to program the android to make the switch?

Greetings	*Leave-takings*
hey	bye
hey there	bye bye
whatdyasay	be seein' ya
howdy	see you
hi	I'll see you later
hello	so long
greetings	goodbye
how do you do	farewell
all hail	adieu
praise be to the Lord	God be with you

PROBLEM 12. Here are some ways to address the same person. What linguistic items in the previous problem can they be matched with? *Mr. President, Mr. Jones, President Jones, Jones, William, Willie, Bill, Billy, your excellency, darling, tiger, daddy, buddy, bud, bub.*

If the android is to behave as human speakers of English do, then it must be able to identify the participants in any speech event it participates in, both absolutely and relatively. It must know not only who those participants are but what roles they are momentarily playing and how those roles relate to its own momentary role. It must recognize the social features of its situation, both absolutely and relatively. It must know not only the literal place it is speaking but also how that place is to be taken. One can conduct a church service from a barbecue pit. But if the android knows only that it is in a backyard and not that the setting is also a scene for a church service, it could speak in ways entirely inappropriate to the context. And the android must understand something about the topic being discussed both absolutely and relatively. Parts of the body, for instance, are spoken of in one way on the screen of X-rated movie houses, in another way with three-year-olds sitting on the potty, in another way yet in medical classrooms.

1.6 Intentions and Outcomes

All this is complicated by the fact that these three variables: participants, topics, and settings, interact with a more important variable, a variable that can override what we might take to be the objective restrictions or options inherent in the selection of particular participants, topics, and settings. That is the intention, the hoped-for outcome, on which the participants base their decisions and interpretations of selection, shaping, and arrangement of their discourse. A speaker may, if he wishes, deliberately violate customary rules of appropriate language. And it is important that we recognize his intentions, or at least assume that he has *some* intention, if we are to make sense of his part of the discourse.

Intention, of course, is prospective, and outcome is retrospective. Intention both anticipates and is simultaneous with the actual selection and arrangement of the components of the speech event as it is being created by a speaker. Outcome is the consequence, the effect of the speech event on an audience. Because intentions and outcomes are not identical but do constitute two species of the principle that organizes a discourse, it would be convenient if we had a single term we could use to refer to what they have in common. It is the principle by which we can, in studying the speech event not as participants in it but as analysts, explain its nature. It is a principle that we as analysts can deal with as if it were simultaneous with the speech event, informing it though not objectively or physically present in it. We shall call that principle the *telos* of the speech event. It is a Greek word for end or aim. Though it may be alluded to, it cannot be found in the discourse, for it has no material existence. We shall use it as a hypothetical construct that will allow us to explain why any particular speech event or part of it assumes its particular form.

The ability to recognize how the telos operates allows us to do three things.

First, in the form of intention, it allows a speaker (or writer) to organize sounds into words, words into phrases, phrases into clauses, clauses into sentences, and sentences into discourses. This operation does not proceed sequentially, as that sentence suggests, but simultaneously, on all levels at the same time. As we utter a word we are simultaneously constructing the phrase it is in, the clause it is in, its sentence, and its discourse. The telos of the work—in the form of intention—guides us in that creation.

In actual speech events, we might be uncertain about what outcome we intend. We might change intentions from moment to moment, or even have conflicting intentions. We might be unaware of or even uncertain about our own intentions. But no complex human event is serially ordered without some sense of potential ending. We arrange the components of every identifiable whole action in anticipation of the whole shape. Starting an utterance, we do not say *the* without knowing that a noun is going to follow; that following the noun there likely will be a verb; and that if there had been an *although* before the *the,* then following the noun and verb there would be another noun and verb: *Although the man left, I stayed.* A sense of ultimate closure infuses every sentence, even if we aren't absolutely sure how a sentence should end. The same is true for a whole speech event.

PROBLEM 13. A way to understand the consequences of not having an organizing, anticipatory intention in creating sentences is to play a parlor game that goes like this: At the top of a piece of paper, write the first word of a sentence. Give it to the next person, who writes the second word. Before he hands it to a third person, he folds over the paper so the first word cannot be seen. The third person adds a third word on the basis of what could follow the second word. He folds the paper again, leaving only his word, the third word, and passes it to a fourth person, who adds a word that might follow the third word, and so on. The game can be played at varying levels of approximation. It could be played by each player writing two words, three words, and so on. The more words, the more sense the sentence will make. The game can also be played with whole sentences to create a narrative or a conversation.

Second, in the form of an inferred outcome, the telos allows us to interpret a speech event as we experience it. We guess at a speaker's intention and may adapt our part of the event to match it or frustrate it. We might be uncertain, mistaken, or even unaware of how a speaker is organizing a speech event as we participate in it with him. But we cannot escape assuming, usually unknowingly, that everything from a greeting to a stretch of continuous discourse hundreds of pages long, makes "sense," is intended to make "sense," and is guiding us toward one or more consequences.

PROBLEM 14. (a) You are standing by a door in a cold room. Someone in authority shivers, looks at you, then the door, and says gruffly, *The door is open.* How do you know what he wants? (b) You are walking down a strange street in a blizzard, when someone wearing nothing but a hockey goalie's mask cartwheels out of an alley and chants *The door is open* five times and cartwheels back into the alley. How do you know what he wants? What is the difference between the two events? What problem are we going to have with our android's understanding these events?

Third, in the form of an understanding of the complete discourse, the telos of a speech event allows us to explain, after the fact, why the various elements of the discourse (which we need not have participated in) take the form and order that constitute that particular discourse. We might be mistaken or uncertain when we postulate that organizing principle. But we cannot escape making such an assumption if we are to make sense of, to explain the details of a discourse. In this last case, the analyst has the advantage of having the whole discourse before him simultaneously to study. In the first two cases, the speaker/hearer can only anticipate the whole discourse. Here, we approach the discourse having it whole and complete before us, completely understood.

So if our android is going to make people believe it is a real person, we will have to build into it the ability to perceive intentions and to interpret speech events in terms of those intentions. We will also have to figure out a way to make it behave as if it had intentions of its own, because others will respond to it as if it did.

We have come a long way from packing the android's memory circuits with all the sentences written and uttered since 1850. If we were to succeed in building into it all the abilities that we've described here, we could be reasonably pleased with ourselves. For we would have created, for all intents and purposes, not an android but something that seemed to have a will and a mind of its own—something that qualified for personhood.

2. Speech Events

One of the first problems in any investigation is to identify the boundaries of what you want to investigate. Those boundaries might change as you get deeper into your subject. And you might even have no idea where the boundaries are when you begin. But at some point you have to decide that what you are investigating has an identifiable outer shape to it—perhaps many identifiable outer shapes. Whether we are looking at cells, atoms, neighborhoods, historical events, or ideas—they all have shapes.

The outer shapes or boundaries of any phenomenon are strongly defined by the inner network of functional relationships among its internal parts. A human body is a coherent whole because its internal parts relate more closely to one another than they do to anything outside them. The inner workings of a neighborhood define its outer boundaries more sharply than arbitrary streets or sidewalks. Even events are perceived as wholes because the smaller events that make them up seem to relate more closely to one another than to events before or after the perceived whole.

The same questions confront those who study language. Each of us who has studied a foreign language can recall that initial panic that we would never be able to distinguish individual words in what sounded like a seamless stream of unintelligible speech. We know that the flow of language is made up of sentences and that the sentences are made up of phrases and clauses, the phrases and clauses of words, the words of syllables, and the syllables of individual sounds. But given an unbroken stream of speech, those who do not already understand it would be hard put to divide it into meaningful segments, segments whose internal coherence is greater than their connection to other segments around it.

PROBLEM 15. Suppose you are a Martian linguist trying to understand English. It so happens that you have only written texts which forsome strangereasonhavenospacesbetweenwordshowwouldyougoabo-uttryingtodividethestreamoflettersintodiscretewords?howwou-ldyoubeabletodeterminethatinthesentencesyouarenowreadingt-hatthesequencessofararecorrectbutthatthissequenceendsstrangelyly? How would the same problem be solved in regard to sentence boundaries paragraph boundaries section boundaries act and scene boundaries in plays chapter boundaries in books and multivolume boundaries in multivolume works?

But just as every unit has an internal structure, it is also part of a larger system that comprises it. A human body is part of a system of family, work, and neighborhood around it; a cell is part of a system of organs; and an idea is part of a system of thought or part of a larger individual thought. Nothing, except the universe, perhaps, lacks relationships to larger, comprising structures.

In the same way, sentences are parts of larger events. In some cases, that larger event might comprise just a single sentence. A "greeting" may be just "How are you?" or even "Hi." Other larger events might comprise hundreds of sentences in a written report or a long conversation. The largest speech events, of course, also comprise smaller parts, just as the unit we call a sentence is made up of the smaller units we call phrases, clauses, and words.

Unfortunately, while we have a well-developed vocabulary for describing the parts of words and the parts of sentences, we have no similarly well-developed vocabulary to name either whole speech events or their parts. We have some general names for the most common types of speech events: greeting, conversation, marriage ceremony, prayer, joke, riddle, put-on, interview, lecture, cheer, speaking in tongues, invocation, staff meeting, argument, bedtime story, introduction, thank-you note, invitation, RSVP, oath-taking, confession, eulogy, sermon, summons, singing the national anthem, quiz program, commercial, poetry reading, inaugural address, state of the union message, press conference, leave-taking, baptism, asking directions, ordering a meal in a restaurant, job interview, and doctor's consultation. Each of these has a greater internal coherence than external coherence. Each has a relatively well-defined beginning, middle, and end, constituting a discrete whole. Each depends on language.

The most institutionalized and ceremonial speech events have well-defined parts. Each section of traditional Protestant church services has a name: sermon, benediction, offering, doxology, hymn, prayer, etc. Technical articles published in scientific journals have formal parts: title, abstract, introduction, procedure, results, discussion, summary, and references.

But less institutionalized, though no less organized, speech events like conversations are less clearly understood. Between greetings and leave-takings, there are *turns,* or stretches of speech that each participant alternately offers the other. There are interrupters like *oh, excuse me, now just a minute, wait a minute,* and so on. There are invitations for the other to speak such as *What do you think?* There are requests for confirmation: *Right? OK? You know?* But beyond that, the structure of conversation is only dimly understood.

One of the main tasks of contemporary research into these matters, into what has come to be known as the ethnography of speaking or writing, is to identify and analyze these speech events, these social moments that are accomplished by verbal interaction and that are shaped into coherent wholes by some intention, by the telos of the event. It is the degree to which we understand smaller events relating to some governing intention that we synthesize the smaller speech acts into the unity of a speech event.

2.1 The Structure of Speech Events

In order to think clearly about speech events and about the ways the texture of language reflects them, we have to understand how their parts function. The major components of every speech event include: (1) the telos of the event; (2) the participants that create it, its setting, and its subject matter; and (3) the particular forms of language and rhetorical structure that manifest the event in words, sentences, paragraphs, etc.

Before we discuss these components in detail, though, we have to recall that all this is embedded in cultural contexts that define and limit these components in different, often entirely idiosyncratic, ways. It is not a given of human verbal intercourse that we have to be reticent in a religious setting or noisy at a sports event. Different cultures require different kinds of verbal behavior in the presence of death, sex, strangers, superiors, combat, eating, etc. Different cultures even have different attitudes toward the use of language in general. Some value the extensive and elaborate use of language; for others, the less speech the better.

PROBLEM 16. Here are pairs of words that we use to describe the use of language in English. After each of those pairs are some other words that we stereotypically associate with one or the other of the first words. What do our stereotypical associations suggest about our particular values and language use?

a.	talkative, silent:	strong, weak girl, boy	c.	terse, verbose:	reliable, flighty mature, immature
b.	taciturn, voluble:	silly, wise husband, wife	d.	loquacious, succint:	intelligent, foolish aunt, uncle

Are there any words with positive associations that refer to the expansive use of language? Are there any words with negative associations that refer to the reserved use of language? What are the stereotypical linguistic associations we make with these ethnic groups? American Indians, Indian Indians, Irish, Swedish, Jewish, Italian, New Englanders, Southerners. With these roles? Uncle, aunt, cowboy, con man, football coach, taxi driver, waitress, waiter, barber.

We can schematically represent the parts of a speech event and how they theoretically relate to one another with a diagram such as shown in Figure 2.1. The bold arrows in Figure 2.1 both point in the same direction, originating in the telos of the event and ending in the manifestation, because the diagram is a model that represents the components in an idealized, logical hierarchy of explanatory importance. The arrows go from the most global feature, the telos of the event, to the most detailed and local. This is a symbolic representation of the fact that, for example, the global intention to find out how you are feeling ordinarily calls for one kind of role rather than another: I become a questioner rather than a stater; you become an answerer rather than a listener. The intention to find out something ordinarily calls for one kind of sentence structure rather than another: *How are you feeling?* rather than *You are feeling how?* And that question calls for a falling rather than a rising intonation:

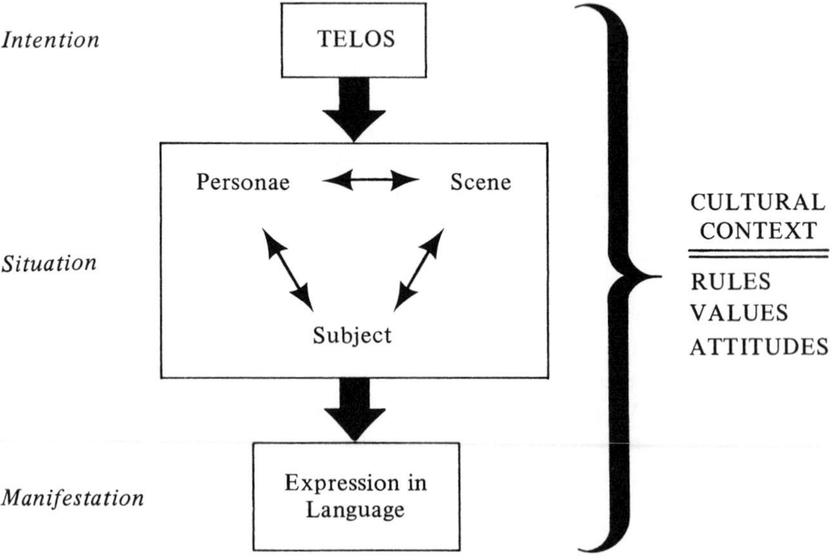

Figure 2.1. ***A Speech Event.***

How are you fee ling? not: How are you fee ling?

The tune is a consequence of the sentence structure. The sentence structure is a consequence of the question. The question is a consequence of an intention to find out how you are.

Now, this is *not* necessarily how we understand real speech events as we participate in them. The diagram is an idealized representation of the event. In real life, we use all sorts of simultaneous cues to guess what the intention of a speech event might be: the look on a speaker's face, the surroundings, or even the time of day. A half-understood grunt from a husband or wife awakening at 6:30 AM is (or may be) understood as a friendly greeting; the objectively same grunt at the dinner table might be interpreted quite differently. We don't work directly backwards from the most physical aspects of the manifestation. We don't first process the phonology, then the syntax, then the words, etc. We process at all levels simultaneously, using all the information available to us, including probabilistic guesses as to what kind of information is ordinarily transmitted in a given context. If we are sitting in a restaurant and someone next to us says something, we are likely to interpret what we hear with reference to what we think we are likely to hear in such contexts. If someone asks us, *Is that salt?* we are more likely to take the sentence as manifesting the speaker's intention to ask us to pass the salt than as the act of a foreign student practicing questions in English. The cultural context delimits the kinds of intentions that are possible, and we use those contexts to interpret the sentence. If the person sitting next to us pointed to the white stuff in the little glass bottle and asked *Is that silt?* we would, hearing *salt,* unhesitatingly answer yes, and probably do something about it.

And in the same way, this model does not perfectly represent how we create speech events. Sometimes we begin with intentions independently of everything else and proceed to make choices down the line. More often the presence of another person, a particular setting, etc., leads to an intention. Good writers often reject one sentence structure and choose another because the rhythm of a sentence isn't quite right. And perhaps the rhythm suggests an idea, which may change the intention. Actual speech behavior is not as neatly organized as that idealized model would suggest.

The model represents not the way speech events come into existence or how they are literally decoded by participants. It is intended to represent a logical hierarchy of relationships, an idealized event understood as a whole, complete entity—a stretch of internally coherent language that reflects some organizing principle; and that we, with the benefit of having analyzed the whole discourse, are able to explain.

There are three hierarchical levels to account for in explaining a speech event, each succeeding one being strongly determined by the preceding, all simultaneously infused by the first. We have already discussed the first and most important level—the level of intention and outcome.

2.2 Personae, Scenes, and Subjects

At the second level of analysis are the three necessary situational components of every speech event: personae, scenes, and subjects. Personae are the persons transformed into the roles that they play to one another; the scene is the conventionalized time and place the event occupies; and the subject is the express ideational, referential content of the sentences, the meanings being transmitted. There can be no speech event without someone to create it, without some place and time where it can be created, and without some reference. But the importance of the personae in determining the form and structure of the event is greater than the importance of the scene and subject because the relationships among the personae can vary so greatly.

2.2.1 Participants and Personae

To emphasize the dramatistic nature of these relationships, we have called the participants in the speech event personae rather than persons or participants. Personae suggests more clearly the distinction between the real people participating in a speech event and the roles that each person must play. At one moment in a conversation, I might be primarily friend-of-other-person; at another moment, employee-of-other-person; at another moment, brother-in-law-of-other-person. The role relationships, the relative personae that the participants must assume, are defined by the telos of the event, by the intention and understood expected outcome shared by speaker and listener; and each influences how we use language to one another.

But we have to keep in mind that speakers are also people who bring to their temporary roles a range of linguistic variables that are determined by their geographical, ethnic, and social backgrounds. These are fixed characteristics, or a fixed range of variable characteristics that a speaker calls on when he adopts the different personae of different speech events.

We all acquire our language in a particular place. Many believe that everyone but them speaks in a dialect. In fact, every form of spoken English bears the traces of some local geographic area, particularly in pronunciation. In the United States, Northerners from around the Great Lakes are conscious of the different vowel sounds used by Eastern New Englanders, speakers from the Carolinas, Georgia, and vice versa. From region to region, the vocabulary of casual speech also differs. What is called a dragonfly by many speakers in the northern parts of the country is a darning needle in parts of New York State, a snake feeder in parts of Pennsylvania and West Virginia, a snake doctor in eastern Virginia, and a mosquito hawk in the Eastern Carolinas. And from region to region there are in casual speech a few grammatical differences: North of a wavy line running through New Jersey, Pennsylvania, Ohio, Indiana, and Illinois, one is likely to hear *He hadn't oughtta do that;* south of that line, *He oughtn't to do that.*

For the most part, these differences occur only in unselfconscious spoken English and occasionally in casual writing. In even moderately careful writing, regionalisms tend to disappear in favor of more generally used forms. Rarely if ever found in writing for public consumption, regardless of the participant's geographical origins, are forms such as *ett* for *ate, seed* or *seen* for *saw,* or *div* or *duv* for *dived.*

A more consequential sort of linguistic variation but one whose range of varieties is still relatively fixed in the behavior of the individual is that which reflects social and ethnic classes. Every community of any size and complexity stratifies itself by class according to such features as wealth, education, occupation, family background, ethnic origin, race, religion, inherited social position, and so on. And while it oversimplifies matters to partition the members of a society into neat categories such as lower class, working class, lower-middle class, and so on, such categories often do serve as useful groupings to study how people from different backgrounds speak. The fact that linguistic differences roughly parallel these classifications suggests that social groupings based on wealth, education, and so on is more than a capricious partition.

The range of words available to various social classes varies at the extremes of very local words at the one end and learned words at the other, though not as greatly nor with the significant consequences that some would have us believe. The great mass of the most common words in the language, the words that constitute over 80 percent of the words we use, are shared by all classes. As a consequence of their education, most upper-middle-class speakers of English have in their productive vocabulary a few more learned words than lower-class speakers and can recognize more when they read or hear them. But depending on the age and background of a lower-class speaker, he may have more local words in his active vocabulary than does an educated upper-middle-class speaker. As a speaker adopts different personae for different intentions, he may choose among the words. But the *range* of words is determined by his experience as a person.

Pronunciation and syntax also differ among social classes of the same geographical dialect. In New York City, for example, upper-middle-class speakers regularly pronounce [r] more often in words like *bar, hear, card,* and so on than lower-class and working-class speakers. They also substitute [t] and [d] for the initial sounds in words such as *thing* and *this* less often, use something close to an [e] sound (as in *beg*) for the vowel in words like *bad, hag,* and *sad* less often. In Detroit, upper-middle-class speakers regularly pronounce each consonant in consonant clusters at the ends of words such as *desk, twist, round,* and *build* more often than speakers from social classes below them. In Norwich, England, each successively lower class drops initial [h] in words such as *hat* and *house* more frequently, pronounces the full -ing [iŋ] sound at the end of a word such as *running* less frequently, and more often substitutes something called a glottal stop for medial [t] in words such as *butter, latter,* and *letter.*

The same kinds of variables appear in syntactic patterns used by different social classes. In Detroit again, upper-middle-class speakers as a group tend to use nonstandard negative forms such as *I can't eat nothin'* almost not at all; lower-middle-class speakers use them about one in every ten cases where a nonstandard form is possible; the upper half of the working class about four times in every ten opportunities; and the lower half of the working class about seven times in every ten opportunities. Other grammatical features such as subject-verb agreement and the lack of a genitive marker in phrases such as *the man('s) book,* follow similar distributional patterns.

PROBLEM 17. To this point, we have been programming our android in terms of a simple dichotomy: grammatical vs. ungrammatical, acceptable vs. unacceptable. By grammatical, recall, we mean those linguistic patterns that one ordinarily hears from speakers of a particular group. For most upper-middle-class speakers in Detroit, *I ain't got no money* would be entirely ungrammatical since they would never say it. But if we use *grammatical* to mean only what is habitually said and not what educated upper-middle-class speakers would prefer to hear, then for lower-class speakers in Detroit, *I ain't got no money* is entirely grammatical. Yet so is *I don't have any money* because they say that too. The distribution of forms we have been describing here introduces a quite new problem in programming our android. What new concept do we have to introduce into its program if our android is to sound like a member of the Detroit working class, one who says both *I ain't got no money* and *I don't have any money?* How do we bring together the idea of a fixed range of linguistic variables and the matter of personae? Do the double negatives by that worker reflect the persona he might at any moment adopt, do you think?

In order to create such variables in the speech of our android, then, we have to introduce into the program a statistical routine that will require the android to use certain linguistic features at frequencies that statistically correspond to the behavior of the speakers it is supposed to simulate. But even though we express those features as statistical variables, their boundaries are fixed insofar as they must identify the android as a member of a particular social class. Their selection depends on how we understand the particular persona adopted in a particular speech event.

For example, all of us are able to utter the words *Dr. Smith* and *Joe* as forms of address for the same person. If your neighbor were *Dr. Joe Smith* and you counted the different ways in which you addressed him, you might discover that you called him Joe 100 percent of the time. But you might also discover that one of his patients at the hospital called him Dr. Smith 100 percent of the time and that one of his colleagues called him Joe 40 percent and Dr. Smith 60 percent of the time.

PROBLEM 18. If we were programming our android to simulate the speech of the medical colleague, what would be wrong with simply programming it to utter *Joe* the first four out of every ten times it saw your neighbor and *Dr. Smith* the next six times? What variables in the speech event relate to the choice between the two?

Every speaker of a language learns to select certain variables from his repertoire of fixed variables not randomly but appropriately to his perceived role, his assumed persona in the speech event he is a part of—to his audience, to his context, and to his intention. Our changing roles require us to adjust our language to suit our understanding of the role of our listener and how he relates to us. One obvious way is by what we call a person: *Dr. Smith* or *Joe,* depending on whether we are speaking to him alone or in the company of his colleagues on a public occasion.

Other languages have much more elaborate systems of deference and address that reflect social relationships and class structure. In addition to formal and informal names, Korean indicates the relationship between speaker and listener with six different verb endings, ranging from intimate through familiar, plain, polite, and deferential, to the most formal relationship, authoritative. Since every Korean verb form used to address a person must have one of these six endings, no Korean speaker can escape varying his language to fit his audience.

At one time, English had a slightly more elaborate system than it does now, incorporating name and title as in modern English, but also including a pair of opposing pronouns, *you* and *thou,* that paralleled the *tu/vous, du/Sie, tú/usted* in French, German, and Spanish. *You* was used to show respect by a speaker from a relatively lower social class or level of authority to a relatively higher addressee, a child to his father, for example; generally among upper-class speakers to one another; and, in situations where *thou* would otherwise have been expected, to communicate a haughty distance. *Thou* was used generally between lower-class speakers; to express intimacy between equals; to express authority or the higher social level of a speaker to a socially lower addressee; to children, animals, the feeble-minded, the dead, and more often than not, to wives, who were expected to return *you* to the husband. When used in place of an expected *you,* it also expressed insulting contempt.

PROBLEM 19. Shakespeare provides some good examples of the distinction between *you* and *thou.* Here are some condensed passages from the last scenes of *Henry IV, Part 1.* Take any of the characters, assume it is our android, and explain what would have to have been programmed into it to make it behave as it does in regard to its use of *you* and *thou,* names and titles.

From Act V, scene iii. *Douglas, a rebel, is hunting for King Henry IV on the battlefield. Blunt, disguised as Henry to mislead the enemy, meets Douglas, who thinks he is Henry:*

Blunt: What is thy name, that in battle thus/Thou crossest me? . . .
Douglas: . . . I do haunt thee in the battle thus/Because some tell me that thou art a king . . . The Lord of Stafford dear to-day hath bought/Thy likeness, for instead of thee, King Harry,/This sword hath ended him. So shall it thee . . .

Scene iv. *The King and Prince Hal, his son, meet.*

King: I prithee, Harry, withdraw thyself; thou bleedest too much . . .
Prince: I do beseech your majesty make up,/Lest your retirement do amaze your friends.

In this next passage from scene v, the Prince meets Hotspur, leader of the rebels.

Hotspur: If I mistake not, thou art Harry Monmouth.
Prince: Thou speak'st as if I would deny my name.

Hotspur: My name is Harry Percy.
Prince: . . . I am the Prince of Wales, and think not, Percy,/To share with me in glory any more.
Hotspur: . . . Harry . . . the hour is come/To end the one of us; and would to God/Thy name in arms were now as great as mine!

They fight and the Prince kills Hotspur

Prince: . . . brave Percy. Fare thee well, great heart;/ . . . Adieu, and take thy praise with thee to heaven.

Obviously, every speaker with an intention that can be realized only by flouting the conventions for the use of *you* and *thou* can do so. Douglas, thinking Blunt is King Henry, violates both the rule calling for the respectful *you* from subject to king and the rule calling for the proper form of the first name with the title *King: . . . for instead of thee, King Harry . . .* The disrespectful *thee* is appropriate to an insulting challenge. So is the diminutive *Harry* instead of the more respectful *Henry*. Contrast this with the way the Prince uses *you* to his father. The important point here is that language varies according to the social variables in the role relationships of the speech event—role relationships adopted to fit the telos of a challenge, an insult, requests, meetings, and farewells.

PROBLEM 20. Identifying the social relationships that determine levels of linguistic formality is extremely complex. Obviously, one person can assume different roles: Joe Smith can be Doctor Smith or Uncle Joe. In some few cases the role and the person become almost indistinguishable: The Pope drops the use of his surname and adopts a name out of history to become Pope John or Pope Paul. The President of the United States remains Mr. President even in those situations where one in the same relative position of power in a corporation would receive a first name. We must distinguish those enduring or semipermanent characteristics of speech that characterize his geographical and social origins, his relatively longer enduring roles, and the momentary and transitory roles. At the time of writing the President is from upper-middle-class Georgian life; he is also the President, an enduring role; but he can simultaneously be in the transitory role of a person-telling-a-joke or a friend-in-conversation. And all this can be further complicated by his being a male speaking to a male or a female, much younger or older, and so on. Each role affects every other, synthesizing into a very complex role.

Here are some enduring and transitory roles. How would the way you spoke to someone playing these dual roles be influenced by those role combinations? *Enduring roles:* your-instructor-in-this-class, your-closest-relative, the-person-you-see-most-often-in-a-commercial-establishment (waiter, clerk, gas station attendant, etc.), Elton John, O.J. Simpson, John Wayne, the Pope, the President. (Obviously, even these enduring roles can be combined.) *Transitory roles:* seatmate-on-a-bus, person-whom-you-ask-for-directions, your-hold-up-victim, joke-teller, person-you-apologize-to-for-spilling-food-on, person-you-thank-for-introducing-you-to-very-large-audience-of-adults, person-you-bump-into-in-public-washroom.

PROBLEM 21. We have been proceeding as if there were a simple pair—a person and a role—catalyzed into a persona by a telos, and that each persona in a speech event is such a pair alternately speaking and listening, or just speaking or listening. But the situations can often be much more complex than this. Who are the speakers and audiences in the following speech events?

1. The press secretary to the President is reading an announcement to assembled reporters live on national television.
2. A minister on Sunday morning before a packed church begins: *Dear Lord, you know that all of us are great sinners.*
3. An actor on TV speaks to himself: *To be or not to be, that is the question.*
4. A parent reads from the Bible to a child: *Honor thy father and mother: that the days may be long upon the land which the Lord thy God giveth thee.*
5. A panelist on a stage in front of a packed auditorium answers a question put to him by another panelist. The panelists are both politicians running for office.
6. Someone in a fundamentalist revival meeting suddenly begins "speaking in tongues."

In many cultures, a dramatic way to signal social relationships between speakers is for a speaker to switch linguistic codes entirely, to shift to the other speaker's dialect, or even his language. Or in an ostentatious way, not to switch to his dialect, or even to switch away from it. In Paraguay, for example, more than half the population speaks both Spanish and a native Indian language, Guarani. When a bilingual Paraguayan wishes to signal a formal role relationship with another speaker because of that speaker's responsible social position (schoolteacher, government official, etc.), he speaks in the official language, Spanish, the language of national affairs. But when he wishes to be intimate, he speaks the native language, Guarani. Speakers choose on the basis of how their roles relate to the roles of their audience. A situation a bit like that may be developing in some of our larger cities, where Spanish is becoming more and more a second language, with bilingual Spanish-English speakers able to switch languages, depending on the perceived role of whom they are addressing. If a few generations from now, many parts of our country become as thoroughly bilingual as, say, Miami, Florida, it is not impossible that many speakers of Spanish descent would come to behave linguistically as speakers in Paraguay do, with Spanish the equivalent of Guarani, and English the equivalent of Spanish.

A somewhat analogous problem is that of standard English and various minority dialects. A current debate in national educational circles is whether or not it is psychologically sound, morally defensible, or for that matter even politically possible to teach speakers of nonstandard dialects of English to speak a standard English dialect. An argument in its favor is that when speakers of a minority dialect have to deal with speakers of standard English in relatively formal or official contexts, they can switch from their familiar nonstandard dialect to standard English and thereby not be penalized for their socially unacceptable English—socially unacceptable to standard speakers, that is.

2.2.2 Setting and Scene

By setting, we mean the physical setting, the literal place and time of a speech event. By scene, we mean what the conventionalized understanding turns a setting into, into the scene where the event appropriately occurs, a distinction that parallels that between person and persona. The setting of the altar of St. Peter's Basilica in Rome on Easter Sunday would be the unlikely scene for a commercial and a very logical scene for a mass. Similarly, a most serious and solemn ritual could be conducted in the setting of a barnyard transformed into a scene for a religious service. What is important is the intention governing the moment, the understood shaping telos that transforms a physical setting, place, and time into an appropriate scene.

PROBLEM 22. Some scenes are more likely to be called into existence in some settings than in others. Below are listed several settings and several scenes. How would the formality or informality of speech be determined by their intersection?

Settings: football stadium, classroom, street corner, local bus, cross-country bus, public toilet, office, bedroom, lunch counter, mountain top, church, stable, hospital room, funeral parlor, movie theater. *Scenes:* the scenes for public prayer, interview, greeting, joke, academic lecture, marriage ceremony, debate, community sing-along, graduation, casual conversation, challenge to a duel, request for directions.

PROBLEM 23. To understand how complicated the selection of appropriate language can be, correlate setting/scene combinations with person/persona combinations. What must the android be taught in order to do this, to select the appropriate language in such situations? What would it have to "know" for example, in order to be an upper-class Bostonian in the role of greeting a colleague in church? at a football game?

Just as different relationships among participants require different dialects, sometimes even languages, so can different settings and scenes. In Paraguay, again, most bilinguals will choose to speak Guarani in the countryside but in the city will choose Guarani or Spanish on the basis of the perceived social relationship and intention shared by the speakers. In Israel, one is more likely to hear Hebrew in a public scene and a native language in private than vice versa.

2.2.3 Subject and Topic

The last component of the triad is the subject, and here again, we can, though much less clearly, occasionally distinguish the immediate topic from the real subject. An invitation for a date to come up to a woman's apartment for a cup of coffee might be just that, or it might be an invitation to spend the night. A political speech about the evils of socialism might really be about preventing the spread of public housing into the suburbs.

Some subjects, of course, tend to be discussed in a limited range of styles, though the particular decisions in regard to style involve the interaction of person/persona, setting/scene, and topic/subject. A discussion in a bar between close friends about sex with the intention of amusing one another will call for a style quite different from a discussion of the same subject with a different intention in a priest's office. Other subjects are less open to stylistic variation. For most people talking about the death of a loved one demands a more careful style.

In American English, William Labov, a sociolinguist who interviewed New Yorkers in their homes to gather data on social variation in language, found that his informants tended to speak in a more casual style when they spoke of their childhood games or moments when they thought their lives were in danger. In a study of how New England children use *-ing* or *-in'* at the end of progressive verbs, J. L. Fischer found one child to give the participial endings on words like *criticizing, correcting, reading, visiting,* and *interesting* as *-ing,* while for verbs like *punch, flub, swim, chew,* and *hit,* he gave it as *-in'*.

PROBLEM 24. Why might *correcting* be pronounced with [ŋ] and *swimmin'* with [n]?

In those same societies whose speakers switch dialects and languages according to the participants and different settings, those same speakers also switch codes for different topics. In Paraguay, if a discussion in a nonrural area occurs in an informal atmosphere between intimate friends, a nonserious topic will call for Guarani; a serious topic will elicit the first language the participants learned, whether it be Spanish or Guarani. In Norway, depending on a variety of other considerations, those who speak two particular Norwegian dialects will discuss personal and homely topics in one, official and formal topics in the other.

PROBLEM 25. Modern English reflects an earlier situation not unlike many of those bilingual situations we have been describing. After the Norman Conquest in 1066, Anglo-Saxon England was entirely dominated by French-speaking Normans. From the twelfth through the fourteenth centuries, the law, religion, government, entertainment, culture, and so on were discussed and written about largely in French (though most of the earliest writing was done in Latin), at least among those who were—or aspired to be—closer to the Norman upper classes than the Anglo-Saxon lower classes. In the following list of word pairs, the first is native English, the language of the conquered, and the second is French, the language of the conquerors. Can you speculate why these pairs exist?

calf	*veal*	*swine*	*pork/bacon*
cow	*beef*	*deer*	*venison*
boar	*brawn* (the meat of the boar)	*sheep*	*mutton*

PROBLEM 26. Here is another problem along the same lines. Compare these occupations.

From Old English words	From borrowed French words
farmer	*tailor*
woodsman	*vintner*
fisherman	*butcher*
shepherd	*physician*
hunter	*barber*
skinner	*attorney*
miller	*haberdasher*
baker	*merchant*
cook	*butler*
maid	*servant*

Why the difference in origins?

PROBLEM 27. List twenty-five parts of the body. Look up the etymologies. Why are some native Anglo-Saxon and other borrowed from Latin and French? Why are there two words for some parts?

womb	*uterus*
wind pipe	*pharynx*
guts	*intestines*

One particularly striking way in which subject interacts with personae and scene in regard to the choice of words is called *euphemism,* from Greek, meaning to speak well. A euphemism is a term we use to refer to something whose more common name evokes too many offensive associations among the personae in a particular setting: *puke, shit, cancer, spit, pus, snot,* and so on. Compare *regurgitate, feces, growth, expectorate, matter,* and *nasal mucous.*

In English, we can create euphemisms in five ways. First, we can borrow a word from Latin, French, or Greek, a word whose formal, learned associations will to some degree mask the offensive associations of the thing the word refers to.

PROBLEM 28. Use your dictionary to discover what words we have borrowed from Greek, Latin, or French so that we do not have to use the following words when we feel they must be avoided: *sweat, pee, die, false teeth, kill, belly, bad breath, screw.*

Second, we can use a general rather than a specific word (which is itself often a borrowed word). *Pus* is a kind of matter, *rape* is a kind of assault, *tuberculosis* is a kind of condition, *dying* is a kind of expiring. But rather than say *pus, rape, tuberculosis,* and *dying,* we prefer those more general terms, *matter, assault, condition, expiring,* terms that do not precisely identify the kind of assault, the kind of matter, the kind of condition, the kind of expiration. We can add to the general term a modifier to create a phrase that more precisely specifies the referent. Gonorrhea is a kind of *disease* which we can identify more exactly as *social disease* (like measles, the flu, and other diseases we contract from others, if somewhat more distantly); feces is *waste* which we can identify more exactly as *human waste* (like heat, sweat, dandruff, and exhaled carbon dioxide); rape is a kind of *assault* which we can identify more exactly as *criminal assault* (like hitting someone on the head with a hammer or pushing him under a subway train). In order to precisely identify these concepts, we would have to add a third modifier: *venereal social disease, solid human waste, sexual criminal assault.*

This process can analyze a concept into its semantic components and then name the components rather than the concept as a whole. If *father,* for example, were a dirty word, we could analyze the concept into its semantic parts: the meaning of *father* includes the fact that the referent must be male and must be a parent. *Male parent* names those two components with two borrowed words. If *parent* were a dirty word as well, we could analyze it into its semantic components: a parent is in the immediate ascending generation, in direct lineal relationship with the offspring. This would produce the elaborate euphemistic phrase for *father: male relative of immediate ascending generation in direct lineal relationship with offspring.*

PROBLEM 29. Make up euphemisms in the way just described for these words: *politician, war, prison, poor, criminal, debt, work, study, marriage, divorce, children.*

A third kind of euphemism is the use of the name of something contiguously related to another in order to refer to that other. We can talk about *the crown* and mean the king, about *hands* and mean the crew of a ship, *heads* and mean the whole herd of cattle. Going to the bathroom precedes urination, but the action of going to the place, *go to the bathroom,* comes to name the following action, the action performed in the place. Sleeping with someone presumably most often occurs after sexual intercourse, but the action of sleeping comes to name the preceding action, the act of sexual intercourse. A memorial is something that elicits a memory. A tombstone or grave marker or gravestone causes a memory. Since the associations with *tombstone* are not pleasant, a consequence of a tombstone, to memorialize, provides the name for that stone: *a memorial.*

PROBLEM 30. Make up euphemisms in the way just described for these concepts: *undertaker, prostitute, toilet, false teeth, menstruation, constipation, die.*

A fourth less frequent kind of euphemism is metaphor, the use of a word naming something somewhat like the thing whose "real" name is being avoided. A pimple is called a *blossom* because it is little and red. A tomb is a *resting place* because the individual inside is lying in it with his eyes closed. A navel looks a little bit like a button, so it becomes a *belly button.* Most of our current obscenities and a good deal of our slang is based on metaphor.

A fifth kind of euphemism is phonetic modification. We use initial letters to name the referent: *VD, BM, TB, SOB, WC, BO,* and *GD.* Or we use rhyming syllables, distortions, and diminutives: *doo doo, poo poo, pee pee, wee wee, fanny, hickey, shucks, shoot, cripes, darn, sam hill, doggone.*

PROBLEM 31. Is the subject alone sufficient to require the use of a euphemism? In what way would person/persona, setting/scene, topic/subject, and telos interact to determine whether or not a euphemism were used?

PROBLEM 32. What would an android have to know to use euphemisms correctly? What would it have to know in order to create one?

PROBLEM 33. Is one method of devising euphemisms more likely to lead to a more formal style than another? To a less formal style?

2.3 Levels of Style

Our discussion of English style has touched on a few problems of pronunciation, some of word choice, and a few involving grammar. Sentence structure itself, of course, is also a component of style. We can write simple little sentences with no subordinate clauses. These sound pretty informal. The writer doesn't plan too much ahead. He doesn't worry about contractions or whether he's going to accidentally split an infinitive or whether the end of a sentence is where a preposition will end up at. Not many sentences begin with long introductory clauses. Usually, they have a short introductory phrase. If they have anything at all. In very intimate spoken and written styles, we use pieces of sentences. Because we think we're relating to our audiences pretty closely. Just enough to make us clear. We drop whole parts. Leave lots unsaid. Understand? No? Mmmm.

But if one's ability to compose one's sentences equals one's desire to sound the organ chords of a swelling cadence that reverberates through the meticulous and balanced architecture of an ornate period soaring to the reaches of the rhetorical empyrean, then one cares not that a turn of phrase may strike as archaic the ears of those more pedestrian readers unable to recognize an echo of Cicero or ascend to the stately grandeur of a Dr. Johnson, that his sentences roll on, clause balanced against clause, phrase balancing phrase, each harkening to the rhythm and tone of another, harmonizing part with part until one's mind reels, yet still following the syntax, absorbing the thought, feeling along one's nerves the crescendo of member mounting upon member, clause upon clause, sentence upon sentence, in an arching trajectory through a grammatical and semantic history created by two thousand years of Western literary tradition.

In ordinary writing, of course, we look for the middle ground, sentences that are not obviously rhetorical, but not chatty either. We choose words from that middle group, ordinary words that for the most part we would expect to find in a well-edited newspaper or magazine. Our mean sentence length for expository written prose is about twenty-one words. But some sentences will be longer and some shorter, depending on our intention. And unless we were raised in a very strict grammatical tradition, artificial rules such as not beginning a sentence with a coordinating conjunction hold little weight. Today's middle written style may be just a bit more formal than the style of this chapter.

Like class structure, discretely definable levels of style must arbitrarily divide a continuum that in reality ranges imperceptibly from the very intimate to the very formal. Sentences can gradually become longer or shorter throughout an essay. The frequency of formal words (*inter, locomote, cognizance*) can vary not absolutely but relatively against the frequency of more ordinary words (*bury, move, understanding*). There might be no balanced parallelism among the parts of a sentence. Or just a hint of balance and antithesis—just enough to suggest that the writer knows where he wants to go and that he can control the structure of phrase, clause, sentence, and paragraph well enough to get there.

So schemes to categorize styles must slice the continuum arbitrarily. There are several, no one of them persuasive enough to dominate the field. Different dictionaries label words in several different ways. The greatest of the English dictionaries, the Oxford English Dictionary, labels some words as literary, common, or colloquial with slang, dialectal, archaic, vulgar, technical, and scientific as subcategories. But this system confounds levels of style (colloquial and common) with subject matter (technical, scientific, literary) with local appropriateness (dialectal, archaic, vulgar).

William Labov, who has done some of the most innovative work in linguistic variation, distinguishes four levels of spoken style: casual, careful, reading, and word list—levels defined by the contexts in which he elicited language samples in his interviews. Interviewees used casual speech before the interview proper, during interruptions, or when recalling a moment in which they thought their lives were in danger—all situations where the role relationships were casual and relaxed. Subjects used careful speech when they were conscious of being interviewed by a linguistic scholar. Reading style was used when they were reading from a printed text; word list style was their most careful pronunciation, reading words from a list that sounded much alike, such as *bed–bad, cart–cot*.

In fact, however, no good system has yet been devised that will unequivocally assign any given stretch of speech behavior to a discrete, definable level of style. In most cases, we have to be flexible, referring to more or less formal styles, more or less intimate styles. Between these two, intimate and formal, we can often identify styles we might want to call casual and informal. But they are by no means objectively identifiable in real speech behavior. And this is largely because our understanding of what the level of style *should* be is often enough for us to take the objective speech in that sense. It is the telos of the speech event again infusing the event.

Large concepts such as intelligence, literature, goodness, and the English language are not easily defined. But within the first three, we can accept a principle of individual variation that does not violate the defining principles of what we mean by intelligence, literature, and goodness. It is less easy for us to accept the idea that within something we call the English language there can also be a good deal of legitimate variation. Too many among us assume there is one and only one form of correct English.

And yet each of us talks our way through every day, switching styles with an ease and flexibility that would bewilder us if we had to think about it. Each new situation requires that we choose anew from a repertoire of linguistic forms that best fit the telos of the speech event that we participate in. The repertoire itself depends on influences ranging from geography, social class, and education to sex, personality, and occupation. But regardless of the different repertoires and regardless of the variations those repertoires make available, we all still speak English.

So as we come to master the "English language," what we really master is its styles as well as its grammar, its varieties as well as its shared features. The concept of a language as a fixed and complete entity is often a useful fiction. But the reality of language is variety.

Suggestions for Further Reading

In addition to the suggestions given at the end of the other chapters in this book, four other references are particularly useful.

Bauman, Richard and Sherzer, Joel, eds. *Explorations in the Ethnography of Speaking*. London: Cambridge University Press, 1974.

Hymes, Dell. *Foundations in Sociolinguistics*. Philadelphia: University of Pennsylvania Press, 1974.

———. *Language in Culture and Society*. New York: Harper & Row, 1964.

Shopen, Timothy. *Languages and Their Speakers*. Cambridge, Mass.: Winthrop Publishers, 1979.

Style

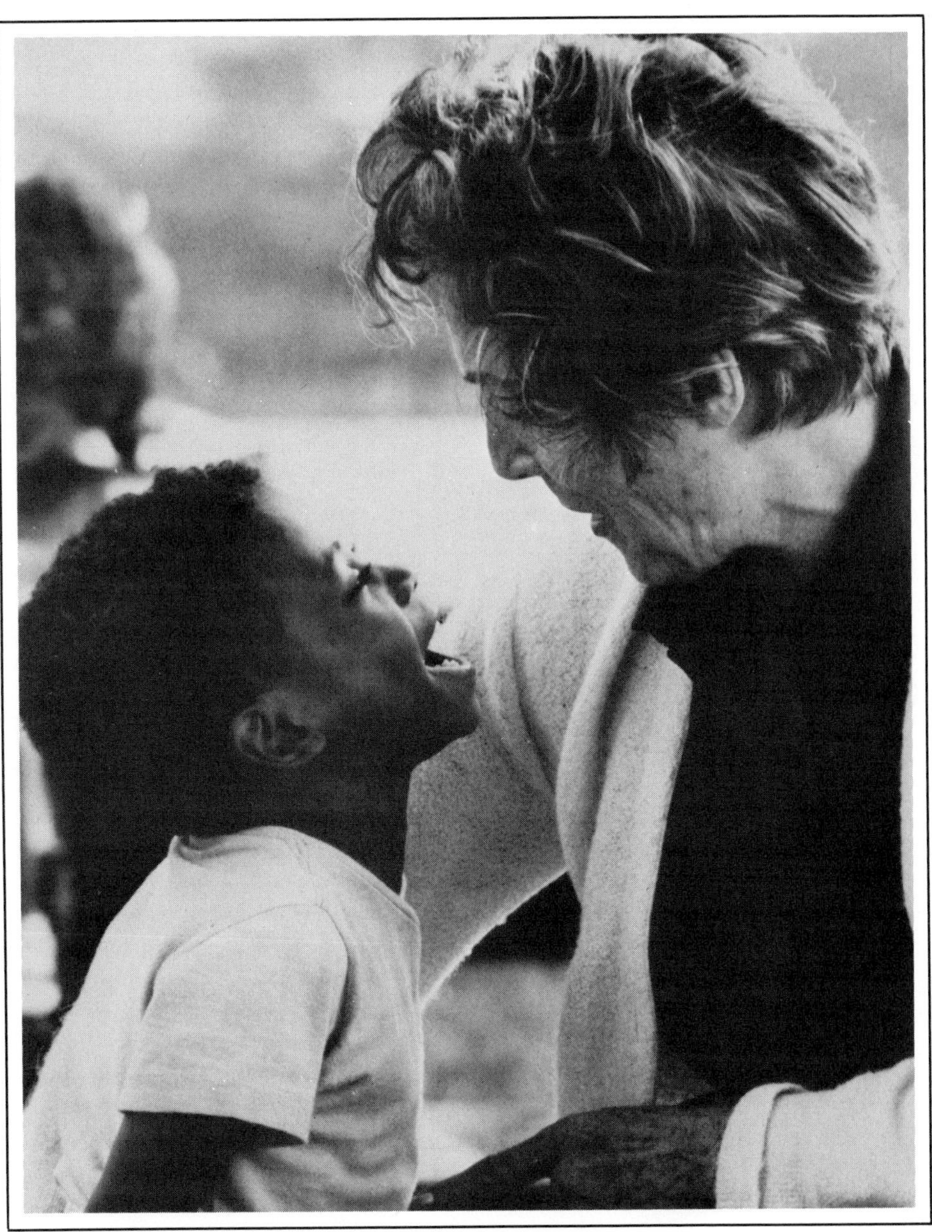

Chapter 3

Styles

Ann D. Zwicky

Ann Zwicky is a teacher at Ohio State University of beginning anything—so far linguistics, French, English composition, English as a second language, and remedial writing. She is interested in the overlap of linguistics and stylistics. She is currently collaborating with Arnold M. Zwicky on a study of the style and content of restaurant menus, a topic that combines two major interests, language and food.

1. Introduction

You probably don't speak to your grandmother exactly as you do to the neighbor's two-year-old, or the same to your minister as to your roommate. You wouldn't write your reason for requesting a loan in exactly the same terms on a bank form as in a letter to your brother. While you may be aware of making a special effort to produce your best language along with your best manners for some people—a prospective employer, for example, or a prospective in-law—you usually change styles automatically and effortlessly, without giving it a thought. In fact, most people change styles so unconsciously that they may be unaware that they ever do so. Some people deny that they *have* different styles on the grounds that it would be insincere—a form of play-acting—to speak differently to different people. In reality, adapting your spoken or written style to your audience is like choosing the right tool for a job. You can't eat bouillon with a fork or sirloin steak with a spoon. And you may have eaten your peas with a spoon when you were three years old, but you wouldn't feel comfortable doing it at a dinner party now. If your four-year-old cousin asks you why your begonia needs light, you can't explain it with the one word "photosynthesis," but you would include that word in your answer to the same sort of question on a botany exam. You may tell your mechanic that one of the wires seems to have come loose from that funny-looking black thing, and he may respect the depths of your ignorance by replying to you in similar terms, but if he talks that way to his assistant, you may begin to doubt his competence. Common sense makes you choose simple words to speak to a small child and use appropriate technical words, if you know them, to speak to an expert about his field. "Putting on airs" is not the only way to change your speech style, and it isn't even one of the most common.

Most of us are not aware of our own speech as part of a dialect, perhaps because we've heard "dialect" used to mean something like "substandard English" or "outlandish speech." People say things like, "I couldn't understand a thing he said; he speaks some kind of funny dialect." The statement that he speaks a dialect is sure to be true, because everybody speaks some kind of dialect. We grow up speaking the dialect of the region we live in and the social group we live among. If we decide for some reason to get rid of our native dialect—perhaps because it's too Southern or too New Yorkish or just too unlike the way our new friends speak—we can only replace it by another dialect. If we pattern our speech on that of network television announcers, we may have some right to say we speak "Standard American English," but that is really just another dialect. It can be called "standard" because it is widely acceptable but not because it represents *the* language in some special way. Because people who do not originally belong to its region have come to adopt it, a standard dialect eventually ceases to identify speakers regionally, but this doesn't mean that it is intrinsically better than any regional dialect.

We don't have to change our dialect to change styles. Most of us make our style shifts largely within the bounds of our native dialect, but some people become *bidialectal.* They speak a standard dialect at work or with strangers, but a regionally or socially marked dialect among friends and "homefolks." A bidialectal person can usually choose from a range of styles within each dialect, but he can also change his style by switching from one dialect to another.

Even those of us who don't have two entirely different dialects may have a set of pronunciations we avoid when we're on our guard, but slip back into when we're relaxed. The same person who says to a personnel interviewer for IBM that he's from "Columbus, Ohio," with clearly pronounced *o*'s everywhere they're spelled, may say "Clumbus, Uhayuh" [kləmbəs əhayə] when he's among friends.

Various speech styles differ in at least three major ways: in vocabulary, syntax, and phonology. Probably the most obvious of these and the one we are most aware of is vocabulary. Almost everybody learns "bad words" at an early age. Four-year-olds come home proudly from preschool with brand new words like "son-of-a-bitch," and even if they can be persuaded not to use their store of adult shockers, seem endlessly fascinated by their own taboo words like "wee-wee" and "poo-poo." Although nearly everybody outgrows this stage, most of us do occasionally use some kind of "bad language"—some words or expressions we wouldn't want to say in front of the primmest person we know. Because of the forbidden aura around words that have to do with sex and excretion on the one hand and God and religion on the other, we are particularly aware of this part of our vocabulary. We sometimes talk about it as if it were the whole of speech; in fact, "Watch your language!" usually just means "cut out the naughty words." In practice, however, many other sectors of our vocabulary change with our speech style as well.

In addition to "bad language," we often have a set of words or phrases that belong to "best language," a set we keep for our most formal and impressive occasions as we might keep our best china. Not everybody has best china, of course, but most of us do have best language. You may find that you save your best for formal writing. Look for it in term papers or English compositions or the kind of description of your aims and ambitions you often have to write on college or graduate school applications. Poetic words like *myriad* or scholarly-sounding ones like *multiplicity* might belong to this section of vocabulary.

In between these two levels, nearly everybody uses some technical language, or *jargon*. Many of us are more or less fluent in a number of different jargons. Every job and every field of study has some technical terms of its own. So does every hobby and every sport. Many technical terms escape from their own fields and come to be used generally. The space program has given us all "countdown," "A-OK," and "blast-off," for example, and even people with no interest in baseball know how it feels to "strike out." Within its own area, technical jargon is clear, expressive, and economical; for outsiders, much of it usually remains incomprehensible. If I tell you that a protopodite is the basal portion of a biramous crustacean appendage, you may still not have any idea how to recognize one. Both of these characteristics can be useful. Thieves' argot was a technical language invented to keep outsiders from overhearing anything useful. Other professional jargons are sometimes used to confuse or impress people outside the profession. "Rhinitis" sounds a great deal more impressive than "a runny nose." "Rhinoplasty" sounds a lot more complicated and serious than "nose job." When the dermatologist says you have "dermatitis," it sounds like a real diagnosis by an expert; if he called it a "rash" you wouldn't be so sure that he knew more about it than you did.

Sometimes technical language just gives a different label to something we have an ordinary name for. Your "cilia" are just your eyelashes, for example, just as your "rhinitis" is only a runny nose. Sometimes technical language names something for which everyday language lacks a name, like the little cleft that runs from your nose to the middle of your upper lip. Often technical language marks distinctions that ordinary language ignores. A horse breeder raises Thoroughbreds, Standardbreds, Morgans, Appaloosas, or Arabians. In his fields he sees mares with foals. The foals are colts or fillies. When they grow up the fillies will be mares; some of the colts will become stallions or horses, but others will be castrated to make them geldings. For the unhorsy outsider, all these animals are merely horses. "Scarlet" and "crimson" are both "red" to many people who can tell them apart perfectly well—and so are "garnet, magenta, vermillion," and "claret." However, if you are a professional decorator, or even if you are just trying to buy a cushion that will match the exact shade of red in the upholstery of your sofa, "red" becomes too broad a term to be useful.

If you think you don't use any technical language, this is probably because your particular jargon is widely shared among people you know. If you can watch a baseball or football game on television and understand the commentary, you understand at least one form of jargon; if you can go on to discuss the plays yourself, you speak that jargon. To become completely convinced of this, try to describe a baseball or football game to a foreigner who knows nothing about the sport, or try to read a detailed account of a match in some sport unfamiliar to you—perhaps cricket or polo—remembering that its technicalities are no worse than those you've mastered for baseball. (There is a fine, rather untechnical, description of a cricket match in Chapter 18 of Dorothy Sayers' *Murder Must Advertise*.)

Here is another example of cricket talk, from an Australian player of the sport named George Lombard:

> The way the fielding team positions itself depends on the kind of bowler the batsman is facing. For example, a right arm leg-spin bowler bowling over the wicket to a left-handed attacking batsman with a weakness outside the off stump would need a slip and a gully and a ring of fieldsmen in the deep on the leg side saving the boundary; however, if the same batsman were facing a fast-medium right arm inswing bowler, there would be a need for two or three slips, a deep third man, a gully, point (optional), cover, and deepish mid-off, with a man at deep fine leg and another at a wide mid-on position.

Besides technical language, most people speak at least two levels of slang: the nearly neutral everyday language that's just a little too informal for letters of application and the like (*fridge* and *t.v.* belong to this vocabulary) and the more specialized, perhaps shorter-lived "trendier" slang of their own particular group at a particular time. You might call the two sets "common" slang and "in-group" slang. "Get off my case" is an example of the latter where I am living now; it means approximately "stop nagging at me." Some slang is very short-lived, like "Twenty-three skiddoo!" but some lasts long enough to become accepted in the stuffiest circles. "Fan" appeared as a slangy shortening of "fanatic" in the late sixteenth century, and today we have fan letters, fan clubs, and even fan magazines for all kinds of things from baseball stars to rock groups. Slang, like technical language, can be used to keep insiders together and to exclude outsiders. Cockney rhyming slang is an extreme example of this. It originally consisted of replacing a word or expression with an expression that rhymed with it: "wife" became "trouble and strife," while "hat" was "tit-fer-tat." But then the resulting phrases, although unconnected in meaning with the words they stood for, still offered cues to their *sounds,* so the slang makers went one step further and deleted the rhyming word. Thus your wife becomes your "trouble," while your hat is your "titfer." On the other hand, slang terms often move readily from dialect to dialect. Some originally Black slang is now very popular with Americans of all races. Non-Cockneys often learn and use bits of rhyming slang for fun.

Many of us also have at least some bits and pieces of a private language peculiar either to our own families or our closest friends. This kind of intimate vocabulary may be based on long-outgrown baby talk, the malapropisms of eccentric aunts, quotes from favorite books, punch lines of family stories, or even a deliberate code. In my own family, just the phrase "To me . . ." with a rising tone on *me* is a warning that bragging is unbecoming. It is a quotation from a letter to my uncle, who was organizing an amateur show. "Why not let Miss X sing?" it said, "To me, she has a lovely voice." Unfortunately for her aspirations, Miss X was recognized as the writer of the letter. One of the most widespread family codes—"m.i.k." for "more in the kitchen" vs. "f.h.b." for "family hold back"—is so well known that it's probably useless now.

Many English speakers also draw on a stock of foreign words and phrases. People whose parents or grandparents speak another language at home may use expressions from that language only in casual or intimate conversation. They may have some favorite foods, for example, which they can refer to only in another language. Those who have traveled abroad may use foreign phrases to add elegance to their more careful conversation or to their writing. Some people with no Jewish background like to use Yiddish phrases because they sound "citified" or "show biz."

Every speaker is able to draw at will from all these varied vocabularies whatever seems appropriate. As long as the choices *are* appropriate, neither the speaker nor the hearer is likely to notice that he dips into a number of different vocabularies within a single conversation.

To find your own personal vocabularies, try some of the following exercises.

1. Suppose you were to drop a cup of coffee, leaving a pool of coffee and broken china at your feet. What would you say to express your annoyance? (a) if you were alone; (b) if you were with your parents; (c) if you were with your roommate; (d) if you were at a reception for a clergyman, or a bank president, or anybody you personally would consider very respectable. Write down what you think you'd say in each case and compare. (Since so much of style depends on who you are and what your social relationships are, we have been imagining a specific someone as our reader, and that is a particular kind of college or university student. Other readers can think of what they would do in that role, also imagine situations in their own lives comparable to ones we suggest here.)
2. (a) Watch a sports event on television and write down all the technical terms you notice. Separate them into those you use yourself, those you understand but might not use, and those you don't understand (if any). *Or* (b) Read one assignment for a subject you are studying and write down all the technical terms you find in it.
3. Look over any term papers you have written or any other formal writing you've done. Write down any words you find in your writing that you never use in ordinary conversation. Connectives like *ergo, therefore,* and *nevertheless* are good words to look for, and so are poetic or literary words like *valor* and *evanescent*. Scholarly work may make you come up with *dichotomy* or *seminal*. Your own "best" words may, of course, be nothing like any of these.

2. Pronunciation

We may be less aware of changing our way of pronouncing things than of changing our choice of words, yet our phonology does change with style. A number of studies have been made of "casual" or "fast speech" phonology. For people who are not linguists, the most obvious feature of casual speech is probably "dropping your *g*'s" in words that end in *-ing*. We all know about this, because most of us have had teachers who told us not to do it. Even people who spend their lives telling other people not to at least occasionally "drop their *g*'s" in expressions like *going fishing*. (Linguists use quotation marks around the phrase "dropping *g*'s" because what happens phonetically is a change from [ŋ] to [n], with no [g] involved in either pronunciation.) If you listen very carefully, you will find that even people you think *never* drop their *g*'s (you may be one of them) do so sometimes, and even people you think always drop them put in a few. Men are generally said to drop more *g*'s than women and boys to drop the very most.

You've probably heard that Cockney speakers "drop their *aitches*"—and sometimes put them in where they don't belong. You may not be aware of dropping your own aitches, but all English speakers, including both the most untraveled Americans and the most cultivated Oxford graduates, drop some. The initial *h* of pronouns like *he, her,* and *him* tends to disappear, especially when it is preceded by a consonant sound. Try saying "Don't let her hit him" at ordinary conversational speed, and see how many *h*'s you honestly hear. Get your friends to say it and see if you hear their *h*'s. Of course, through the years some have become completely mute, like the one in *honest.* Some speakers never say *h* before a *y* sound, and so don't have it at the beginning of *human, humor,* or *huge,* but this is part of a regional dialect and not a matter of style.

Speakers of many dialects replace the *th* pronunciations in words like *ether* and *either* with *t* and *d.* You have probably heard them unfavorably characterized as "dese and dose" speakers. Whether or not you say "dese and dose," you may sometimes drop the first sound of *this* or *that* completely. Young men, in particular, do this often in casual speech. Everybody does it in the phrase "atta boy"; "that's the boy!" would sound ridiculously affected as a shout of encouragement.

You may have been taught that it's informal to use contractions, but this is really only true of written style. In speech, it is extremely formal, even stilted, not to use contractions. The ordinary contractions like *he'll, she'd, won't,* and *can't* are neutral in style. In tag questions, like "Herbert could do that, couldn't he?" the contraction of *not* is almost obligatory. "You are studying English, are you not?" could only be a non-native speaker's question—or one by a native speaker being extremely highbrow. In really casual speech, we make nonstandard contractions in addition to the ordinary ones. In ordinary fairly careful style, we say "he'd" for "he would" or "he had." In casual speech, we say "he'd've" for "he would have," and in the most informal style, that becomes "he'd'a." A sentence like "It would have been funny" can come out as [id əv bin fənīy], with "it would" reduced to "it'd" and then "id," and "have" reduced to something that sounds just like "of." Children often write *of* for *have* because they sound the same in casual speech.

Unstressed syllables are lost in some words in any but supercareful pronunciation. Almost nobody regularly pronounces three full syllables in *every, opera,* and *camera*. In really casual speech we lose many other syllables, so that we say things like "'lo," "bye," and "'k'you" for "hello," "goodbye," and "thank you." "Going to" and "want to" will be reduced to "gonna" and "wanna," and we'll make various other reductions.

The process of contraction goes so far in really intimate conversation that we get down to vocal signs we can say with our mouths shut and really can't satisfactorily spell at all. "Hmm?" with a rising intonation is "what?" "Mn-hmm" is "yes," and "uh-unh" with a glottal stop in the middle is "no." We can more or less hum the whole sentence "I don't know," particularly if we shrug our shoulders as we do it.

People often disapprove officially of casual speech patterns as "sloppy" or "careless" speech, but they're really economical and efficient when used where they belong. With close friends a very careful, formal style is wounding—as rude as the most casual speech style would be in addressing a prospective employer we'd just met. We usually enunciate very carefully with our families only when we're angry and want to show the distance we feel from them.

So far we've discussed mostly sounds that are reduced or lost in casual speech. Another phonological process that becomes more widespread in casual speech is assimilation—one sound becoming more like a neighboring sound—in English, usually the one after it. Some assimilations are reflected in our spelling; when we put somebody *in prison,* we *imprison* him. The *n* of *in* brought into such close contact with the *p* becomes an *m*. The *in* of *input* keeps its *n* in writing, but in any but the most painfully careful pronunciation, it sounds like *m*. A vowel followed by a nasal consonant is always at least somewhat nasalized, not only in English, but very probably in all languages of the world. The vowel of *can't* is always slightly different from that of *cat*. Sometimes the physical difference between the words *cat* and *can't* is entirely in the nasalization of the vowel of the second. This is so automatic a process that for the most part we don't recognize it, but the difference is there and always shows up on equipment that is designed to measure it. As we speak faster and more carelessly, we tend to make more and more assimilations without meaning to. You may find it hard to believe you make any extra assimilations even in fast speech. To be convinced at least that *other* people do, read aloud at moderate speed to a friend the words "Empire Stape Building, Hybe Park, carbboarb box" and ask him to repeat what you said.[1] For most people these pronunciations sound perfectly fine at normal speed because they are used to

1. These examples are from G. W. Turner, *Stylistics* (London: Penguin Books, 1973), pp. 11, 239.

hearing them that way and making the necessary mental corrections. Listen carefully and try to catch yourself or your friends in unsuspected assimilations.

Here are some things you might do to find out more about casual phonology:

1. Ask five or more people to count from sixty-five to eighty-five. Then ask each one to read the number seventy-seven from a card. Tell them it's a class project or a psychological experiment, but don't explain until after they've finished just what you're looking for. Concentrate on the way they pronounce "seventy." You should hear pronunciations from carefully enunciated "seventy" to something very much more like "sebmty." Some people may also drop the *v* entirely and say something that sounds like "senty." For each person you ask to count, have a piece of paper with two columns headed "assimilated" and "unassimilated"; write the numbers from seventy to seventy-nine down the margin, and then seventy-seven again. Make a mark for every pronunciation of *seventy* in one column or the other. Add to the page the sex and approximate age of the person you asked and how well you know him. When you've finished, write a short summary of your results.
2. For several short periods during the next few days, try to count occurrences of *-ing* and *-in* endings—*doing* vs. *doin* and so on, and note the approximate circumstances of your counting. You can jot down on a piece of scrap paper something like "Linguistics class, 9/17/80" with a column for the teacher and another for students, or "conversation, 9/18/80" plus a set of names like "me, Jane, Tarzan" and then tally *-in*'s to the left and *-ing*'s to the right under each name, for example. At the end of your observation period, figure the percentage of forms counted with *-in* and the percentage with *-ing*. Check to see if the percentage is noticeably smaller for more formal situations, like classes, or for female speakers. Then make a general statement about *-in* and *-ing* in current English usage. Include any special observations of your own that seem relevant. (See Chapter 6 for how to do a more extensive study of these pronunciations.)

3. Syntax

The process of contraction in casual speech leads to syntactic changes as well as phonological ones. Some words seem to be phonologically eroded to almost nothing, and others are deliberately dropped. We use more sentence fragments and leave out more unnecessary words. *I* and *you* as subjects tend to disappear, especially when they would be the first word of a sentence. The verbs *to have* and *to be* drop out, especially when they are auxiliaries rather than main verbs. "What are you doing?" becomes "Whatcha doin?" and "goin a town," is a perfectly good answer. A noun phrase often stands alone. "Nice day" is a standard conversational opening. "New car" can be a shortened version of "I have a new car," "You have a new car," or "That's a new car" (at the neighbors') or even of several more complicated sentences, depending on the situation. The circumstances of our speech fill in their own details and tell the person we are talking to exactly what we mean. Very intimate speech may be characterized by extremely abbreviated sentences in which normally vital bits of information are left out. "Did you put in my . . . ?" "Yes."

In casual speech we may use constructions we would avoid in writing or in speaking to an audience. "Bill and me are going" is normal in casual speech for many people who would write "Bill and I." "Where's it at?" is good casual style for many who would say "Where is it?" if they were speaking carefully. I usually say only "who" in conversation, but I often write *whom,* even in letters to friends.

Some types of sentences are usually reserved for casual styles. One process that is characteristically informal is topicalization, which pulls the object to the front of the sentence: "That I'd like to see!" Another is called the *alpha-tag*. An ordinary tag question, called a *flip tag,* is a statement with a question "tagged" on: "You know Rosie, don't you?" or "You don't want any more, do you?" These questions have negative tags ("don't you?") with positive sentences, positive ones ("do you?") with negative sentences. The alpha-tag is a positive tag added to a positive sentence: "You're buying a borzoi, are you?" as opposed to "You're buying a borzoi, aren't you?" Ordinary tag questions are conversational, but neutral in style. Alpha tags are markedly informal. They may be pointedly sarcastic, or they may just be conversational openers.

There may be a number of constructions that we save for writing or for very formal speech that don't fit our everyday usage. One of these is the subjunctive. The subjunctive is technically a verbal *mood* contrasted with the indicative. The indicative is prescribed for statements of fact, and the subjunctive for wishes, suppositions, and other nonfactive uses. Many people now don't use the English subjunctive at all, or if they do, reserve it for their most formal style. Only the "contrary-to-fact" subjunctive in clauses like "If I were rich" occurs at all regularly in speech or informal writing, and even that seems to be getting rarer. Forms of the subjunctive other than *were* in *if* clauses usually occur only in fixed phrases of extreme formality, such as a lawyer's "if it please the Court" or a written petition's "we hereby request that this *be* done." Sentences that begin with a subjunctive element—"Be he live or be he dead, I'll grind his bones to make my bread!"—are almost never heard in modern speech and rarely even seen in writing.

In writing or in prepared talks we are usually careful to vary our sentence structures; in casual speech we'll use simpler structures and reuse them more often. Sentences that contain a number of clauses strung together by *and* are usually informal. On the other hand, sentences with subordinating structures are usually formal. For a sentence to begin with a clausal or sentential subject, as this one does, is a mark of formality. It is perfectly neutral for a written or spoken sentence to begin with *it* and have its sentential subject placed after the verb, as this one does.

Choices about where to put negative markers often affect the tone of a sentence. Sentences with double negation—"I didn't do nothing"—sound colloquial or, for some dialects, ungrammatical, although most children go through a stage of marking a sentence as negative at every possible point; and in many languages (French and Russian, for example) that is the correct way to express negativity. Sentences with a negative adverb at the beginning and the auxiliary verb placed in front of the subject, as if in a question—"Never had he seen a more hideous sight"—are very formal, probably because they show such a wrenching of normal word order. As long as you can preserve normal word order, it seems stylistically neutral to mark negation as early in the sentence as you can. Sentences with negative subjects—"Nobody came" and "Nothing happened"—are perfectly ordinary, but when those same negative pronouns come after the verb—"I saw nobody" or "He touched nothing"—they sound rather formal. "I didn't see anybody" and "He didn't touch anything," in which the negative element is attached to the verb rather than expressed in the object, seem to represent the most neutral style for these sentences.

"Who did you see?" and "Who did you go with?" are of ordinary conversational style. "Whom did you see?" and "With whom did you go?" are notably formal. "George and Eric, whom you met last week" seems normal to me, but many people avoid *whom* altogether. Putting in relative pronouns where it would be equally correct to leave them out marks a sentence as formal. "I enjoyed the book you lent me when we were here last week" is less markedly formal than the same sentence with "which" or even "that" added.

The use of passive rather than active constructions is generally formal, and so is a very *nouny* style. For example, that last sentence would sound less formal written this way: "When you use passive constructions rather than active ones and write in a very *nouny* style, you usually sound formal." Both passives and nominalizations (nouns made from verbs, as *nominalization* is made from *nominalize*) can be used to avoid putting in pronoun agents, which cause trouble of various kinds. The first sentence of this paragraph contains no pronouns or *agents* or *actors*. Some handbooks and some teachers advise writers to avoid the pronoun *I* in any but the most informal writing. But the "editorial we" can be confusing, especially in articles or books with more than one author, where it might be a real *we*. Writers also sometimes include their readers in a *we* ("As we will see again in a later chapter . . .") and sometimes do not ("We find this solution unsatisfactory, for reasons which we will discuss below"). Writers may eliminate *we* as well as *I* by the extremely formal device of writing third-person phrases like "in the opinion of the present author" to avoid saying "I think." (*I think* the formal expression sounds awful, so this is probably a good time to repeat that "most formal" and "best" aren't necessarily the same.)

Authors may address their readers as *you,* which creates a somewhat informal, person-to-person tone. Early novelists often spoke directly to "dear reader," but this and "gentle reader" are long out of style. In some languages the most formal or more respectful way of addressing somebody requires the substitution of a third-person form like *he* or *she* for any second-person *you* form. This kind of deferential speech occurs very rarely, if at all, in modern spoken English (you may possibly have heard a movie butler say something like "If Madam will step this way . . ."). But third-person address is sometimes used in textbook writing: "The interested reader should consult the supplemental references at the end of this chapter." This creates a whole new problem, because if the interested reader is pronominalized, he or she (unlike *you*) must have a marked sex in English.

There are a number of answers to that problem. The traditional one is to say that *he* is unmarked in English, because it can be used either for a male person or for an unspecified person, whereas *she* can apply only to a female. Most people are less convinced of this than the authors of the Ohio statute that states that "No person shall be forced to undergo an abortion against his will." An increasingly popular solution in spoken language is to use a *plural* pronoun—"Somebody left their galoshes", "Nobody seems to know where they are going"—but most grammarians still frown on this in writing. Nobody seems to be happy with E. Nesbit's solution of writing sentences like "Everybody put on its hat"; perhaps it threatens our pride in our humanity too much. "He/she" is a fair solution for official forms, but it sounds awkward. Some people write "s/he," but it has no pronunciation.

Perhaps the most effective is the most explicit, "he or she," which sounds all right in any but casual styles, and as long as it is not repeated several times in close succession. Some modern feminists have proposed the introduction of new neutral pronouns; *co* is one form that has been suggested. This solution seems unlikely to be accepted, because the pronouns have been a closed class of words too long to accept new members readily.

For most American speakers, *you* is a normal indefinite pronoun, as in "You can lead a horse to water, but you can't make him drink." *One* in this sense is still the prescribed form, but it is generally reserved for extremely formal usage. In British English, *one* used to be a polite substitute for *I*, but it is now considered funny—old-fashioned at best, and probably affected.

We in place of *you* occurs only in very special conversational styles—usually nurse to patient or teacher to children—and is probably meant to indicate friendliness and empathy, although it is generally accompanied by some element of coercion.

Another syntactic element that reflects styles is the choice of certain sentence types, which are sets of sentences whose form is related to their major uses. The major sentence types in English are *declarative, interrogative,* and *imperative.* Declarative sentences are most straightforwardly used to make statements, interrogative sentences to ask questions, and imperatives to give orders, but it is obvious that these are not the only functions for which we use sentences. We use sentences not only to exchange information and to command action, but also to establish contact, to make jokes or play games, to pray, to make requests, to promise, threaten, cajole, insult, and so on. We don't have anywhere near enough sentence types to serve all our communicative needs, so the ones we have must be versatile. "How do you do?" has the form of a (rather peculiar) question, but it functions as a greeting formula to which the most common response is an identical "How do you do?" Both "Have a good day!" and the Southern "Y'all come back, now!" have the shape of imperatives, but they act as leave-taking expressions: neither expresses any real hope of influencing the future behavior of the person addressed.

Some sentences have the special property of doing what they say. "I promise to pay for the penguins," is both a declarative sentence and a promise. Saying "I promise" performs the act of promising. "He promised to pay for the penguins," a very similar sentence, is a declarative sentence, but is not in itself a promise. "I'll pay for the penguins" can be an offer or a promise; "You'll pay for the penguins" is a prediction or a threat.

The meaning of a sentence is limited by the understandings of the words that make it up, but it is not absolutely determined by them.

That is, in ordinary English, "I'm very fond of apples" can never mean "Throw me a grapefruit," or "My grandmother wears a wig"; but it can be either a statement about the speaker's preferences in fruit or an indirect request for an apple, and one can imagine situations in which it would have still other meanings. The speaker could be talking about what kind of tree to plant or what wallpaper pattern to choose for the kitchen (red apples or ivy on a lattice). He could even be explaining his good health by an indirect reference to the well-known proverb "An apple a day keeps the doctor away."

Just as the same sentence type may fulfill different functions, different sentence types may fulfill the same function when we have a choice of different ways to convey the same message. English offers a number of different ways of making requests, for example. The most straightforward requests take the form of imperatives, or orders, with *please* added: "Please close the door" or "Close the door, please." Neither of these is noticeably formal or informal; you could say either to a close friend or a perfect stranger. If you wanted to be especially polite, you could phrase the same request as a question: "Would you mind closing the door?" Sometimes the force of a request can be conveyed indirectly by a statement like "There's rather a draft in here with the door open." People often prefer the indirect approach when they're afraid of being turned down. Then if they don't get what they wanted, they still haven't been directly refused. Straight commands with no *please* attached are generally considered rude unless they are given by somebody formally in charge, like a military officer, or somebody informally in charge in an emergency. "Call the fire department!" isn't rude. In some situations, particularly rather intimate ones, even harsh words may have a softening effect on commands, and "Shut the damn door" may be no worse than a friendly request.

It is generally informal, outside of the Socratic dialogue, to answer a question with a question. Sometimes it is just a way of putting off an answer until you have further information: "Are you coming?" "What time is it?" Sometimes the second question is the answer: "Are you coming?" "Why not?" In some really casual styles a question/answer like "Is the Pope Catholic?" means "yes," while one like "Does a chicken have lips?" means "no." This sort of response can be risky if you aren't sure the people you're talking to are used to it; not everybody understands that kind of answer.

The strong influence of the circumstances of speech makes it very difficult to generalize about sentence types and formality. The standard way to answer a question is certainly to use a declarative sentence. On the whole, it seems reasonable to predict that the most neutral way to formulate a request in English is to use a question, rather than an imperative with or without *please,* or a statement of conditions which might prompt a request. In English conversation it is most acceptable to be neither too direct nor too indirect. Notice, however, that even the most formal written style uses direct imperatives. I wrote "notice" in the last sentence, not "perhaps the reader would be interested in noticing" or "would you please notice"; writers do not hesitate to order their supposed readers about.

Here are some projects to try to become more aware of the interactions of style and syntax:

1. Compare some sample of informal writing with a sample of formal writing by the same person. You might use a term paper of your own and an unmailed letter to a close friend. Perhaps you have a letter *from* a friend and a sample of some more formal writing by that person, such as an article from a school paper. Or you could look at published correspondence of some twentieth-century writer or scholar (F. Scott Fitzgerald and Virginia Woolf are two among many writers who have had at least some of their correspondence published) and compare the private letters with the professional prose of the same writer. Choose short samples of writing—not more than one printed page long—but try to choose representative ones. If you are looking at a piece of fiction, try to choose a page that is mostly narrative, without too much dialogue. Look at the number of passive sentences versus the number of active ones in the two samples. Count the number of whole sentences and the number of sentence fragments or sentences with some element left out in each. What punctuation marks are used in each sample? What is the average length of a sentence in each? Are there any constructions that show up often in one sample but aren't present at all in the other? How many sentences in each begin with something other than the subject? How many contain subordinate clauses? Finally, try to make some general statements characterizing the differences and similarities you find in the two writing samples.
2. Try to get through some "service encounter" like buying your lunch in a cafeteria or asking for something in a store without making any direct requests. Without being impolite, try to avoid adding *please,* since it marks questions as requests. "Could I have a slice of tomato on my hamburger, please?" must be a request, although without the *please* it might have been a real question. Write down what you said, and what the results were. Did your indirect requests succeed, and if not, why not?
3. In a conversation with your roommate or a relative or someone else you know well and often talk to, ask at least two questions using *whom* instead of *who* ("With whom are you going out to-

night?" "Whom did he ask to the party?" "To whom are you writing?") and use at least one sentence with *one* instead of indefinite *you* or *I* ("One doesn't often see those anymore"). If you don't get any reaction the first time you do this, repeat the experiment. Describe your experiences.

4. Scales of Formality

So far we have been talking about style as if there were four relatively easily defined stylistic levels of language: formal, neutral, casual, and intimate. No matter how you name your levels, they are not really separate categories, and they overlap in unexpected ways. A very large segment of our vocabulary is neutral in feeling and can be used appropriately in any style. "Car" is more formal than "heap" or "wheels," less formal than "automobile" or "limousine," but it is acceptable at any stylistic level. Abbreviations like "t.v." and "fridge" are now usual in neutral as well as casual and intimate styles. Technical terms like "carburetor" may reach all levels of style because they have no nontechnical equivalent. We may know only technical words or only informal words for some things—my husband always says "lythrum" for the spikes of pink flowers at the bottom of our garden, but the only name I can usually remember for them is the common name, "loosestrife."

Often we may deliberately change styles, not because of a change in our situation, but because of a change in our feelings. We may speak formally to our family or our most intimate friends when we are angry or embarrassed. It's a commonplace of family relationships that a mother's calls escalate from "Jimmy!" to "James!" to "James Altman Kimball!" When your mother gets to the most formal form of your name, you know she's serious. The same implications hold for adult life. "Good morning" said by a wife to her husband may be less cordial than an inarticulate grunt, given the right circumstances. We may choose to speak casually or even intimately to a stranger on an airplane to be reassuring or to a stranger in the next car to be insulting.

For a number of body parts or functions we seem to lack neutral words, so that we have only medical terms or euphemisms on one side and slang terms (often vulgar) or nursery words on the other. "Micturate" is a very technical term for the only slightly less technical "urinate," "void" is so elliptical only nurses understand it, "wee wee" is childish, "piss" is rude, and phrases like "go to the little girls' room" and "wash up" are coy and run the risk of not being clearly understood. In a case like this it's hard to find a term that really fits a neutral style, so we have to mix in a term from whatever other style seems most natural for us.

Sometimes we mix styles deliberately. Somebody explaining a highly technical process may use very informal terms like "this little doodad" to lighten the terminological load a little. Politicians often inject a few "down-home" phrases into even their most formal addresses to remind their constituents that they are still "just folks." Preachers and teachers may try to show young people that they understand their problems and can still "speak their language" by using popular slang expressions. This kind of style mixing succeeds in its aims only if it is well done and doesn't sound too self-conscious. Done badly, it becomes embarrassing.

Speakers or writers who are attempting to use an unfamiliar style may slip uncontrollably in and out of it. A late nineteenth-century American poet, Julia Moore, wrote about Lord Byron, "Such obloquy he could not endure,/So he done what was the best."[2] We are appalled and delighted by the discord between her highflown choice of words (*obloquy* and *endure*) and her very casual use of syntax (*he done*).

Eliza Doolittle, in *My Fair Lady,* said to her aristocratic companions at the races at Ascot, "Gin was mother's milk to her; in my opinion, they done the old lady in." Eliza spoke with the perfect enunciation and flawlessly aristocratic pronunciation Professor Higgins taught her, but both the expression "do her in" and the past tense "they done" belong to a different linguistic level.

These last two examples illustrate stylistic clashes. Such discords are usually funny, but they also serve to make stylistic elements stand out in a way they wouldn't in a more homogeneous discourse. Nobody who has read Julia Moore can continue to assume that vocabulary alone can make a style; the clashing syntax stands out too clearly.

Clare Silva and Arnold Zwicky[3] have suggested that degrees of discord could be measured by assigning formal elements values between 0 and plus 10, and casual elements values between 0 and minus 10 (neutral elements would be valued at zero). The degree of stylistic deviance of a sentence would then be judged as the difference between

---

2. D. B. Wyndham Lewis and Charles Lee, eds., *The Stuffed Owl: An Anthology of Bad Verse* (New York: Capricorn Books, 1962), p. 237.

3. Clare Silva and Arnold Zwicky, "Discord" in *Analyzing Variation in Language,* edited by Ralph W. Fasold and Roger W. Shuy (Washington, D.C.: Georgetown University Press, 1975), pp. 203–19.

See also: Arnold Zwicky, "Note on a Phonological Hierarchy in English" in *Linguistic Change and Generative Theory,* edited by Robert P. Stockwell and Ronald Macaulay (Bloomington, Ind. : Indiana University Press, 1972), pp. 275–301. Arnold Zwicky, "On Casual Speech" in *Proceedings of the Eighth Annual Meeting of the Chicago Linguistics Society,* edited by Paul M. Peranteau, Judith N. Levi and Gloria C. Phares (Chicago: Chicago Linguistics Society).

its most extreme elements—a sentence which contained both a minus 10 item and a plus 10 item would have the highest possible discordancy value of 20. Such a sentence would probably sound ludicrous, while a sentence with a discordancy value of 2 to 5 might sound relatively normal.

The problem, of course, is how to assign values. The subjunctive at the beginning of a sentence (“Were you to ask . . .”) is obviously very highly marked—maybe plus 10. “Does a chicken have lips?” may be at the other extreme, a minus 10. In between these extremes lie a number of puzzling questions. “Wanna” in “Do you wanna go to California?” seems slightly less casual than the very same reduction at the end of the sentence “Do *you* wanna?” Obscene expressions may be minus 10 in some company, only about minus 7 in others. Deletion of *be* and the subject *you* in “Coming?” results in less informality than the deletion of *be* alone in “He coming?”

In spite of all these perplexities, it is possible to assign discord values to sentences that present stylistic clashes, precisely because the sense of clash illuminates the difference between the elements that characterize various styles.

In both of the examples of stylistic discord we have seen, a relatively formal tone was clearly intended. Julia Moore’s vocabulary matched the gravity of her subject matter—the life and death of a great poet—but her syntax (and her art) failed to live up to it. Eliza Doolittle’s pronunciation and intonation suited the occasion and her company, but her subject matter and her syntax didn’t. If Eliza had stayed at home with her Cockney dustman father, her subject matter and her syntax would have been appropriate, and her new high-class accent would have been the discordant element. We have to remember that there is no one style that is always and everywhere the best choice. A learned word can be as discordant at a pep rally as slang in a sermon.

The appropriate style for anything a speaker says—any *speech act*—always depends on the interaction of the setting, the participants involved, and the speaker’s intention. Of these, the speaker’s intention is always the most important element. We can tell with some certainty that Julia Moore wanted to write a serious poem, even a tragic one, and that Eliza Doolittle meant to contribute an apt anecdote to a conversation among stylish people. Both failed in their intentions.

In some cases a speaker may use language that seems inappropriate to the setting of the conversation and to his role in it, yet which fulfills his intentions perfectly. When my daughter’s junior-high-school music teacher stands in front of a classroom full of riotously noisy eighth graders and says slowly and clearly the one word “sex,” she usually accomplishes the aim of getting everybody’s attention. If she said, “Now I want you all to sit still and listen,” her words would sound more appropriate, but they wouldn't be as effective. If I want to insult a bishop it may or may not suit my intentions to address him as "Your Grace."

The observation that a given expression may have different values in different social or syntactic contexts gives us a clue about value assignments. The values must be relative, rather than absolute, and we will want to take into account as much relevant context as we have. In a sentence like "That is a foxy lady, is it not?" the uncontracted *is* in the main part of the sentence and the wording *is it not* for *isn't it* are noticeably formal elements. We might assign the first uncontracted *is* a value of plus 4, or four degrees more formal than a neutral style, and the very stilted *is it not* a value of plus 8. *Foxy* and *lady* might seem to represent a clash as word choices, but we know that this is a fairly common expression, so we can consider the phrase as a whole. Suppose we assign it a value of minus 7, or seven degrees *less* formal than a neutral style. The choice of *that,* rather than *she* or *Marybelle,* may be considered as neutral, since anybody might use it to talk about a stranger in a public place, so we can assign it a zero. Similarly, since the subject of the sentence determines the pronoun in the tag question, we can pass that *it* as neutral. Then the widest difference of values in the sentence is between the minus 7 of *foxy lady* and the plus 8 of *is it not.* To get the absolute difference between these two we add their values, disregarding their signs, and get a total clash of 15.

This kind of discordancy value doesn't tell us anything about whether the clash is caused by the formal or the informal elements. We have to consider everything we can find out about the setting, the people taking part in the conversation, and the speaker's intention. Suppose we know that the speaker of our clashing sentence was a college student sitting in a student hang-out with a close friend. He is commenting on the looks of another student who has just walked in. We can assume that his intention goes with *foxy lady,* and that it's the formal elements in the sentence that cause the clash.

What if we know that the speaker is a guest at a glittering ball where he knows very few people and is speaking to a stuffy, bemedaled old gentleman about an imposing lady in an emerald tiara? Then a very formal tone would suit the occasion, and it's *foxy lady,* the informal element, that is out of place and clashes with its surroundings. He should have said something more like "extremely attractive woman."

Suppose our speaker is a freshman at a reception for new students at a large university and he is talking to a dean to whom he has just been introduced about a woman faculty member. Then *is it not* sounds unnaturally formal, while *foxy lady* sounds impudent and rude. The clash is just as evident and the sentence is just as out of place as ever, but we can't identify either the formal elements or the informal ones as the cause of the incongruity; we have to say that both contribute almost equally to the discord.

In each of the following sentences, identify each stylistically marked element and assign a number to it. Then find a discordancy value for each sentence. Finally, imagine a situation in which somebody might have used the sentence and imagine the intention of the speaker; then say which elements in the sentence are inappropriate. You will probably want to "juggle" your numbers a bit as you progress in the exercise, since the values are comparative.

1. What is going down?
2. Never did he go for hard rock, you know.
3. That is a hot one, is it not?
4. Have not seen George around for a long time.
5. That Gregory was a pot-head was unsurprising to his mentors.
6. Could you possibly shut your big fat yap?
7. With whom was you figuring on sallying forth?
8. Whaddaya mean, you won't lemme request that I be allowed to graduate early?
9. Speaking as a psychiatrist, I would diagnose him as nuttier than a fruitcake.

As a further exercise, set up *different* imaginary situations for five of the preceding sentences, so that the clashing elements are not the same ones you identified the first time.

As a final exercise, try the following:

1. Suppose that you are a student in physical education. You are engaged to a student in economics named Elizabeth Manley or Albert Manley (choose one, according to your sex). How would you introduce your sweetheart to: (a) an old friend (of your own sex) at a barbeque or a beer party; (b) a class of ten-year-olds you are teaching to swim; (c) your grandmother at a family dinner party for Thanksgiving; (d) your advisor in the lobby of a movie theater; and (e) the president of your university at a formal reception for a visiting dignitary. What elements change in your various introductions? Which ones, if any, stay the same? Look for differences in address terms (kids, Granny, Dean Williams, etc.); in titles (my advisor, my grandmother, my fiancee, my old man, etc.); in sentence types ("May I introduce . . . ?", "I'd like you to meet . . ."; etc.); and in order (who is introduced to whom). You may find other differences as well.

2. Get three friends to do the same exercise, or compare papers with three other students in your class. How do the answers differ from each other? Is there any one category of possible usages in which you find an especially large number of differences? Who shows the widest range of changes? The narrowest? Are the answers noticeably more alike for people of the same sex, or not?

Suggestions for Further Reading

The most readable introduction is G. W. Turner's *Stylistics*. A good textbook with useful exercises on rhetoric and style is *The New English* by Joe Williams. A short book which has become a classic as a discussion of conscious decisions in style is Martin Joos's "The Five Clocks."

In the area of less conscious choices that contribute to style, the notion of *sociolinguistic variables* is of central importance, and here the section of this volume by that title is recommended, as well as William Labov's *Sociolinguistic Patterns*.

Joos, Martin. "The Five Clocks." *International Journal of American Linguistics* 28, no. 2 (1962). Bloomington, Ind.: Indiana University Research Center in Anthropology, Folklore, and Linguistics.

Labov, William. *Sociolinguistic Patterns*. Philadelphia: University of Pennsylvania Press, 1972.

Turner, G. W. *Stylistics*. London: Penguin Books, 1973.

Williams, Joseph M. *The New English*. New York: Free Press, 1970.

Chapter 4

The Organization of Discourse

Charlotte Linde

Charlotte Linde is a partner of Structural Semantics, a consulting firm which is applying techniques of discourse analysis to industrial and governmental communication problems. She has taught linguistics at the City University of New York, Naropa Institute, and the University of California, Berkeley, and has been a visiting scientist at the Max Planck Institute Project Group on Psycholinguistics, Nijmegen. Her research interests involve the structure of such ordinary discourse types as planning, reasoning, and life stories.

1. The Discourse Unit

Let us begin our investigation of the organization of discourse by looking at the following piece of verbal communication:

(1) and finally he came home and in the

Without knowing anything else, we know that this is not all that was said. This may be a piece of a sentence, but it is not a piece that makes any sense. An example of a natural piece, or constituent, is this:

(2) And finally he came home and in the process evidently got lost twice.

Example (2) is obviously a complete sentence, and a rather complex one. Even an example as compact as this should make it clear that not all strings of words, whether invented by a linguist or actually uttered by a speaker, are useful to analyze. We need pieces that are natural pieces, units out of which speakers actually construct conversation.

We are used to the idea of the sentence as a unit. It is less common to consider larger units in spoken language, but we can examine these in just the same way. That is, although (2) is an adequate sentence, it is clear that the speaker did not begin with this sentence, nor end with it. Sentence (2) forms a part of a larger unit, which is as tightly structured as its component sentences. The example is taken from a story told in response to the question "Have your kids ever gotten lost?"

(3) It was last weekend on the Promenade. They had a Promenade art show and he went up with a little girl who's twelve down the block, two houses down. She asked him to do something and they split and when he came back to what *he* thought was the point where he left her, he couldn't find her. And he looked and he looked and he looked for her, and finally he came home and in the process evidently got lost twice, but he did make it home.

Example (3) also represents a natural unit, with a definite beginning and end, and a great deal of internal structure. And on yet another level of organization, it is part of a still larger unit, a question-response pair. This chapter will deal with units like (3), discourse units.

Unlike the analysis of sentences, the study of discourse units is just beginning; however, one reason for this is the traditional analysis of written language, to which we have all been exposed in school. The work of teaching English grammar, of teaching people how to produce acceptable written English, has usually consisted of analysis of sentences. We are taught to name parts of speech—nouns, verbs, etc., the smallest building blocks of sentences. We are taught to recognize intermediate units of sentences, such as main clauses, dependent clauses, adverbial phrases, participial phrases, etc. And we are also taught something about the kinds of relations between a sentence and its parts. That is, a noun may be the subject of a sentence, an adverbial phrase may modify the verb, etc. Although it is often not clear to students why they have to learn these things, or what theory these facts are supposed to illustrate, the grammar usually taught in school adds up to a theory (however vague and incomplete) about the primacy of sentences and their structure.

Our school training, though, gives us no tools to deal with example (3). We might analyze it as a kind of paragraph, but the analysis of paragraphs is much less clear-cut than the analysis of sentences. There is currently no theory of paragraphs and their parts which is nearly as elaborate as a theory of sentences. Many writers often have trouble recognizing whether a group of sentences really forms a good paragraph. It is one of the hardest problems in teaching writing.

At this point, we must distinguish between written and spoken language. Even though there are differences between written and spoken sentences, we can use the notion of sentence for both written and spoken language. But the notion of paragraph, as it has been taught, appears to be applicable only to written language. In general, the grammar taught in school is taught to improve writing. So we must look elsewhere for a description of units like example (3).

Theoretical linguistics appears to be a good place to look for a discussion of the units of spoken language. In the twentieth century, linguistics has focussed either on particular spoken languages, as in the American Structuralists' descriptions of previously unknown languages, or on language in general, as in the current theories stemming from the work of Noam Chomsky. However, here too we see a focus on the sentence as the basic unit of analysis. Zellig Harris, summarizing the position of the American Structuralist school, argues that the concentration on the sentence is a matter of convenience.[1] The tools applicable to the analysis of sentences could be used on larger units. Since the problems of greatest interest to this school, the predictable co-occurrence relations between words and pieces of words, happen within the sentence, most work was restricted to the sentence. The sentence was the object of study because it was not necessary to look at anything larger.

Chomsky also takes the sentence as the primary unit of analysis. Furthermore, in focussing on competence, the speaker's knowledge of whether or not a sentence is grammatical in his language, Chomsky has introduced a normative element into linguistics. Rather than accounting for how people actually use language, the linguist determines whether a given sentence is judged to be part of the language, or whether there is something wrong with it which keeps it from belonging to the language. He must then produce a grammar that will describe and explain the structure of those sentences which fully belong in the language. This grammar is supposed to account for both its spoken and written forms.[2] However, speakers' intuitions about the grammaticality of a sentence of English are often heavily influenced by what they have been taught about "correct English," a notion that essentially involves standard written English.

If we wish to investigate how people really use language, there are a number of approaches which can be taken. One is to consider the social effects of speech—how people persuade, request, agree, refuse, insult, promise, etc. These questions lead immediately to a consideration of actions accomplished in the social arena. We would then look at such speech acts as promising, betting, christening, etc.

1. Harris, "Discourse Analysis," pp. 355–83. (Full references not given in footnotes will be found in the Suggestions for Further Reading at the end of the chapter.)
2. Chomsky, *Syntactic Structures; Aspects of the Theory of Syntax.*

This is an approach that forms the basis of an entire school of linguistic philosophy.

But there is another approach. It does not immediately look to the social consequences of linguistic acts but rather at the major linguistic units which people produce. People narrate stories, tell jokes, give recipes, plan their activities. Each of these is a linguistic unit, as well as a social unit, and it appears that they have more salience for the speaker than do smaller units. That is, as speakers, we are far more aware of undertaking to tell a story than we are of undertaking to produce a sentence.

Two immediate questions we have to ask about any linguistic unit are the nature of its boundaries and the nature of its internal organization. The question of boundaries is one which is important to us both as analysts of language and as participants in conversation. As competent members of our social groups, we are able to recognize these boundaries. For example, we usually know that a speaker has begun a joke, and we are socially required to recognize its end by laughing or demonstrating some other form of appreciation. As we shall see in the analysis of a number of different discourse units, it is the fact that speakers and hearers treat these discourses as units that allow us to recognize their unity.[3]

We also must consider the internal organization of the discourse unit. The component sentences of (3) are clearly organized very tightly. This can be shown by an attempt to rearrange its clauses. The reader is invited to try to do so. It may be possible to start with the second sentence and follow it with the first: "They had a Promenade art show. It was last weekend." But any other reorganizations seem to destroy the coherence of the discourse. It is important to discover what principles of organization are used to achieve this coherence. One very obvious principle in (3) is its temporal organization. The order of the sentences reflects the order in which the events seem to have occurred. Consider (4), an excerpt from (3).

> (4) . . . and he went up with a little girl who's twelve, down the block, two houses down. She asked him to do something, and they split.

Reading or hearing this, we assume that first he went with the little girl, then she asked him to do something, and after that they split. This principle of temporal ordering of main clauses—matching the order of clauses to the order of events they describe—may seem to be too obvious to discuss. But it is necessary to specify this as a major princi-

3. B. Wald, "The Discourse Unit" (unpublished manuscript, UCLA, 1977).

ple of coherence of English stories, since it is not the only logically possible relation which could hold between sentences. Even in English, we can have other interpretations of the temporal relation between the events referred to by a series of sentences:

(5) a. She sang and he accompanied her on the harpsichord.

b. I yelled and I screamed and I jumped up and down.

In both of these examples, the most natural interpretation is that the events are simultaneous.

These might seem like minor exceptions to the temporal ordering principle. But we must be careful not to draw universal conclusions about discourse from examples in a single language. If we compare an English narrative structure, whether oral story, novel, movie, etc., to the plot of a Javanese shadow play *(wayang),* we find an enormous difference. Becker in his study of the structure of *wayang* has shown that temporal organization is not the major principle of coherence. Rather, these elaborate puppet plays are organized by the coincidence of events in several different realms: human, demonic, and divine, and by the requirement that actions be presented in a fixed series of places.

> An American who seeks character development in *wayang* is going to be disappointed in all but a few *wayang* stories, while a Javanese who seeks complex coincidences in all but a few American movies (those few being comedies like the Marx Brothers' *Animal Crackers*) is going to be disappointed. . . . What in the *wayang* plot are significant coincidences, in the Western plot are crudities, violations of the basic notions of unity and causality. In *wayang,* we might say that Gatsby, Godzilla, Agamemnon, John Wayne and Charlie Chaplin—or their counterparts—do appear in the same plot: and that is what causes the excitement—that clash of conceptual universes is what impels the action.[4]

Although temporal ordering is an important way of organizing discourse, it is not the only one. Another extremely common form of organization in discourse can be described as a tree structure. A tree is a formal structure which can express any kind of relation of dominance or inclusion. Let us begin with an example taken from a description of a typical family dinner.

(6) OK. Some kind of meat, a starch, like rice or potatoes, um a vegetable, green vegetable or a salad, and something

4. Becker, "Text-Building, Epistemology, and Aesthetics in Javanese Shadow Theatre."

that that the kids will eat like corn or some, something like that. And that's about it. Usually no dessert. I don't make dessert.

Although (6) may appear to be quite simple, it is actually a very tightly structured discourse. Its boundaries are clearly marked, the beginning by *OK,* and the end of the description of the meal proper by "And that's about it.". We can display the information that the speaker has given to us in the form of a tree, Figure 4.1.

This diagram displays the major categories that we can expect to appear in a typical family dinner, and in some cases, gives examples of what specific foods fill these categories. It also represents the parts of the discourse. The cultural information which Americans share with the speaker includes the knowledge that a dinner typically consists of a meat, a starch, and a vegetable. Each of these categories can be represented by a number of specific foods. For example, "a starch" may be rice, potatoes, or a number of other things that are not mentioned in this discourse but which would be equally appropriate. Each category may be divided into smaller sub-categories. For example, the category "vegetable" is divided by the speaker into things that kids will eat, and by implication things like green vegetables and salads, which they won't eat. "Dessert" is a particularly interesting category in this discourse. Why did the speaker include dessert at all in her description of her family dinner, if she does not make it? Clearly, she shares with us the expectation that a meal typically includes dessert and so uses the negative statement to contrast her actual practice. (This use of negation

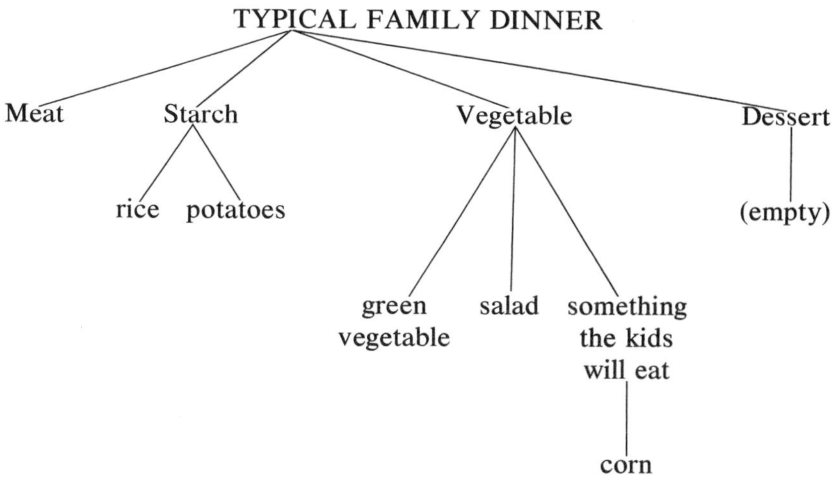

Figure 4.1. ***The Structure of a Typical Family Dinner***

as a marker of deviation from expected events or norms is extremely widespread. We will come back to it in the discussion of narrative structure.)

The discourse unit in (6) clearly marks dessert as a special category by separating it from the other parts of the meal. *And that's about it* is obviously a closing. Yet it does not end the unit; it is followed by a mention of the absence of dessert. We might at first be tempted to analyze the first closing as an error, but in fact it serves as a boundary between the parts of the meal which are actually present and a final part of the meal which could be expected but which is absent.

Figure 4.1 represents one tree structure that emerges from the discourse in (6). Certain other analyses are possible. For example, we might have done a further analysis, like Figure 4.2, in which Meat, Starch, and Vegetable are all members of a larger category of "Main Course."

Setting up the category of Main Course corresponds to our knowledge about typical meals, but there is no direct evidence for it in the discourse.

The tree structure representing this meal description is only one example of the many uses and kinds of tree structures. The most obvious linguistic example is the tree postulated for the structure of sentences, which indicates the sub-parts of the sentence and their relations to one another. Some other examples are the Dewey decimal system for classifying the subject matter of books, the standard Linnean biological classification, and organization charts for large groups like

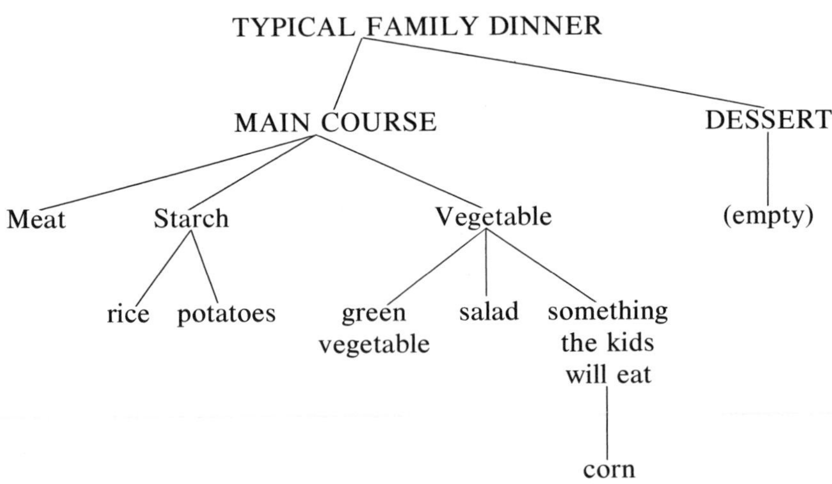

Figure 4.2. ***The Structure of a Typical Family Dinner Revised***

the United Nations. For an example like (6), we may ask whether the tree structure tells us anything about the discourse itself, or whether the discourse shows a tree structure only because the information itself is tree structured. But, for (6) we cannot settle on an answer. Later, in Section 4, we will see an example in which the discourse structure can be represented as a tree, even though the information underlying it is *not* tree structured.

Temporal organization and tree organization are principles of structural organization. They are equivalent to the organization of sentences into subject and predicate. But obviously the content of a discourse is an equally powerful means of achieving coherence. We expect that any discourse will be "about" something; we cannot just string together any sentences and get a coherent discourse, even if those sentences share referents. One strong form of organization which the content of the discourse provides is a contrast between the state of affairs expressed by the discourse and the beliefs that the speaker holds about the way that things ought to be.

There is a clear example of this in (6). The speaker tells us, "Usually no dessert. I don't make dessert." Her description of a typical dinner assumes that it is normal for it to include dessert, and so she reports the way in which her behavior differs from this norm. This statement probably also contains an implicit claim that she is actually doing a good job of feeding her family by not giving them dessert, since there is another norm that desserts are not good for you. It is impossible to establish this point from (6) alone. But we can get confirming evidence from other speakers answering the same question about family dinners. For example, (7) concludes a discussion of family dinner.

(7) . . . and we have dessert depending on whether we're feeling fat or thin at that point. Generally not of late. We always have fruit, incidentally. I mean there's a basket in the kitchen that always has fruit in it.

This speaker is clearly assuming that dessert is bad for you, but fresh fruit is good. The reader may enjoy examining this norm further by listening to how people discuss desserts. "It's a sinfully rich chocolate cake," "I was really wicked this weekend, I had pie, and an ice-cream sundae," etc.

Particularly when we come to the analysis of stories, Section 3, we will see that cultural expectations about the way things ought to be will play a large role in explaining what the point of a story is and how the speaker chooses to tell it. In fact, cultural expectations are present in every type of discourse.

Let us summarize the kinds of questions that we will ask about discourse units. In Section 2, we will consider the question of how the unit begins and ends. In Section 3, we will consider how beliefs and attitudes of the speaker and hearer are used to structure the discourse unit. In Section 4, we will look further at the question of the internal structure of the discourse unit and the effect it has on the structure of the sentences which comprise it.

2. A Highly Structured Discourse Unit—The Joke

One dimension along which discourse units differ is the degree to which they are personally created by the speaker. At one end, there are units like the Pledge of Allegiance or the Lord's Prayer—forms that are totally fixed. Other highly formal discourse units, like the christening of a ship or a State of the Union address, while not as frozen, are still extremely constrained in both their form and content. At the other end of the scale, we find stories of personal experience, which allow for a great deal of individual creativity. Somewhere between these two points lies the joke, which allows for a great deal of creativity in style of delivery, but which has a limited form.

One factor that defines the form of a joke is that it has a definite beginning and ending. There are formulaic beginnings which signal that a joke will follow. "Stop me if you've heard this one, but . . . ," "Did you hear the one about the man who . . ." "A funny thing happened. . . ." Not all jokes begin this way, but when we hear any of these, we know that a joke is being signalled, just as we know that "Once upon a time . . ." signals the beginning of a fairy tale. These formulaic beginnings are all structural indications of the kind of unit the speaker intends, rather than markers of content. There are also certain subjects that are standard topics for jokes, and these too can serve as signals that a joke is intended.

(8) It seems there was a priest, a minister, and a rabbi . . .

This standard cast of characters signals a joke, while the introductory "It seems there was . . ." merely signals the beginning of a unit, probably a joke, but not necessarily.

Jokes also have obligatory endings, a unit which is commonly called the "punchline," the part which pulls the joke together and makes it funny. (It is impossible to discuss here what makes jokes funny. A number of extremely serious works have been published to answer this question.[5]) The punchline also has an important structural property. It must be the last part of the joke; nothing must follow it. Therefore, for the social interaction of joke telling to be successful, it is the job of the speaker to make it clear that the punchline has been reached, and it is the job of the hearer to indicate that he has realized this, by laughter, groans, or the production of another joke.

Often, jokes are spoken of as being "funny stories." We will examine the structure of stories in Section 3, but at this point, we can examine at least a few properties of jokes, both structural and social, which differentiate them from stories of personal experience. Some jokes, like elephant jokes, knock-knock jokes, riddles, and other types which have a Question-Question-Answer structure, are easily distinguishable from stories. Other types of jokes appear to have a narrative structure—they have characters, scenes, and a sequence of events. But certain factors distinguish them from stories.

One is the person in which they are told. Stories are most often about personal experience, and so are told in the first person. Jokes are told in the third person: "This man goes into a bar . . ." This is not only a third person, it is an extremely abstract third person. We know nothing about him at all. He is not someone the hearer knows ("You remember Albert, the one who never took a bath") nor is he someone of interest because he is related to the speaker ("My cousin Herbie . . ."). The one exception to this is in the performance of professional comedians, whose special position permits them to tell what are formally jokes in the first person.

Another social characteristic of jokes which differentiates them from narratives of personal experience is that they are taken as fictional. The truth of a story can be challenged, but it is obviously inappropriate, at the end of a joke, to object, "That's not true. He did *not.*" This is something that children have to learn. We can sometimes observe young children asking after a joke, "What happened then?" indicating that they have not yet learned that they are to take the events of a joke as unreal.

The social use of jokes in conversation also reveals a great deal about the nature of these units. One of the strongest arguments we have for treating jokes and stories as units is that participants in a conversation treat them as uninterruptable units. Roughly speaking, once a speaker has begun a discourse unit and the hearers have recognized that he has begun it, he has control of the floor until he finishes. This does not mean that everyone else is silent throughout. The other

5. The classic work is Sigmund Freud, *Jokes and Their Relation to the Unconscious* (New York: Norton Library, 1960).

participants often contribute remarks of appreciation, comments, questions, side remarks, etc. But the person producing the unit has the floor in the sense that he has permission to finish the unit which he has begun; the subject will not be changed until the unit is complete. This point about the noninterruptability of discourse units is of particular interest, because it forms a sharp contrast with the rules for the exchange of the floor in other kinds of conversation. The normal rule is that one of the hearers may begin speaking at a point when the speaker has come to the end of his sentence, or to a point which is a possible end of the sentence, even if not the one intended by the speaker. Formally structured discourse units like the joke or the story enlarge the scope of this rule. Rather than having the floor for the duration of the sentence, the speaker may continue for the duration of the discourse unit.[6]

Before the speaker obtains the floor to deliver an extended unit, there may be negotiations about whether or not he will get it. One possible issue may be whether the situation is an appropriate one for jokes. Another issue may be whether the hearers already know the joke. It is a convention that a joke is funny for a hearer only once, and so he has a right to stop the telling if he knows the joke. This idea is reflected in formulas like "Have you heard the one . . ." and "Stop me if you've heard this one." One way for the hearer to prove that he has heard the joke already is to tell or summarize the joke which he expects is intended, thus gaining the floor himself. Another way to reject the intended joke is to tell another, obviously bad joke, as an example of the kind of joke that can be expected from the speaker.[7]

These negotiations take place before the beginning of the unit. But sometimes it is not until the middle of the joke that the hearer identifies the joke being told as one he knows. It seems to be impolite to stop the speaker at this point; in fact, there seems to be no socially acceptable way to do it. Rather, the hearer will permit the speaker to continue to the end and will duly laugh at that point. Sometimes, particularly if there are other hearers as well, the person who has recalled the joke will begin to laugh in the middle and will continue to laugh until the end. He may even chorus the punchline or part of the punchline. But he will not end the telling in the middle.

EXERCISE. Listen to jokes as they are told by people you know and by professional comedians, preferably on television or in person, rather than on records. What kinds of differences do you observe in

6. For an extensive discussion of this process of turn exchange, see Sachs et al., "A Simplest Systematics for the Organization of Turntaking for Conversation, pp. 696–735.
7. An extended and elegant analysis of such negotiation can be seen in Sachs, "An Analysis of the Course of a Joke's Telling in Conversation," pp. 337–53.

how the jokes are introduced? What kinds of differences are there in how the characters in the joke are identified? It would be particularly interesting to find examples of professionally told jokes retold by your friends. Television talk shows and the monthly joke sections of magazines like *Playboy* are good sources for this kind of retelling.

3. A Personally Creative Discourse Unit—The Narrative

Although jokes obviously differ from teller to teller, they are not fully creative discourses. That is, it is rare for a speaker to invent a joke. Let us now consider a less restricted discourse unit, the narrative of personal experience.

The minimal definition of this unit is that it is a form that retells past experience by matching the sequence of clauses to the purported sequence of events.[8] Before a unit can be considered a narrative (in English) it must have at least this feature of temporal ordering. Usually narratives contain much more structure as well, but temporal sequence is the defining characteristic, or the obligatory principle of coherence. Example (9) is an instance of a minimal narrative.

(9) Well this person had a little too much to drink and he attacked me, and the friend came in, and she stopped it.

Here we are given nothing more than four events and the order in which they happened. It would have been perfectly possible for the speaker to have given the same events without matching the order of clauses to the order of events—without making it recognizable as a narrative.

(10) A friend of mine came in just in time to stop this person who had a little too much to drink from attacking me.

These narrative clauses, past-tense main clauses that give the events of the experience, form the skeleton of the narrative. But normal narratives contain other parts as well, which are outlined below. This division into parts has not been made according to any predetermined scheme for the logically necessary parts of a narrative. Rather, it has been established through the empirical examination of a great number of narratives. In addition to narrative clauses, these parts are:

8. The definition of the form of narrative is taken from Labov, "The Transformation of Experience in Narrative Syntax," pp. 354–96.

1. *Abstract.* Often speakers begin with a few clauses which summarize the entire story, as in (11).

> **(11)** I once had to have my number changed because someone was bothering me. They were very good, they did it very quickly.

In some cases, the narrator stops and is prompted by the hearer to continue. This is particularly true in stories like (11), which were given in response to an interview question. But in ordinary conversation, the abstract may serve as the basis for negotiations similar to ones discussed for jokes. In other cases, both in interviews and in ordinary conversation, the narrator goes on immediately from the abstract, without any prompting from the hearer.

2. *Orientation.* Often there are a number of clauses, either at the beginning or after the abstract, if there is one, which serve to identify the characters, the time, the place, and the surrounding activity. The narrative given in (3) begins in this way, without an abstract.

> **(12)** It was last weekend on the Promenade. They had a Promenade art show.

The speaker was asked about whether her children had ever gotten lost. There is no need for an abstract, since we know what sort of a story it will be. The main character has also been established, so the orientation gives the time, the place, and the situation.

3. *Coda.* Narratives are often, though not always, concluded with a coda, a signal that the story is over. A very common coda is "That was it." This is a pure ending signal; it does nothing but indicate the close of the unit and is found in many other types of discourse units besides narratives. Other codas, like (13), may give the effects of the event:

> **(13)** And it worked out very well.

The coda may also bring the speaker back to the present, as in (14).

> **(14)** So we've been here for five years now.

EXERCISE. In (15) identify the abstract, orientation, narrative clauses, and coda. (There will be some material left over, which we will discuss later.)

(15) I've had one bad experience in sixteen years, and I think that's pretty good.

(*Interviewer:* What happened?)

I was walking down the street before we moved in here and some guy came up to me with a knife, and you know, said he wanted money, and I clunked him on the head with my purse and bit him on the hand and he finally went away. (Laughs) And that's the only time I have ever had any bad experiences.

The units which we have been examining are sequential units—beginning, middle, and ending, with some reversals and overlaps. We must now examine a component of narrative that has no fixed place in the sequence, but which may occur anywhere. This is the evaluation—the speaker's way of conveying what the point of the story is, why the story is worth telling. The minimal narrative in (9) lacks such an evaluation, and as a result, seems odd. These are dramatic events, but the story is not dramatic, since the speaker gives no clue about what her attitude is, how she wants us to feel about these events, or why she bothered telling it.

There are a number of devices that a speaker can use for indicating why a story is worth telling. One is external evaluation. The narrator steps outside the story to tell the audience what the point is. There is an example in (15), "I think that's pretty good" (to have only one bad experience in sixteen years). The next stage in integrating the evaluation into the story is to report the evaluation as an emotion which occurred at the time, or to quote another character giving an evaluation. A less direct form of this device is to narrate some action that occurred as a response to the main events, which will give the hearer an idea of what those main events must have been like. Thus in (16), the end of a story about being caught in an electrical blackout, we are told something about the participants' reaction to these events that portrays them as exciting.

(16) And we all finally made it home to my house and we all stayed up half the night just talking about it.

Many of these devices appear as full sentences, and as such, interrupt the flow of events. But we can also find evaluative devices which are integrated into narrative clauses. For example, in (16) "We all finally made it home to my house" is a narrative clause, telling a final event in a sequence. But it contains a number of devices which tell the hearer not only what happened, but also what kind of an event this was. The adverb *finally* implies that the process was long and difficult. The choice of the verb in *made it home* also implies difficulty. Compare the effect of (16) with (17), which is more purely narrative, without evaluative force.

(17) And we all went home to my house.

Another similar device is repetition, as in this excerpt from (3).

(18) And he looked and he looked and he looked for her.

The speaker is not only reporting what the child did, she is making the point that he really did his job and behaved in a proper way.

It would probably be impossible to give a list of all the syntactic and lexical choices that a speaker could use to produce an evaluative effect. It is much more interesting to examine evaluation as a function. There are at least two such functions that we can distinguish. One is to establish reportability, and the other is to refer to values and norms about the way things should be. Reportability contrasts the ordinary and the extraordinary. Completely ordinary events cannot be made into a narrative; the speaker cannot justify holding the floor with something that might elicit the response "So what?" Thus it would ordinarily be socially impossible to narrate the sequence "I saw John today and he said hello to me."

This might make social sense, however, if John were known to be someone who scorns all social conventions and never greets anyone. It would, of course, be possible to make up any number of possible circumstances under which such a sequence would be reportable. The important point is that it is necessary to construct some interpretation and, if necessary, make it available to the listener with an evaluation device. By comparison, a sequence like "I got hit on the head with a beer bottle and they took me to the hospital, and I had to have fourteen stitches" requires no additional justification at all for its narration.

There is no fixed scale to determine how reportable the events of a narrative must be; it is determined by the speaker and the hearer and their relation to one another. People who see one another every day, for example, coworkers in an office, may relate stories of relatively low reportability which they would not bother to tell to close friends whom they see less often. There are also differences in the degree of reportability of first-person and third-person stories. I can tell a relatively commonplace story about myself. But if I am to tell a story about a friend of ours, it must be more reportable than the most commonplace story which I can tell about myself. This is all the more true for third-person stories about someone not known to the hearer. I can tell a story about someone my listener does not know only if the events involved are quite out of the ordinary. In effect, there is a continuum of the reportability or degree of interest regarding characters which runs: first person—known third person—unknown third person. The greater the reportability of the character, the lower the degree of reportability of events need be, and the less evaluation is required to function as a reportability device.

This continuum obviously omits the second person. Normally, we do not tell our listener a story about himself, since by convention, a story imparts new events and we may assume that a person is the best authority on the events of his life. It is when he is not that we get second-person stories. One such case is parents telling children stories about their behavior as babies. These, presumably, are events that are too early for the child to remember. This appears to be one way in which parents impart to children mythologies about their characters: "Even then, you were a stubborn kid." Another example is the situation in which the hearer does not remember an event he was a participant in. A third case is the one in which both the speaker and the hearer remember the events, but they interpret or remember them differently.

In addition to the relative reportability of their events, narratives are also made coherent through moral comments about the way things are, the way things ought to be, and the kind of a person that the speaker is. Evaluation devices express these concerns as their second kind of function. Consider example (3) again. The protagonist is the speaker's nine-year-old son. This story appears to be rather short and sparse, but in fact it is full of evaluative devices, both in choice of words and choice of incidents. Most of these devices make the same point—everyone behaved well, everyone did just what he should.

(19) . . . and he went up with a little girl *who's twelve* down the block, two houses down.

By including information about the age of her son's companion, the speaker indicates that she was not irresponsible in sending her young son out alone to get lost.

(20) *She asked him to do something* and they split.

He did not just wander off; he was obeying a perfectly reasonable request.

(21) *. . . and when he came back to what he thought was the point where he left her,* he couldn't find her.

He tried his best to find her. It was nobody's fault that he failed; it was just a mix-up. The mother and son are portrayed as moral and reasonable people doing what ought to be done.

We can look for this form of evaluation both in the events that people narrate and in the points that they make with them. For example, people frequently tell stories about hospitals in order to demonstrate the well-known awfulness of hospitals. However, if the awfulness is well known enough, it then becomes possible to tell a hospital story whose point is that, surprisingly, everything went well.

It is not always possible to predict from the events of a narrative what the direction of the evaluation will be. Consider again story (15). These events are certainly reportable—a woman foiling a would-be mugger by violence. Yet, there is something odd about this story. We would expect that events like these would be turned into a narrative whose point is to demonstrate the courage, cleverness, and resourcefulness of the speaker. Yet she does not do this. We might argue that she is achieving this effect by indirection and understatement; the events are so striking that they need no further evaluation. But in fact what the speaker is doing is a good deal more complex, and in order to understand it, we need to know something about the speaker and something about the constraints of the interview situation. The speaker has been seriously involved in community politics for at least fifteen years. The interview was about urban neighborhoods. She used the questions as a way of making a number of points about her neighborhood that are very important to her. Again and again she returned to the theme that the neighborhood is rich in human resources, that it is not as bad as people say, that the attempts of community members *can* change things for the better. A story about being mugged in the neighborhood pulls in the opposite direction, and so she tells it to make the point that one not very serious incident in sixteen years is not really bad, rather than making the most of the incident to enhance her own picture of herself.

This is a clever solution to the problem of presentation, but why did she tell the story at all, if it posed a problem? She began by answering a question about whether she was satisfied with the police protection.

(22) . . . I have *never ever* in this neighborhood felt unsafe. I walk at four o'clock in the morning by myself, always have. I've had one bad experience in sixteen years, and I think that's pretty good.

She is making her point about how good the neighborhood is, but in the course of doing so, she has made a claim about having had a bad experience. When asked about it, she is under some pressure to prove that she really did have one. This appears to be a constraint operating both in the interview situation and in everyday conversation as well. If someone is asked "What was the worst fight you ever had with your parents?" he has an acceptable mechanism for avoiding the question by claiming that no such thing ever happened. But if he is asked "Did you ever have a really bad fight with your parents?" and answers "Yes," it is extremely hard for him to refuse to answer a question about an incident whose existence has been admitted.

EXERCISE: Divide the following narrative into its parts. Which events are presented as reportable? What norms about the way things should be is the speaker presupposing? What kind of person does the speaker present herself as?

(23) (*Interviewer:* You were telling me about this apartment. How did you find it?)

Well, we uh arrived in, first of all moved to New York with a moving van that not only had all the standard garden tools uh it was, I guess, well I said in the beginning that we intended to live in the city and I wanted to . . .

(Interruption)

(*Interviewer:* So how did you find this place?)

So we came to New York, the only person we knew in New York was a cousin who lived in Berkeley Heights, New Jersey, ironically. So we had agreed to talk with them about where to live and they thought Berkeley Heights was the place to live. But because of this conversation with the other friend, I wanted very much to come to the city. So we took the train in, and the train ride itself was one reason why I felt we should not live in New Jersey, that it was a difficult, the train was very bumpy, it was a, it was not the express kind of train that you might have had in the morning. And I just felt that my husband's effectiveness would be diminished by that train ride. So that was negative number one, and then negative number two, we got to the city and we really loved Brooklyn Heights. We thought it was charming. We liked the architecture and the scale and we stumbled into a house that belonged to U———, who was one of the first people to start the brownstone renovation, as it turns out, in Brooklyn Heights, and she took an interest in us, and began to make phone calls about finding a place to live, and we tried a couple of them out and they were both very expensive and not very attractive and so about five, we settled down for a cup of coffee in a drugstore and the pharmacist strolled over and we told him our problems and he said he knew of an apartment. And he sent us over there and we knocked on the door and the super said, no they didn't have any apartments, and we said "But this person told us that you did." And so it turned out it was one of those very involved New York situations where they, the people who had the apartment, wanted to get another apartment and they could only do it if they rented theirs but there were a couple of friends. Well anyway the husband was called of the current lessee and said the first person to take it gets it. So we were shown the apartment and uh it seemed very expensive, it was $175 a month which compared to to, I can't remember now but I think I paid 115 a month for a far more attractive and newer, I think the worst thing about New York to us was the fact that everything was so old. The kitchen was dilapidated, bathroom was not very attractive, and so uh we debated the hundred and seventy-five dollars and the whole urban move for a few minutes, and my husband, who is very conservative, said "Well let's go and think it over." So we walked down to the Sound and I said "Listen. From what we've seen today, this looks like a very good deal." And I said "What we'll do is we'll stop the first three people who come along and we'll ask them if an apartment of that size at that rent is a good deal. If it is, I think we should go back and take it." So we did that.

(*Interviewer* (laughs): This is an *enterprising* story.)

We stood on the sidewalk, we stopped three people, we said "Listen, we don't know a thing about New York, we found this four-and-a-half room apartment for $175 a month with nice big rooms, should we take it?" And everyone said "Sure you should take." So we walked back in and we said "We'll take it." That's how we landed in—Ironically, one of the people we asked was the husband of the lessee, who said later he thought people who were so naive as to ask that, he should have said "By all means, don't take it, that's outrageous." But anyway we took it, they became very good friends of ours in the end. And that's how we

> landed in New York. We really didn't intend to live there very long but we lived there four and a half years. I believe it was, before we moved.

Here we have a story about the experience of finding an apartment. Like most such experiences, it is not intrinsically interesting; it is the job of the narrator to make it interesting. The narrator of this story succeeds in doing this both by recounting a complicated series of events, and by the use of an elaborate evaluative structure. It would have been possible for her to tell this as a story with few events: meeting the pharmacist, being the first to ask for the apartment, and getting the apartment. The much more complicated series of events which she does narrate serves as an indirect corroboration of a number of her main points—that getting an apartment in New York is difficult, and that she and her husband, although naive, were able to succeed because they were both lucky and enterprising.

As your analysis has no doubt shown, the evaluative structure of this narrative is extremely rich. The speaker has succeeded in making the events of her story reportable by shaping them so that they all have social meaning. That is, the events and the descriptions of this narrative all make some point about the way New York City is, or about what apartment hunting is like, or about the ways in which people should act in new and unfamiliar circumstances. This makes the narrative interesting to a wide potential audience, since it is not merely a story about her own particular experiences, but about a world which we share with her.

The problem of why a narrative is told raises a number of interactional issues that can only be touched on here. A narrative is not just a unit with its own internal structure; it is also a part of other ongoing processes. One is the speaker's presentation of self and his activities as constituting a coherent and worthy person. Another function of the narrative is its role in the conversation, the interview, or whatever other interaction is going on. The narratives presented in this paper all come from interviews, where they functioned as responses to the requests of the interviewer. In conversation, they are sometimes produced in response to a request, sometimes self-generated and sometimes produced in response to a preceding story. The narrative may form a part of a larger pattern, being used to agree with or argue with some previous point made in the conversation.

But one thing that emerges clearly from the way that narratives are treated in interactions is that they are units which are significant to the participants. Once a narrative is begun, it will be completed. If it is interrupted by an external event, it will be resumed; and if a new participant enters, the story will be summarized for him and then continued. Often after an interruption, the hearer will prompt the speaker to continue. Narratives thus have very great powers of cohesion in an interaction; they strongly require completion. A narrative about a relatively unimportant event may be resumed long after it was interrupted.

4. Information and Discourse Unit—The Apartment Description

The discussion of narratives paid little attention to how the information of the narrative is chosen. The notion of reportability distinguishes a small number of unusual or highly salient events from all the other things going on. But it is clear that reportability is not a fact of the physical or even of the social world, but rather is something that is accomplished by the narrator. That is, the job of the narrator is to find a way to make events reportable. One thing that distinguishes a good storyteller is that he can turn seemingly minor events into a story. (Listen to the best storyteller you know to observe the kinds of events from which his stories are constructed.)

Even the notion of 'event' itself does not have a pre-existing reality but is created by the speaker as he constructs his units. All of these factors make it extremely difficult to study how the speaker chooses the information of the story, especially since these stories involve past happenings to which we have no direct access.

However, we can study the choice of information by investigating another discourse unit, the description of apartment layouts. The descriptions given here formed part of an interview in which the speaker answered the question "Could you tell me the layout of your apartment?"[9] These discourses are also produced in natural conversation and appear to have much the same structure. Let us begin by considering two examples:

(24) I'd say it's laid out in a huge square pattern, broken into four units. If you were looking down at this apartment from a height, it would be like, like I said before, a huge square with two lines drawn through the center to make like four smaller squares. Now on the ends, in the two boxes facing out on the street, you have the living room and a bedroom.

9. The results of this research are presented and discussed in Linde, *Linguistic Encoding of Spatial Information,* and in Linde and Labov, "Spatial Networks as a Site for the Study of Language and Thought."

In between these two boxes, you have a bathroom. Now between the next two boxes facing on the courtyard you have a small foyer and then the two boxes, one of which is a bedroom and the other of which is a kitchen and then a small foyer a little beyond that.

(25) That one was also a one-bedroom apartment. It was a brand new building. We were the first occupants in that apartment. You walked in the front door. There was a narrow hallway. To your left, the first door you came to was a tiny bedroom. Then there was a kitchen, and then bathroom, and then the main room was in the back, living room, I guess.

Although both (24) and (25) clearly answer the same question, they illustrate very different strategies for choosing and presenting information. We can characterize (24) as illustrating a map strategy. The speaker begins by giving the outside configuration of the apartment, then sketches in the internal divisions, and finally labels the internal divisions. This is fairly close to the procedure by which people actually draw maps. In contrast, (25) uses what we can call a tour strategy. The description takes the hearer on an imaginary tour of the apartment. The tour proceeds room by room, building up the knowledge of the layout by a successive naming of each room and its position. The imaginary tour may also contain some mention of actual motion through the layout, as in "You walked through the front door."

Our analysis of these descriptions will consider only the tour strategy, the most common strategy, representing 96 percent of the descriptions collected. There are good reasons why the map strategy is rare. Speakers use the map strategy only when the apartment they are describing has an outside shape which they can name. But even if the shape of the perimeter is nameable, speakers still may not use the map strategy because they do not know its outside shape. This lack of knowledge becomes evident when the speakers are asked to draw the apartment; they often make mistakes and then comment that they are considering the outside shape for the first time. This is not surprising. In an apartment dweller's experience, an apartment is something which has an inside and no outside, unlike a house, which one can walk around.

Another reason speakers prefer the tour strategy has to do with the temporal structuring of narratives (discussed in Section 3). The tour strategy transforms a spatial configuration into a temporal sequence. This permits the speaker to use the temporal order of language as an organizing principle for presenting spatial patterns. The map strategy has to create its own organization; it cannot use a necessary structure of language. Because it uses this temporal organization, the tour strategy may be considered a pseudo-narrative. A pseudo-narrative is a discourse structure that uses the sequence of clauses to mirror a sequence of events that has not happened in the past. It is, of course, true that the speaker has toured the apartment. But there are features of the spoken tour which are not part of any actual sequence of events. For example, at the end of a description of a long hall or a sequence of rooms, the spoken tour jumps back immediately to the beginning of the hall or sequence of rooms, a maneuver which could not have been part of any actual tour through the apartment. Other examples of pseudo-narratives are some forms of directions (such as cooking directions), stories about hypothetical events, sequences of typical events in the simple present tense or the general past tense, and definitions of words expressed as sequences of hypothetical events. Examination of the apartment layout descriptions shows that they share a number of properties with the narrative proper besides the simple use of temporal sequence.

1. *Summary.* The tour may begin with a summary, which corresponds to the abstract section of the narrative. The summary may describe how many rooms the apartment has, how many people live in it, what special features it has, or what the quality of the apartment or the building is. Example (26) shows some examples.

(26) That one was also a one-bedroom apartment. It was a brand-new building. We were the first occupants in that apartment.

That was one of those cold-water tenements, old, cold-water tenements they called them, I think, and the building was about one-hundred years old. I think it was one, what they call a railroad flat. Long and narrow.

There are three rooms.

There were three of us living in it.

Oh it's wonderful.

2. All these apartment descriptions begin with an entry into the apartment. This section corresponds to the orientation of the narrative, establishing the starting point from which the description will proceed. The entry section may specifically mention the entry, or the front door, or may establish entry through mention of the first room, as shown in the examples of (27).

(27) The entrance is into the kitchen.

You entered into a tiny little hallway.

Well you walk in the door.

When you opened the front door, you stepped into the living room.

You walk into a long hall.

You walked in and you walked directly into like a living room.

3. *Tour.* After the entry, the tour proceeds room by room through the apartment, mentioning each room and its position, like the narrative clauses of a narrative.

4. *Closing summary.* The tour may end with an optional closing summary, which corresponds to the coda of a narrative. This may give the number of rooms or occupants, may evaluate the apartment, or may simply be a formal indication that the tour is over. Examples are shown in (28).

(28) So it's three bedrooms. We use it for three, but it's actually a one-bedroom apartment.

It was very very tiny.

And that's it.

That's how it sets up.

5. *Evaluation.* Unlike narratives, the apartment descriptions need not contain an evaluation to be socially coherent. However, some speakers do include evaluation. This may be an evaluation of the entire apartment or of the building, placed in the opening or closing summaries. The speaker may also comment on the quality of a single room. These comments are either integrated into the sentence introducing the room, or follow it in the next clause. There are no instances in which the entire sequence of rooms is given and then followed by a sequence of evaluations. Examples are given in (29).

(29) You entered into a *tiny little* hallway.

And it comes into a *nice-sized* living room that also doubles for a dining room, *that has very very high ceilings that give a real sense of space.*

And the kitchen was off to the left. *And it was a good-sized kitchen, it wasn't fantastic but it was there, you know.*

This discussion of the form of the tour has included a number of points about the information chosen. We can now consider directly the question of how the speaker chooses information. First, the request for a layout influences the information chosen. The speaker knows many things about the apartment that the question does not call forth—how it

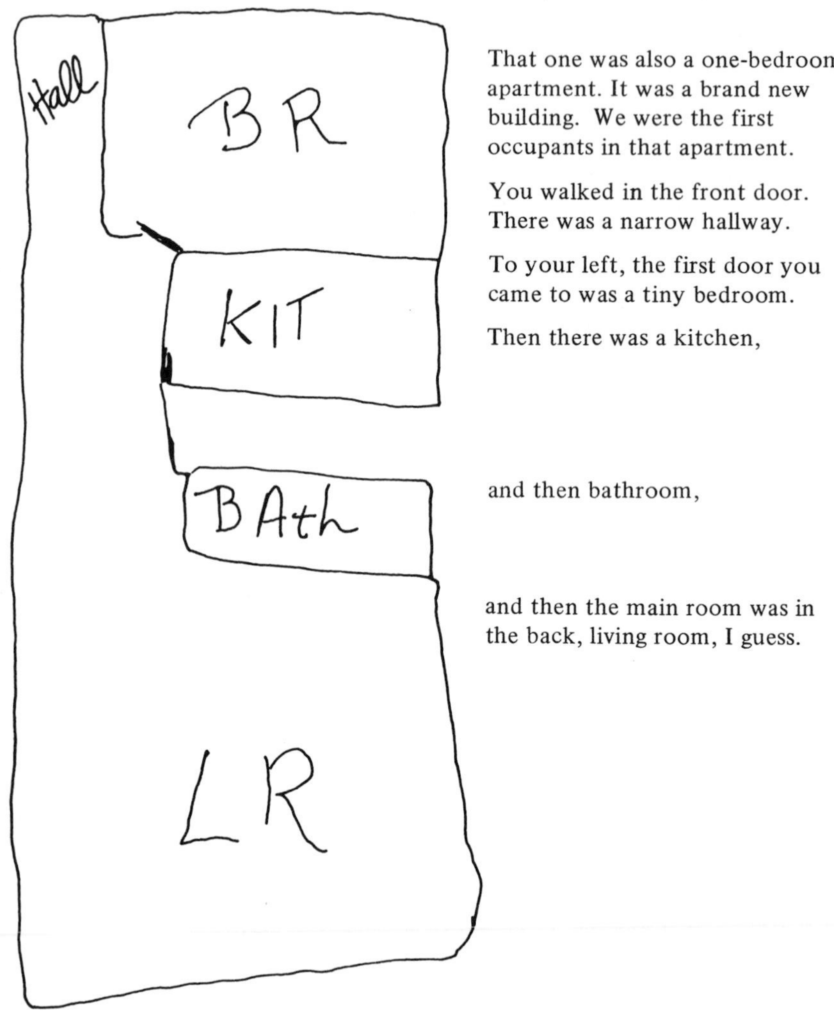

Figure 4.3. ***Floor Plan of the Apartment Described in (25) As Drawn by the Tenant***

is furnished, how he feels about it, what it costs. The answer will mainly consist of spatial information, but even so, the speaker does not use all of the spatial information available to him. A major point is that the tour consists of a route through the apartment, which will indicate to the hearer a way of entering all the rooms. It is important to understand that this actually is the information that the tour is intended to convey. If we look at (25) and try to draw a floor plan of this apartment, we find that we cannot arrive at a single map. We lack too much information about the outside configuration of the apartment, the size of the rooms, the shape of the rooms, and the way they fit together. Figure 4.3 shows the map that the speaker himself drew; clearly the description, reproduced next to it, does not uniquely determine the map.

At this point, we might be inclined to say that (25) is actually a bad description, and (24) is much more accurate. But this suggests that the majority of speakers produce bad descriptions. Rather than draw this conclusion, we must reconsider our assumptions about what the speakers are trying to achieve. If we find a great deal of regularity in a discourse type that speakers produce, we must assume that they are doing something well. It is our job as analysts to discover what it is that speakers are actually doing, rather than assuming that they are doing something else badly. What the speakers are doing well is that they give complete information about the existence and position of the rooms, so that we can trace a route through the apartment.

Let us now examine the formal structure of the information. The speaker has in his memory a three-dimensional experience of his apartment. The map represents a geometric, two-dimensional abstraction from this. The narrated tour represents a further abstraction, which reduces the rooms to points and the relations that exist between each point and the next. Thus we can represent the information of (25) as the tree structure of Figure 4.4.

The tree in Figure 4.4 is somewhat different from Figure 4.2. Figure 4.2, which shows the divisions of a typical family dinner, displays relations of class inclusion; that is, each item in the tree is a

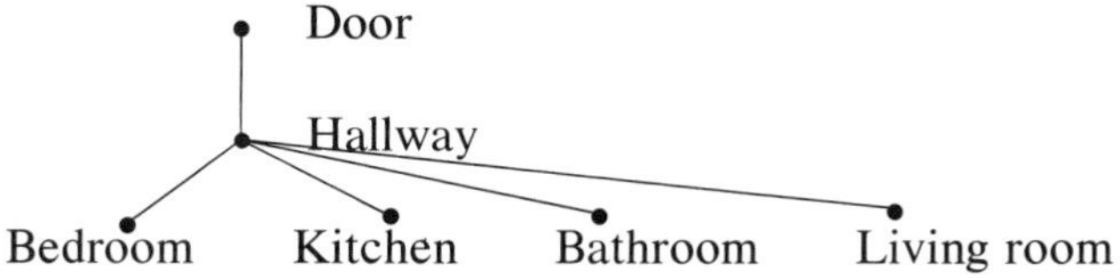

Figure 4.4. ***Formal Structure of the Information of an Apartment Description.***

member of the class indicated by the node above it. In Figure 4.4, the relation of dominance in the tree is used to indicate physical precedence in the spatial organization. Each room is physically further from the door than the place indicated by the node above it. The tree shows that from the door you have to go through the hall to get to the rooms.

The tree structure thus emerges as the underlying organization of the apartment layout descriptions. It might seem that this is a fact about apartments rather than a fact about apartment descriptions. But we can see that this is not the case by looking at apartments with alternate routes, apartments with one or more rooms that have more than one entrance. Speakers always describe only one route and only rarely mention the existence of alternatives. It is not intuitively obvious why this should be so. The fact that a room can be reached in two different ways may be a striking feature of an apartment, one which should be mentioned to give an adequate description of the layout. But the form of description actually given corresponds to the formal definition of tree structure, which forbids loops. That is, speakers take physical structures like Figure 4.5, and describe them like Figure 4.6 or Figure 4.7. Formally, Figures 4.6 and 4.7 are trees, and Figure 4.5 is not.

We have been looking at the structure formed by the rooms of the apartment and their relations. Let us now examine in greater detail one particular type of information, the notion of a room. To some extent the definition of a room is given by the physical world; it is an enclosed space of a given size. (There are a few borderline cases in which the size of a space makes it possible to call it either a room or a closet. Here function, a notion of the social sphere, determines how the space is identified.) The various sub-types of rooms represent distinctions made in the social rather than the physical sphere. The first major division of rooms is into bathrooms and all other rooms. This division is necessary because of the somewhat surprising fact that it is not obligatory to mention the bathroom when describing the layout. Some speakers do, others do not. Notice that this special treatment of bathrooms is not peculiar to apartment descriptions. Bathrooms are also

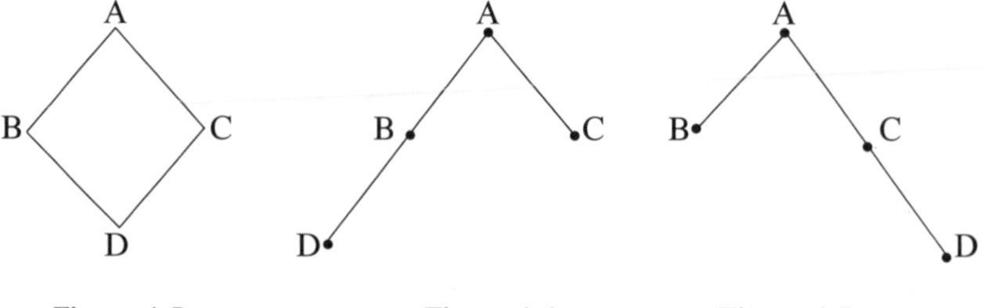

Figure 4.5 Figure 4.6 Figure 4.7

not included in room counts. That is, a three-room apartment will contain a living room, a kitchen, a bedroom, and a bathroom.

The next division that we can make is the distinction between major and minor rooms. Major rooms are those rooms that an apartment is expected to have—kitchen, living room, bedroom, and for some speakers, dining room. Minor rooms are all others, rooms that an apartment may or may not have—study, playroom, den, laundry room, etc. This distinction is reflected in speakers' descriptions of apartments.

EXERCISE: Consider the examples in (30). Each of these sentences represents the first mention of a room in the discourse. These sentences are a representative sample of the data. In these apartment descriptions, the use of the indefinite article *a* does not necessarily indicate that there is more than one of the noun introduced. Thus *To the right is a bedroom* does not necessarily imply that there is another bedroom somewhere else. Which articles are used to introduce major and minor rooms? In what positions of the sentence are the rooms introduced?

(30)a.

1. You walked into a little kitchen.
2. From there you come into the living room.
3. Directly in front of you was a living room.
4. The entrance is into the kitchen.
5. In the back of the apartment was the bedroom.
6. Toward the front there was a huge bedroom.

b.

7. The kitchen is just when you come in.
8. The bedroom was at one end and the bathroom was at the other.
9. And then the two bedrooms are in the back.
10. And the kitchen's on the left.

c.

11. And there's a dressing room, which is about two by four.
12. To the right is a large study, or office.
13. And there was a small sleeping alcove off that.
14. And then you walk straight into a big den.

The examples of (30) show that minor rooms are introduced only with *a,* the indefinite article, while major rooms are introduced with both the indefinite and the definite article. This pattern results from the general pattern of use of the articles. Typically, the indefinite article introduces noun phrases presenting new information, information not previously mentioned in the discourse; the definite article introduces noun phrases presenting old information, something already mentioned. Thus, we expect sequences like "You walk into *a* living room. Off *the* living room is a bedroom." In this example, the noun phrase *living room* is treated as new information the first time it is mentioned and as old information after that. However, the status of information includes more than merely whether or not a noun phrase has been used in the conversation. Information is a social as well as a discourse notion. Even if a speaker and a hearer are strangers to one another, they share knowledge and assumptions about the way they expect the world to be. One such set of assumptions is the knowledge of the kinds of rooms that apartments can be expected to have. Thus the speaker has a choice. In introducing a major room, he may treat it as old information and use the definite article, because it can be assumed that an apartment has a kitchen, for example. Or he may treat it as new information, since it has not yet been mentioned in the discourse. Both strategies are coherent, since information is not a brute fact about the world, but rather is constructed by the participants of the conversation. In contrast, minor rooms are always introduced with the indefinite article. It cannot be assumed that an apartment has a den or a playroom, and so the fact that it does is new information.

The examples of (30) also show that assumptions about the nature of information affect not only the choice of individual items like articles but the structure of sentences as well. We find that major rooms are introduced both in the subject position, as in the sentences of (30)b, and in the predicate, as in (30)a, while minor rooms are introduced only after the verb, as in (30)c. This also results from the nature of the information of the two types of rooms. Generally the subject position is used for the placement of old information. One reflection of this strategy is the very high proportion of pronoun subjects, since pronouns by definition replace some noun phrase which either can be assumed or has already been mentioned in the discourse. This function of the subject position can be checked by looking at any of the narratives given in Section 3. (There are exceptions, in which new information is placed in subject position: these exceptions are much more frequent in writing than in speech.) Given this function of the subject position, to place a minor room in the subject position would be to assume that its existence is to be expected. Consider the effect of someone saying "The aviary is to the left." If this is the first mention of the aviary, the sentence suggests that the speaker assumes that of course one has an aviary. The examples of (30)c do not make such an assumption.

We see then that the description of an apartment has both a physical and a social component. There is a set of physical facts about the separated spaces of the apartment and their relations that the speaker must describe. But there are also cultural conventions about which spaces are rooms, which rooms are expected, which rooms are unusual, etc.; and these cultural conventions must also be reflected in the description. Both types of information influence how speakers describe apartments.

5. Conclusion

We have seen that discourse units have an internal structure that is as regular and accessible to study as the structure of sentences, and that this study must proceed from the examination of actual texts rather than from intuitions of what might be possible. These units are organized by a number of formal and cultural principles of coherence, including temporal ordering, tree structure, and a whole net of social assumptions about the way things are and the way things ought to be. Finally, we have seen a few of the many possible examples of how these principles work to select the kind of information the speaker gives and the structure of the sentences in which he gives it.

My original interest in discourse structure and much of my understanding of it comes from William Labov. I would also like to thank Joseph Goguen, Livia Polanyi, Deborah Tannen, and Benji Wald.

Suggestions for Further Reading

The Structure of Narrative

Becker, A.L. "Text-Building, Epistemology, and Aesthetics in Javanese Shadow Theatre." In *The Imagination of Reality: Essays on Southeast Asian Symbolic Systems,* edited by A.L. Becker and A. Yengoyan. Norwood, N.J.: Ablex Publishing Co., 1979.

Labov, William. "The Transformation of Experience in Narrative Syntax." In W. Labov, *Language in the Inner City,* pp. 354–96. Philadelphia: University of Pennsylvania Press, 1972.

The Structure of Jokes

Sachs, Harvey. ''An Analysis of the Course of a Joke's Telling in Conversation.'' In *Explorations in the Ethnography of Speaking,* edited by Richard Bauman and Joel Sherzer, pp. 337–53. London: Cambridge University Press, 1974.

The Structure of Apartment Descriptions

Linde, Charlotte. *Linguistic Encoding of Spatial Information.* Ph.D. dissertation, Columbia University, 1974.

Linde, Charlotte and Labov, William. ''Spatial Networks as a Site for the Study of Language and Thought.'' *Language* 51, no. 4 (1975): 924–39.

Turntaking and Control of the Floor

Sachs, Harvey; Schegloff, Emmanuel; and Jefferson, Gail. ''A Simplest Systematics for the Organization of Turntaking for Conversation.'' *Language* 50, no. 4 (1974): 696–735.

Syntactic Theory

Chomsky, Noam. 1957. *Syntactic Structures.* The Hague: Mouton.

———. 1965. *Aspects of the Theory of Syntax.* Cambridge, Mass: MIT Press.

Harris, Zellig. ''Discourse Analysis.'' In *The Structure of Language,* edited by Jerry A. Fodor and Jerry Katz, pp. 355–83. Englewood Cliffs, N.J.: Prentice-Hall, 1964.

Literary Style

Chapter 5

Literary Style: The Personal Voice

Joseph M. Williams

1. Macrostructure: The Discourse and Its Forms

In all these essays, we've seen how language varies as its social, historical, and geographical contexts vary. But there is another kind of variation that has less to do with these large contexts than with the small, local moment in a sentence—the moment when the writer or speaker has shaped a sentence to lead us to a particular way of understanding a particular idea in the context of other ideas in other sentences. Where variations of geography and social class are largely rule-governed—theoretically if not actually predictably—the local shape of a sentence in any given speech event at any given moment is determined by the intersection of influences we cannot easily predict: the shape of an idea, the nuance of an attitude toward it, a particular intention, a shade of emphasis.

It is true that some writers tend to use certain kinds of sentence structures and words, so much so that often these structures become authorial signatures. Given a sample of prose we had never seen before from Samuel Johnson, Edward Gibbon, Norman Mailer, Oscar Wilde, or William Faulkner, we could guess the author.

But even global traits of style must be locally deployed in particular ways and places to create the particular shape through which a reader perceives the content of an expression. Sentences are the constantly changing syntactic prisms that refract experience into its parts and order them in coherent ways. Indeed, in the most carefully wrought prose, form and content merge into an instance of language in which they are indistinguishable.

We have already sketched in broad outline the theoretical model we shall build on (see Chapter 2). In an idealized speech event, a governing telos of intention/outcome transforms the participants in the event into personae, the setting into a scene, and the content into a subject matter. In this essay, we carry the description to the level of the sentence. Before we reach that level of detail, though, we have to glance at an immediately preceding level—at the abstract form of a discourse, a very difficult and not clearly understood level of linguistic organization and form.

There are two hierarchically related levels within this level: *genre* and *form*. At this level of organization, the potential variables are very great and their dependence on each higher hierarchical level of structure increasingly complex. Theoretically, different personae in different scenes, handling different overt subjects, all infused by different organizing principles, would be manifested in different genres, and each different genre would be manifested by different organizations. We can only glance at the complexities.

1.1 Genre

A genre is a general type of a discourse, a kind of continuous language that has no intrinsic intention, a category of speech or writing that could manifest different intentions. When you combine a specific intention with a genre, you have a speech event. Given the telos that infuses a speech event that we might term "borrowing-money," we could select one from among many genres, depending on different circumstances. We could write a letter; make a direct request; engage in a roundabout conversation; make a speech; sing a sad song; fall on our knees and pray that God will loosen our lender's pocketbook. All these are distinctly different genres of speech events: spoken address, written letter, spoken prayer, sung song, conversation, etc. Which of these genres we can use to manifest the speech event depends on the particular way in which the three components of personae, scene, and subject are infused with the particular intention of the event, all in the context of our cultural conventions.

PROBLEM 1. Genres connect to the internal structure of speech events on the one hand, and to their external contexts on the other. First, the internal structure. Is there any relationship between a genre and the form of sentences manifesting that genre? What kinds of sentences characterize prayers? Next, the contexts. What are the rules for the use of genres; for example, when does our culture forbid various genres? Consider the following: monologue, chant, prayer, song, letter, lyric poem, newspaper column, interview, essay, telephone call, conversation.

1.2. Form

There is one more crucial level of abstraction we must discuss before we get to the structure of sentences, to the explicit *text* of a discourse. Unfortunately, we must use sentences to illustrate it, a misleading procedure because it lets us confuse the ideational, cognitive structure of a speech event with its linguistic structure.

Now in reality, in the actual creation of a discourse—in the one I am creating at this moment, for example—the material manifestation of my thoughts is almost simultaneous with my sentences. I did not, at least consciously, think through to the end of that previous sentence (or this one) before I began writing it. The full, finished, complete idea did not, in truth, pre-exist my writing the sentences that expressed it.

And certainly as readers, we would find ourselves in an odd paradox if we assumed that there existed somewhere on the other side of the page the meaning that each sentence conjures up in our minds. The meaning is simultaneous with our recreating it.

But we are, as it were, out of time when we think about idealized discourses. We will assume in what follows that the meaning, the complete meaning, pre-exists the sentences and that the sentences only figure forth that meaning. So try to conceive of the ideational structure behind the particular sentences used to represent it as having a kind of independent existence. For example, these very different syntactic structures all share some aspect of meaning:

> The boy discovered the money. The money was discovered by the boy. What the boy discovered was the money. It was the boy who discovered the money. What the boy did was discover the money. The boy's discovery of the money occurred. The discovery of the money by the boy happened. The boy's discovering the money . . . For the boy to discover the money. . . .

Behind the diverse grammatical structures of those clauses and phrases is an unvarying core of abstract, cognitive relationships. There is the referent of *boy,* the referent of *money,* and the referent of the act we call *discover.* The cognitive, ideational referents, not the words, are in a constant relationship, regardless of the particular grammatical form of the clause or phrase. What *boy* refers to is always the agent of the action; what *discover, discovered, discovery,* and *discovering* refer to is the action; what *money* refers to is always the goal of the action. But *boy* is not always the subject, *discover* is not always a verb, and *money* is not always an object. Nor does *boy* always precede *discover* nor *money* always follow.

Actually, the problem is even more complex than this, for we also know that neither *boy* nor *money* refers directly to the thing out there in the real physical world, but first to the *idea* of boy or money. Out in the real world, the object to which *boy* relates is an unknowably complex set of cells, molecules, organs, and so on. The concept which *boy* refers to, the idea of a boy that 'exists' somewhere above the level of our eyebrows, is also unknowably complex, abstract, and obscure—but it is not the boy out there. The word *boy* mediates between the two in ways that after millennia of inquiry remain utterly obscure.

Even more obscure are those propositions that are not about things out there—*An apple is on my desk,* but about things going on in here, in the mental activity we might represent as *I think that the problem of cognition puzzles me more than any other.* It is extremely difficult to think about pure cognitive structure independent of language because we cannot stand side by side and jointly point to anything like the apple on my desk. There is simply nothing to show for whatever that sentence about cognition "stands for," "represents," or "means."

But once we can accept the idea that some shared core of meaning can stand behind the different sentence structures (or over them or under them—at least independently of them), we can begin to understand the notion of stylistic variation. Unless you can grasp this principle, our discussion of style will be very difficult to follow.

A narrative of an event is a relatively easy problem to start with. Let us assume that "out there," three things happen in a particular order and that we understand them together as making up a single event. We can represent the three smaller events in three propositions: (1) *John arrived.* (2) *Then George left.* (3) *Then Bill went to sleep.* Let us assume that someone asks about John, and that a telos roughly represented as tell - what - happened - to - John - in - a - direct - manner . . . infuses the personae, scene, and subject and is realized in a speech event whose genre is a narrative answer to the question:

A: What did John do?
B: He arrived before George left and Bill went to sleep.

But suppose the question were about George:

A: What did George do?
B: He left after John arrived but before Bill went to sleep.

In even as trivial a case as this, the organizing principle of the speech event determines the order of elements. The two answers refer to precisely the same set of events, but their structure depends on which question is asked, which in turn contributes to a distinct telos for the answer.

PROBLEM 2. Here are some other answers. What are the preceding conversational questions or statements that would elicit them? What would be the differences in the telos of each of these answers?

(1) No, it was George who left after John arrived but before Bill went to sleep.

(2) What Bill did was go to sleep after John arrived and George left.

(3) No, it was *after* John arrived and George left that Bill went to sleep.

An expository discourse can also be accounted for first in terms of its abstract ideational structure. Here, for example, is a syllogism, a formal structure of deductive logic based on a major and minor premise and a conclusion:

(1) All men are mortal.

(2) Socrates is a man.

(3) Socrates is mortal.

This too has a language-independent cognitive structure which we could represent symbolically. But for our purposes again, we shall use language. In a discourse, these propositions may appear in any order:

1–2–3: Since all men are mortal and Socrates is a man, he must be mortal.

3–2–1: Socrates must be mortal because he is a man and men are mortal.

3–1–2: Socrates must be mortal because all men are mortal and he is a man.

PROBLEM 3. What other combinations are possible? What questions would elicit the various forms of these statements about Socrates and his mortality? How does the effect of each of these statements differ?

PROBLEM 4. Here in very rough summary are the major ideational units that Abraham Lincoln presented in his Gettysburg Address. Could Lincoln have presented these identical ideational structures in a different order? What order is possible? How would the total structure be different? How would the effect differ? Is any order possible?

(1) Our forefathers established a democratic nation 87 years ago.

(2) The Civil War will decide whether a democratic nation can endure.

(3) We are here to dedicate part of a battlefield as a cemetery for those who died in the war.

(4) They died in the war so that the nation would endure.

(5) That we dedicate part of the battlefield for a cemetery is fitting.

(6) We cannot dedicate this battleground as a cemetery.

(7) The men who fought and died and will be buried here have dedicated the battlefield as a cemetery.

(8) The world will forget what we say here.

(9) The world will remember what the men buried here did.

(10) We must finish the work of the men who were killed in the war.

(11) We must dedicate ourselves to the cause for which they died.

(12) We must act so that this nation will endure.

(1) Four score and seven years ago our fathers brought forth on this continent a new nation, conceived in liberty, and dedicated to the proposition that all men are created equal.

(2) Now we are engaged in a great civil war, testing whether that nation, or any nation so conceived and so dedicated, can long endure. **(3)** We are met on a great battlefield of that war. We have come to dedicate a portion of that field as a final resting-place for those **(4)** who here gave their lives that that nation might live. **(5)** It is altogether fitting and proper that we should do this.

(6) But in a larger sense we cannot dedicate, we cannot consecrate, we cannot hallow this ground. **(7)** The brave men, living and dead, who struggled here have consecrated it, far above our poor power to add or detract. **(8)** The world will little note, nor long remember what we say here, **(9)** but it can never forget what they did here. **(10)** It is for us, the living, rather, to be dedicated here to the unfinished work which they who fought here have thus far so nobly advanced. **(11)** It is rather for us to be here dedicated to the great task remaining before us,—that from these honored dead we take increased devotion to that cause for which they gave the last full measure of devotion; that we here highly resolve that these dead shall not have died in vain; **(12)** that this nation, under God, shall have a new birth of freedom; and that government of the people, by the people, and for the people, shall not perish from the earth.

In principle, there is no difference between variable order in a discourse and in a sentence, except that arranging the same ideational elements in a sentence is constrained by the grammar of the language while the order of elements in a conversation or an essay is constrained by the genre of the discourse and the logic of the event. To make sense of a new organization to the Gettysburg Address, though, we would have to postulate a different telos. More importantly, if the new speech had different affective consequences from the original, then we would have to assume that the consequences of the new speech were more evidence of a new principle of selection and organization, of a new telos.

So if the order of elements can differ from text to text and still express the same propositional structures, different orders nevertheless result from different intentions, and, we must assume, will have different consequences. Just as different word orders in answers imply different questions, so do different orders in a discourse imply different intentions and lead to different audience responses. The intention/outcome that we have called the telos of the speech event allows us to explain why a particular order of elements organizes a speech event, rather than some other order which we could speculatively reconstruct.

PROBLEM 5. Rewrite the Gettysburg Address along the lines of a possible rearrangement. A good deal of the text you can retain unchanged, but you will have to change other parts. Why? How do the apparent intentions of the original and your revision differ? (Try beginning with the idea in element (3) or (8) in problem 4; try ending with element (7).)

PROBLEM 6. Which version of these two seems more natural? Why?

(1) An old battered car came down the street when I was walking along Michigan Avenue one night. A man who seemed to

be very confused was driving the car. Perhaps the bright lights blinded him. A car coming from the opposite direction collided with him.

(2) One night, I was walking along Michigan Avenue when down the street came an old battered car. It was driven by a man who seemed to be very confused. Perhaps he was blinded by the bright lights. He and a car coming from the opposite direction collided.

2. Microstructure: The Text and Its Sentences

At this point, we are beginning to deal with text, with the particular structures of particular sentences, with the problems of variation in grammatical structure, with the ways a writer (or speaker) selects grammatical and lexical options from among those linguistic variables a language makes available to him—variables not dependent on dialect or social context but on the particular telos of the speech event he is creating.

As we begin to analyze particular sentence structures, though, we face the problem of terminology. Different kinds of grammars force us to analyze sentences through the different grammatical categories provided by the grammars. If we use a traditional grammar, we must talk about nouns and verbs; subjects and objects; and simple, compound, and complex sentences. If we draw on any of the more modern grammars, we might find ourselves using terminology such as form class, constituent structure, transformation, deep structure, slot, filler, case marking, and so on, terms which various schools of grammar have devised to express their analyses of sentence structure. But these categories do not always serve the needs of those looking into questions of style, needs rather different from those of a grammarian.

Some linguists have begun to push past the grammatical limits of sentence boundaries to investigate the discourses those sentences appear in, and even beyond, to the social contexts in which those discourses exist. They share many of the same concerns as critics of style: to relate particular choices of verbal structures to the largest and most inclusive components of a speech event, to its telos, to its persons and personae, to its scenes and settings, to its subject matter, and in particular to the consequences it has on the audience—especially the ways the audience responds to the particular verbal structures in particular contexts informed by a particular telos.

But while grammatical structure is something every such

analysis of style must at some point account for, not all grammatical structure is relevant to the problem. The fact that in English an article, *a* or *the,* occurs before a noun is an inescapable observation in the study of sentence structure, but is irrelevant to the study of style. What is stylistically significant is that form which is selected when more than one structure is theoretically available.

In what follows, we shall be using a vocabulary that overlaps a bit with traditional grammar and a bit with some of the newer grammars. But because this vocabulary is designed so that we can describe style in terms that include contexts and intentions, and not abstract grammatical structure or proper usage, some of it will be used in new ways.

The first three terms of analysis are *sentence segmentation, lexicalization,* and *grammatical manifestation.*

2.1. Sentence Segmentation

Behind the Gettysburg Address, behind any discourse, is a seamless web of thought, a complex structure of ideational relationships among the concepts that make up the thought of the work. We might think of it metaphorically as some infinitely fine grid of semantic units and relationships which also stand in some relationship to "the world out there." Or in here. The relationships between the elements on that semantic grid and the boundaries of words and sentences are arbitrary and historically accidental; they are not necessarily systematic or intrinsic in the relationship between thought and language. The same content can be represented as one sentence or as many, as one word or as many.

Consider our short narrative again from problem 6. It could have been segmented like this:

> (1) It was one night. I was walking. I was on Michigan Avenue. Down the street came a car. It was old and battered. A man was driving it. He was confused. The lights blinded him. They were bright. A car was coming. It was from the opposite direction. He collided with it.

Or like this:

> (2) One night I was walking on Michigan Avenue when down the street came an old battered car driven by a man who, confused and blinded by the lights, collided with a car coming from the opposite direction.

In the first version, the network of semantic, cognitive relationships and events is segmented into minimally short sentences. In the second, the same ideational content is represented as one long sentence in almost the same ideational order. Since our primary interest in stylistics is at the level of sentences, the amount of ideational structure each sentence represents is relevant in distinguishing simple and complex styles.

PROBLEM 7. What is wrong with the following segmentation? What does your answer suggest about the relationship between sentence segmentation and what is going on "out there"?

> (3) One night I was walking along. I was on Michigan Avenue when down the street came an old battered car. It was driven by a man. He was confused and blinded by the lights. They were bright and he collided with a car. It was coming from the opposite direction.

It is important here to distinguish two kinds of sentences: *orthographic* and *grammatical*. An orthographic sentence is any stretch of words between a capital letter and a period, question, or exclamation mark; the first narrative could have been represented as a single orthographic sentence, *One day something happened: I was walking; I was on Michigan Avenue; a car came down the street; it . . . ;* substituting semicolons for periods changes several orthographic sentences into one orthographic sentence, but it does not change the grammatical structure; the sentence you are now reading is one very long orthographic sentence, for several potentially independent sentences have been linked by semicolons and commas, and this punctuation is facilitated by the grammatical device of coordinating conjunctions (*and, but, yet, so, for, nor, or*), and as a consequence, it seems to go on forever; indeed, it goes on too long to be effective, so it should be divided into smaller segments by periods.

PROBLEM 8. Repunctuate the previous sentence.

A grammatical sentence is any stretch of words which potentially can be set off with a capital letter and end punctuation mark. This is one orthographic sentence but three grammatical sentences: *Tom left, but Bill stayed, and I went to bed.* Periods could have set off each clause: *Tom left. But Bill stayed. And I went to bed.* The rhythm of the two versions is certainly different, but the difference depends only on punctuation, not on differences in grammatical structure.

This next orthographic sentence coincides with a single grammatical sentence: *When Tom left, Bill stayed because I went to bed.* In this case, we cannot set off as independent grammatical structures capable of standing alone sequences such as: *When Tom left. Bill stayed. Because I went to bed.* This time we have clauses connected by *when* and *because,* subordinating rather than coordinating conjunctions. Subordinating conjunctions bind clauses together more tightly than coordinating ones, and so they resist the segmenting effect of periods.

PROBLEM 9. Resegment the Gettysburg Address (problem 4). Combine shorter sentences to make longer orthographic sentences and segment the longer sentences into shorter grammatical sentences. What is the effect?

PROBLEM 10. Here is the first sentence of the Declaration of Independence. Resegment it into at least three shorter grammatical sentences. What is the effect?

> When in the course of human events, it becomes necessary for one people to dissolve the political bands which have connected them with another, and to assume among the powers of the earth, the separate and equal station to which the Laws of Nature and of Nature's God entitle them, a decent respect to the opinions of mankind requires that they should declare the causes which impel them to the separation.

PROBLEM 11. Repunctuate (and if necessary rewrite a bit) this part of a very long orthographic sentence from Norman Mailer's *Armies of the Night* so that it becomes several individually punctuated grammatical sentences. What is the effect?

> In any event, up at the front of this March, in the first line, back of that hollow square of monitors, Mailer and Lowell walked in this barrage of cameras, helicopters, TV cars, monitors, loudspeakers, and wavering buckling twisting line of notables, arms linked (the line twisting so much that at times the movement was in file, one arm locked ahead, one behind, then the line would undulate about and the other arm would be ahead) speeding up a few steps, slowing down while a great happiness came back into the day as if finally one stood under some mythical arch in the great vault of history, helicopters buzzing about, chop-chop, and the sense of America divided on this day now liberated some undiscovered patriotism in Mailer so that he felt a sharp searing love for his country in this moment and on this day, crossing some divide in his own mind wider than the Potomac, a love so lacerated he felt as if a marriage were being torn and children lost—never does one love so much as then, obviously, then—and an odor of wood smoke, from where you knew not, was also in the air . . .

PROBLEM 12. Why are the sentences so short in this passage from Ezra Pound's *ABC of Reading*? Combine several of them into longer sentences. What is the effect?

> Good writers are those who keep the language efficient. That is to say, keep it accurate, keep it clear. It doesn't matter whether the good writer wants to be useful, or whether the bad writer wants to do harm.
>
> Language is the main means of human communication. If an animal's nervous system does not transmit sensations and stimuli, the animal atrophies.
>
> If a nation's literature declines, the nation atrophies and decays.
>
> Your legislator can't legislate for the public good, your commander can't command, your populace (if you be a democratic country) can't instruct its 'representatives,' save by language.

2.2. Lexicalization

The next level of analysis is *lexicalization*. It means simply how a unit of meaning that has been segmented within the whole network of abstract ideational units will be manifested in word-length units. Now again, we must think of the idealized structure of meaning in a text as independent of the words that happen to represent its structure. When we examine the relationship between a word and the structure of meaning that lies behind it, we might think of that word as lying on a network, covering more or less of its specific meaning, implying other aspects of meaning that the word suggests, related to other words in the proposition also lying on that network. *Parent,* for example, would cover more of the network than *father,* though *father* implies part of what *parent* covers. *Parent* covers less of the space than *relative,* but implies some of what *relative* covers. *Daddy* and *pater* cover much the same area as *father,* but all three extend into different affective space. *Male parent* covers much the same ideational space as *father, pater, daddy, pop,* and so on, but all extend into different affective space, all suggest different emotional and social associations in addition to their strictly logical, ideational senses.

When the propositional space is lexicalized, when a segment of that ideational, language-independent space is first segmented into sentence-length units and then mapped into word-length units, each unit can specify relatively small and specific areas, or the same area can be covered by the intersection of groups of more general words. *Father* specifies a small and exact unit. The intersection of *male* and *parent,* more general words, covers the same logical space that *father* covers. Whole sentences can be made up of general or specific words yet mean roughly the same thing:

The criminal	*confessed*	*the murder.*
The individual who performed an action that violated criminal law	stated to some party his responsibility for an action unknown to that party that he	intentionally caused a human being to stop living by illegal means.

Styles differ in how general and how specific a vocabulary a writer selects.

Now we have to become a bit more abstract. At this stage of our analysis, we ought not think just in terms of individual, wholly realized words, for even words can change their form when they become manifested in different grammatical structures, the next stage of our analysis. These two phrases considerably overlap in the ideational space they cover:

(1) We realized that he was disappointed.

(2) There was a realization on our part of the disappointment in him.

Different parts of speech, and different forms of words cover much the same space:

we/our realize/realization he/him disappoint/disappointment

Even the relationship between the words is manifested in different ways. In (1), the relationship between *we,* the agent, and *realize,* the action, is signalled by the fact that *we* is a pronoun and *realize* a verb and that the pronoun comes before the verb. In (2), the relationship is signalled by the phrase *on our part* after the noun-form *realization.* But the abstract relationship is the same.

It is linguistically useful—though conceptually difficult—for us to develop a dual sense not of just fixed, real words, but also of real, spelled words on the one hand, and on the other of potential words, of word-like elements, of lexical units that can be manifested in concrete words in different ways, but all referring to, covering the same ideational space behind the realized sentence. Schematically, the relationship might be represented like this:

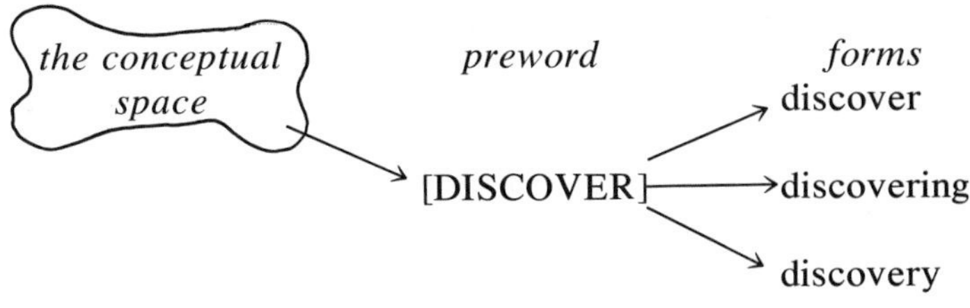

PROBLEM 13. These next phrases and clauses cover a shared aspect of meaning. How do the words covering that same space differ in form?

> I discovered that the world is flat. The discovery that the world is flat is mine. It is my discovery that the world is flat. The discovery by me is that the world is flat. The flatness of the world is a discovery of mine. The flatness of the world is of my discovering.

By first postulating not specific concrete words but more abstract "prewords," we can examine a text in a way that frees us from assuming that the specific forms of the words on the page are the only possible forms in which the words could have appeared. It is only when we can see why a particular form of a word was chosen from among all the possible forms that we shall understand the uniqueness of the particular text. It is only when we imagine another possible state of affairs that we can understand why the given state of affairs is as it is.

PROBLEM 14. Here is the first sentence of the Declaration of Independence, a bit revised (see the original in problem 10). Let us assume that this and the original sentence both convey the same basic ideas. How do the effects of the two versions differ?

> Now and then, one group of human beings has got to dissolve the political bands which have connected it with another one. And it has got to assume among the powers of the world the separate and equal place which the Laws of Nature and Nature's Supreme Being give it title to. Then if it decently respects what thoughts everyone else has about this, it has got to say why it separated itself from that other group.

Some of the ways in which styles can differ lexically, then, are these:

(1) The same ideas can be mapped by several general words:

> The person who assists me would not let me do that which I would have incorrectly done.

or fewer more specific words:

> My assistant prevented me from erring.

(2) The same referents can be mapped by a few general words:

> The room smelled bad.

or by several specific words which can include the general meaning but are more concrete:

> The anatomy laboratory in Gulch Hall was thick with the stench of pickled cadavers.

(3) Ideas can be mapped by words with relatively little social or dialectal weight:

> The man is mentally unbalanced.

or with more:

> This adult male Homo sapiens is afflicted with a neuropsychiatric disorder.
>
> That dude is a weirdo.
>
> That fella's right teched in the head.
>
> Him loco.

There is one more point about the lexicalization of ideational space which we should touch on. In some cases, there happens to be no single word in the language that corresponds to the semantic space we have created, no concrete word for an abstract idea that needs expressing. Often, if we have no form, we need none. We have no specific word like *widow, widower,* or *orphan* to name parents whose children are dead because we do not think about that category often enough to require a word for it. If we did, we would find a word soon enough. This is one reason why we borrow from other languages words like *taboo, tycoon, mafia, guerilla, vigilante, boor, robot, kosher,* and so on. Each of these words seems to fit a semantic space that we previously had no word for.

More often, though, we change the meaning of an old word to fit a new idea. Until the second half of this century, for example, we had no word, no transitive verb (because we needed none) to name the action of putting into a circular path around a celestial body some artificial object. *Orbit,* once a noun, then an intransitive verb, was pressed into use as a transitive verb. A *programmer* was once anyone who drew up a plan. Now we use it specifically to mean the person who tells the computer (another word that has changed its habitual referent) what to do.

One very common way of using words to map unnamed ideational space in new ways is *metaphor,* the use of a word referring to one thing to name another thing, but one with which it shares some affective or ideational space. Some metaphors quickly become part of our daily language. We had no good word for privately revealing to the public secret, usually bureaucratic, information until someone metaphorized *leak.* No word quite expresses the infuriating attention to tiny details like *nitpick,* a word originally meaning to pick the eggs of lice out of one's hair.

But most metaphors have a shorter, more transitory life, one in which they may appear only once and disappear, until they are perhaps reinvented by another writer. This passage is from J.L. Austin, a philosopher:

> We have left numerous loose ends, but after a brief résumé we must plough ahead. How did the 'constantives'—'performatives' distinction look in the light of our later theory? . . . on this point I could do no more than explode a few hopeful fireworks.

Loose ends, plough ahead, in light of, on this point, explode a few hopeful fireworks—all were originally metaphors. The first four are so familiar they they have virtually lost their metaphorical quality. The last is Austin's personal creation. *Fireworks* does not appear in any of the standard dictionaries meaning highly stimulating observations. It means more than that, of course, but then it is exactly the "more than that" which Austin was trying to capture in the metaphor.

Highly metaphorical styles sometimes approach poetic prose, but can also slide into silliness. On the other hand, the extended metaphor can be used effectively. This next is from Henry David Thoreau:

> If the injustice is part of the necessary friction of the machine of government, let it go, let it go: perchance it will wear smooth—certainly the machine will wear out. If the injustice has a spring, or a pulley, or a rope, or a crank, exclusively for itself, then perhaps you may consider whether the remedy will not be worse than the evil; but if it is of such a nature that it requires you to be the agent of injustice to another, then I say, break the law. Let your life be a counterfriction to stop the machine. What I have to do is to see, at any rate, that I do not lend myself to the wrong which I condemn.

PROBLEM 15. Review the Gettysburg Address (problem 4), the first sentence of the Declaration of Independence (problem 10), and a poem of your own choosing. Paraphrase the metaphors into literal language. What are the consequences? That android we were discussing in Chapter 2 would also have to be able to understand novel metaphors. What is required to understand any of the metaphors in those texts? What is required to create a metaphor?

PROBLEM 16. Are some intentions and genres more likely to call for metaphors than others? Consider these: laws, prayers, newspaper stories, newspaper columns, insults, sermons, scientific reports (read some before you answer this one), medical textbooks, writing textbooks, class lectures, automobile repair manuals, telephone books, dictionaries, weather reports on TV, and asking for directions.

2.3. Manifestation

Given a set of potential words representing abstract ideas in abstract relationships, ideas independent of any particular words or particular grammatical structure, we can now investigate how this abstract content is realized in actual sentences. But because we now have to deal with specific features of style, we need some terminology. Some of the terms will be familiar: *subject, verb, object, pronoun; clause, phrase, sentence.* Others will almost certainly be new: *topic, pivot, stress; agent, goal.* Most of these new terms reflect much that we already know about sentences. Their usefulness will lie in their allowing us to talk about it.

Regardless of how complicated any sentence seems to be, it almost always has the skeletal grammatical structure of subject-verb and, if necessary, of complement:

Subject	*Verb*	*(Complement)*
I	itch.	
The man	is	happy.
That ontogeny recapitulates phylogeny in ways surprising to most of us with even a fair understanding of biological processes	indicates	the need for further research into the mechanisms of evolutionary dynamics.

It is on this subject-verb-(complement) structure that we drape a semantic structure, a structure of somebody or something being, doing, or being done to—of ideas relating to ideas. Sentences also have a rhetorical structure, a way of putting old and familiar information early in a sentence, before the newer and unexpected information at the end. We cannot understand how sentences work as complete systems until we understand how these three kinds of structures: grammatical, semantic, and rhetorical interact. And until we understand how sentences work as complete systems, we won't understand style.

2.3.1 The Grammatical Structure: Subjects, Verbs, and Complements We'll begin with the most familiar and objectively definable level of sentence structure, both because it is familiar and because it is the structural backbone of every English sentence. We can describe how to identify the three fundamental parts of an English sentence in a straightforward enough way: The verb is that word that typically uses tense to signal the time of an event. That sentence and this one express propositions in the present tense. We can often identify a verb by changing the time of the sentence to the past if it is present and to present if it is past:

> The verb *was* the word that typically *used* . . .
>
> That sentence (and this one) *expressed* propositions . . .

The word we change is the main verb, if it is alone, or the first auxiliary verb: *is* → *was, uses* → *used, express* → *expressed, can identify* → *could identify, have gone* → *had gone, is coming* → *was coming, has been thinking* → *had been thinking.*

We can identify subjects easily enough by putting *who* or *what* immediately to the left of the verb and then asking the question:

> *What* was that word that typically used . . . ?
>
> *What* expressed propositions . . . ?

The answer is invariably the subject: *The verb, that sentence.*

The complement is whatever completes the structural sense of the verb, if the verb requires that structural completion. In some cases, the complement is a direct object:

> He discovered *America.* You realize *why I left.*

It can also be a predicate complement in the form of a noun, adjective, or prepositional phrase. It follows a linking verb such as *be, seem, appear,* etc.:

> He is *a friend.* They seem *happy.* She is *in the house.*

Verbs such as *discover, realize, is, seem,* and so on ordinarily require some kind of complement after them, as opposed to verbs that refer to actions complete in the subject:

I exist. She disappeared. The star twinkled. The sun shined.

Ordinarily, the subject-verb-complement sequence occurs in that order, but not always:

Complement	*Subject*	*Verb*
George	I	cannot endure.
Complement	*Verb*	*Subject*
Down the street	came	an old car.

It is because of sentences such as the first that we want to avoid defining the grammatical subject as what the sentence is about. In some sense, these sentences are "about" their complements.

2.3.2 The Semantic Structure: Agents, Actions, and Goals

A traditional definition of subject is the "doer" of an action. But there are too many exceptions to that definition to make it entirely reliable. The passive is an obvious counterexample:

The window was broken by the boy with a stick.

And some active verbs allow us to shift into the subject position what otherwise might be expressed as a direct object or as the instrument by which an action is accomplished:

The window broke.

The stick broke the window.

And a few active verbs can semantically reverse an action back toward a subject:

We received a rebuff from the crowd.

He took a punch to the midsection.

We suffered the lashing of the waves

I experienced a fear of the dark.

You will now undergo an examination.

It went through a complete analysis.

Each of these sentences has another active version in which the subject is really the doer:

The crowd rebuffed us.

Somebody punched him in the midsection.

The waves lashed us.

The dark frightened me.

Someone will now examine you.

Someone completely analyzed it.

But regardless of these exceptions, the grammatical subject of a sentence is strongly associated with agency, with a sense of responsibility for the action of a verb. When speakers of English are asked to judge the energy or the animateness of a nonsense word, they assign a higher level of animate agency to that word in the subject position:

The *glorb* smamped the snidget.

than when it occurs in the object position:

The snidget smamped the *glorb*.

At a certain age, children typically mistake the subject of a passive sentence as the agent of the action, interpreting:

Johnny was hit by Mary.

as:

Johnny hit Mary.

And the fact that so few active verbs allow us to put the literal "receiver" of an action in the subject position suggests that English (and many other languages) regularly associate subjects with agents.

In the same way, the verb position typically expresses the action of the agent. Again, there are many exceptions:

We made a decision to leave.

The verb is *made* but the real action, of course, is expressed in the direct object, *decision*. Actions can even be expressed in the subject position:

Our decision to leave then occurred.

But in some basic way, we associate verbs with actions:

We decided to leave.

Now, as you can perhaps sense from these examples, we can refer to the same events ''out there'' in different ways: by manipulating agents, actions, and goals through subjects, verbs, and complements. And as we shall see in a moment, it is partly through this manipulation that a writer can achieve different stylistic consequences.

But before we do that, we have to consider that primary level of reference, what goes on in the world we refer to. If the subject and the seeming agent of an action need not correspond, neither need the seeming agent of an action correspond with the doer or source of an action in the real world of objective experience. For example:

My son defeated me in chess.

is a straightforward, agent-action-goal sequence. But so is the potentially synonymous:

I lost to my son in chess.

We have to say ''potentially'' because it may be that I lost on purpose, that I was in fact the real agent of the deliberate action of losing rather than the receiver of an action directed toward me. In other words, the *I* of *I lost* could be either doer or receiver. What is going on out there in the real world does not necessarily correspond with how we encode those events in grammatical or semantic structure. A seeming active agent in a subject position:

These letters increased in value to me.

may be the real ''receiver'' of an action:

I increasingly valued these letters.

Of course, nouns relate to verbs in ways other than just agency and goal:

Instrument:	Someone will persuade you with this report. This report will persuade you.
Location:	The fugitives found shelter in the jungle. The jungle sheltered the fugitives.

Time:	New problems will appear in 1981. 1981 will bring new problems.
Cause:	He died from pneumonia. Pneumonia killed him.

But when a noun that may "really" be an instrument, location, time, cause, goal, etc. appears in the subject position, that noun unavoidably takes on by association or metaphorical extension a sense of agency. We cannot ignore the stylistic choice that invests a sense of that agency in one rather than another noun phrase. The key stylistic choice is what appears as subject. That choice can emphasize or deemphasize agency; it determines how the rest of the predication will flow.

We can give the most natural correlation between the grammatical structure, the semantic structure, and the referential structure:

The World:	**Reference**	Doer	Action	Receiver
The Text:	**Semantics**	Agent	Action	Goal
	Grammar	Subject	Verb	Complement

This most natural correlation turns out to be a key index of good as opposed to bad writing. There will sometimes be sound reason for deviation from this line up, but *most of the time* writing that is clear, vigorous, and easy to understand will name the real-world doer as the subject and the action as the verb. Complex writing, in the sense of hard to understand, is characteristically deviant from just this principle, and it happens all too often in legal, medical, and bureaucratic prose.

> The government's attempt at an investigation into the corporation's handling of the contract was met by its refusal to allow an examination of its assignment of costs.
>
> The government attempted to investigate how the corporation handled the contract, but it refused to allow the government to examine the way it assigned costs.

PROBLEM 17. Each of the sentences below has a subject that feels like the active agent or perpetrator of the action or state expressed by the verb. In each set, try to identify the real-world, referential doer or source of the action or state. Then try to decide why anyone would want to express that information in a sentence in a way that would or would not coincide with its semantic or grammatical structure. That is, why would anyone want to say *He slowly grew old* rather than *Age slowly overtook him,* or vice versa? You may not be able to decide in some cases.

(1) He slowly grew old. Age slowly overtook him.

(2) A cold hit me. I caught a cold.

(3) Trouble always pursues you. You are always in trouble.

(4) You remind me of your father. Your father resembles you. I think of your father when I see you.

(5) Children fear the dark. The dark frightens children. Fear afflicts children in the dark.

(6) Violence disgusts me. I am disgusted at violence. Disgust overcomes me when I see violence.

(7) The war began on Sunday. Sunday brought the beginning of the war. The beginning of the war came on Sunday.

(8) I came to believe it because of those reasons. Those reasons persuaded me. My belief arose because of those reasons.

(9) We must investigate further now what they have decided. Their decision demands our further investigation. Our further investigation is necessary because of their decision.

(10) Mathematics naturally attracts those minds that seek underlying order. Those minds that are attracted by underlying order naturally turn to mathematics.

(11) We organize how we think on the basis of the great oppositions of nature. The great oppositions of nature organize our thinking for us.

2.3.3 The Rhetorical Structure: Topic, Pivot, and Stress

We avoided defining the subject of the sentence as the doer because there were too many exceptions to make it a useful definition. In the same way, we want to avoid defining the subject of a sentence as what a sentence is about, because sentences can be about different things in different ways. If I say:

I think there's a spider on your collar.

I use the subject *I*, but *I* is certainly not what that sentence is "about." It is about a spider and your collar.

PROBLEM 18. Is there any context in which we could reasonably claim that this same sentence is in fact about *I*? (What question, for example, would make it about *I*?)

In this sense, "about" is not a grammatical term. It is a rhetorical term. But "aboutness" is a complicated matter because there are two kinds of aboutness. It can mean the first main idea in a sentence, the idea that the rest of the sentence comments on or flows from. Or it can mean the most important information in a sentence, the new information that the sentence communicates. For example, each of the preceding sentences is about "about." "About" or "it" or "aboutness" is the subject of each sentence, and each sentence communicates some information about "about." So we can say that the sentences are about two kinds of information—the topic we are discussing: aboutness, and the new information that we want to impart about aboutness.

It would be useful to have some terms to distinguish these different kinds of "aboutness." But before we can do that, we have to notice something else. Just as the subject of a sentence and the agency of an action strongly—though not invariably—coincide, so does the subject of a sentence regularly—though not invariably—coincide with the general subject we are talking about. In fact, we can go further: The first *part* of a sentence regularly expresses old, assumed, given, unsurprising information. The last part of a sentence regularly expresses new, unexpected, unpredictable information. For example, the second sentence of this pair seems a bit more natural than the first:

> A bug-eyed monster visited me in my room last night.
>
> Last night in my room, I was visited by a bug-eyed monster.

And once the new information has been expressed, it thereby becomes old information and appears early on in the next sentence. Which of these two would more naturally follow the second one above?

> He told me that the object of his visit was to find a bathroom.
>
> I was told that to find a bathroom was the object of his visit.

It would be useful to have a term to refer to the first part of a sentence, the position where old information is regularly expressed, and a term for the second part of a sentence, where the new information is regularly expressed. We'll use the terms *topic* and *comment.* These two positions regularly, but need not inevitably, coincide with subject and predicate. Therefore, topic and comment can't be given simple grammatical definitions.

But we also need terms to refer to old and new information. We can't use the same terms, topic and comment, because those two terms refer to structural positions in a sentence. We need terms that refer to the informational aspects of meaning. For old information, we shall use the term *theme;* for new, *rheme.*

PROBLEM 19. For each of the four sentences about the bug-eyed monster, identify topic and comment, theme and rheme. In which do topic and theme coincide? In which do comment and rheme coincide?

In addition to using the subject position to announce a topic and communicate thematic (i.e., old) information, we can call on other topicalizing devices. Some phrases that topicalize their objects at the front of the sentence are *as for, in regard to, speaking of,* and other constructions such as *turning to the question of* and so on. For example,

> As for the style of the book, *Huckleberry Finn* is no less than definitive in American literature.

The sentence flows from a topic that is not the subject of its verb: *the style of the book.* We could have topicalized other elements if they had been thematic:

> As for American literature, the style of *Huckleberry Finn* . . .
>
> As for *Huckleberry Finn,* its style is . . .

But we can assume the writer of the original sentence had been discussing other features of the book: character, plot, thought. These components, including style, constitute the thematic material of the text. And so as he begins to discuss the next in the series of points, style, he announces it as his temporary topic by using a topicalizing phrase and putting it at the beginning of the sentence in the topic position.

In this next example from Benjamin Franklin, the topic coincides with a whole clause:

> With regard to the first [point], that the colonies were settled at the expense of Britain, *topic*

> it is a known fact that none of the twelve united colonies were settled, or even discovered, at the expense of England. *comment*

In this next example from James Baldwin, a prepositional phrase shifted from its normal position at the end of the clause to the beginning topicalizes *traditional attitudes*. Then *I*, reinforced by *personally*, constitutes the topic and subject of the second clause:

> Of traditional attitudes there are only two—for and against, and I personally find it difficult to say which attitude has caused me the most pain.

In each of these examples, the topic expresses thematic (older, more predictable, less informative) information. The rhematic information is reserved for the comment position.

This matter of topic is complicated by the fact that the topic of a sentence may or may not overtly name the more abstract "topic" of a paragraph or of a discourse. Indeed, it is possible to have topics within topics within topics. The topic of this collection of essays is variation in language. The topic of the essay you are now reading is style. The topic of this section is the rhetorical organization of sentences. The topic of this particular subsection is topics. But the sentence you are now reading has as its overt topic *the sentence you are now reading*.

This hierarchical nesting of topics within topics within topics is a very complicated matter, one that is crucial to the organization of every discourse. But as important as it may be, we can only mention it here, if we want to deal adequately with the structure of specific sentences.

And just as there are hierarchies of topics within the paragraphs and sections of a discourse, so do single sentences have sets of topics and comments within topics and comments. In the Ben Franklin sentence, for example, the topic has its own subfield of a topic and comment, and the comment has its own subfield of a topic and comment:

With regard to the first [point], that

topic:	the colonies topic	were settled at the expense of Britain comment

it is a known fact that

comment:	none of the twelve united colonies topic	were settled, or even discovered, at the expense of England comment

The interaction among these elaborately structured hierarchies is, as you might expect, a matter of extraordinary complexity. The complete analysis of even a single paragraph would require many pages. What we can offer here is only the outlines of a model that can be used in the analysis of prose texts and their styles.

PROBLEM 20. How would you explain sentences such as these, typically produced by children?

> My uncle, he works in a bank.
>
> Chicago, my brother went there last year.
>
> Comic books, their stories are silly.
>
> Eating, that's what you do all the time.

PROBLEM 21. As we have said, though, the topic usually appears as the subject. Here is a longer passage, written about 1850 by Alexis de Tocqueville:

> While *the Americans* are thus united by common ideas, *they* are separated from everybody else by one sentiment—pride. For fifty years *the inhabitants of the United States* have been repeatedly and constantly told that *they* are the only religious, enlightened, and free people. *They* see that democratic institutions flourish among them, but come to grief in the rest of the world; consequently, *they* have an immensely high opinion of themselves and are not far from believing that *they* form a species apart from the rest of the human race.

The subjects of the clauses and sentences are in italics: *the Americans, they, the inhabitants . . . States, they, they, they,* and *they*.

You have undoubtedly been told to vary your sentence structure, to avoid beginning several consecutive sentences with the same subject. Here, following that advice, is another version of the same ideational structure as the preceding passage. Which do you think is better written? Why?

> While *common ideas* thus unite the Americans, *one sentiment*—pride—separates them from everybody else. *Many* have repeatedly and constantly told the inhabitants of the United States for fifty years that *the only religious, enlightened, and free people* are themselves. *Democratic institutions* obviously flourish among them, whereas *the rest of the world* brings them to grief; *an immensely high opinion of themselves* conse-

> quently results and *a belief that the rest of the human race forms a species apart from them* almost arises among them.

In the second version, the subject varies constantly: *common ideas; one sentiment; many; the only religious, enlightened, and free people; democratic institutions; the rest of the world; an immensely high opinion of themselves; a belief . . . from them.* But now the topic of the passage is blurred. There is no consistent point of view.

PROBLEM 22. One important function of a topic, then, is to maintain a consistent point of departure through a series of sentences which are unified into a whole by that consistent perspective. The whole passage may focus on the same element (as in Tocqueville), or it may focus on different elements that belong to the same general concept. The topics in the opening sentences of Abraham Lincoln's Second Inaugural Address may at first glance seem to exhibit a blurred focus. Does anything unify them?

> At this *second appearing to take the oath of the presidential office,* there is less occasion for an extended address than there was at the first. Then *a statement, somewhat in detail, of a course to be pursued,* seemed fitting and proper. Now, at the expiration of four years, during which *public declarations* have been constantly called forth on every point and phase of the great contest which still absorbs the energy and engrosses the attention of the nation, *little that is new* could be presented. *The progress of our arms,* upon which all else chiefly depends, is as well known to the public as to myself; and *it* is, I trust, reasonably satisfactory and encouraging to all. With high hope for the future, *no prediction in regard to it* is ventured.

The sentences topicalize *second appearing . . . office, a statement . . . pursued, public declarations, little that is new, progress of our arms, it, no prediction . . . it.* But these elements do in fact constitute a unified set: They are the abstractions constituting the scene and its telos, but not its central persona, a series of choices that directs our attention away from that persona, Lincoln, and toward the setting and subject, the ceremony.

Rewrite this opening paragraph so that the topic and the subject of each clause is Lincoln. For example:

> As I appear here for the second time to take my oath of the presidential office, I have less occasion to address you at length than I did at the first.

What is the difference? Now rewrite it so that the other persona, the audience, is topicalized.

How we select rhematic and thematic information to express in the topic and comment positions of a sentence, then, is not "given" by the content, by the subject matter, but rather reflects higher levels of organization and intention. It reflects what the writer assumes about his audience, what they do and do not know, what information he considers to be more important and less important. We define rheme and theme on the basis of how our telos interacts with the personae of the event, the subject matter, and the scene, and how they together determine form and genre.

Had Lincoln intended to focus on himself as the source of the occasion rather than on the occasion itself, he could have done so through the structure of his sentences, making himself the subject and topic. But that would have required a very different intention, a different telos to infuse through his speech event, a different understanding of the persona he wanted to present (or hide) from his audience, of what he wanted to accomplish through the opening paragraph of that address. In examples such as these, we realize that structure is content infused with intention, that the most global intentions of an author can—indeed must—determine small details of grammatical structure.

But if the topic is important for expressing thematic information, for focussing our attention through a series of sentences, the comment is important for emphasizing new, rhematic information. As a consequence of this double rhetorical imperative—old or assumed information in the topic position, and new or striking information in the comment position—the conclusion of one sentence often leads (as in the sentence you are now reading) to the topic-beginning of the next. And the beginning of that next sentence (as in that beginning) thereby expresses the old information and what follows it, the new. And that new becomes in turn the old, and so on, creating a chain-like series of sentences, the end of one leading to the beginning of the next.

So if the topic is important in controlling our point of view as we move through a discourse, the end of each sentence, indeed, the end of each clause and phrase is equally important in telling us what the sentence is "about" (that second sense of aboutness we mentioned), perhaps more so because the end of each clause introduces and *stresses* the new and presumably most salient information. It is at the end of a sentence where we achieve our greatest emphasis.

That much writing not only blurs the focus of a discourse by capriciously shifting topics from sentence to sentence but also allows its sentences to dribble off into insignificance and anticlimax is a problem with writing today in many instances, which is not good unless there is some reason for it in which case it is acceptable, which would be uncommon for the most part, though, I think.

Unlike the above limp structure, a strong sentence builds

momentum as it moves toward its emphatic conclusion, a conclusion that stresses not what is trivial but what is semantically and rhetorically of greatest significance. Like that one.

PROBLEM 23. Here is another version of the first sentence of the Declaration of Independence. How does its effect differ from the original (in problem 10)? Why? Think of it in terms of *topics* at the beginnings of sentences and *stress* at the end.

> When it becomes necessary for one people to dissolve the political bands with another which they have been connected by and for them to assume the separate and equal station which the Laws of Nature and of the God of Nature entitles them to among the powers of the earth in the course of human events, their declaration of the causes of the separation which they are impelled to is required by a decent respect to mankind's opinions.

These two rhetorical functions, topic and stress, are so important in how we understand a discourse that English grammar provides several ways to manipulate the basic subject-verb-complement sentence structure so that we can topicalize and stress exactly the right elements, so that we can position at the front of a sentence the old information or push to the end the new. Here are some of the more important devices.

The passive. We are regularly advised to avoid passives. But if we followed that advice blindly, we would never be able to topicalize what otherwise would be a direct object or stress what otherwise would be an active subject.

PROBLEM 24. Make every passive sentence in the following excerpt from Walter Lippmann an active sentence and every active sentence with a transitive verb into a passive sentence. How is the passage changed? (Every passive verb and its accompanying form of *be* and every active verb that can be made into a passive are italicized.)

> Freedom of speech *is* best *conceived,* therefore, by having in mind the picture of a place like the American Congress, an assembly where opposing views *are represented,* where ideas *are not* merely *uttered* but *debated,* or the British Parliament, where men who are free to speak *are* also *compelled* to answer. We may *picture* the true condition of freedom as existing in a place like a court of law, where witnesses testify and *are cross-examined,* where the lawyer *argues against* the opposing lawyer before the same judge and in the presence of one jury. We may *picture* freedom as existing in a forum where the speaker must *respond* to ques-

> tions; in a gathering of scientists where the data, the hypotheses, and the conclusion *are submitted* to men competent to judge them; in a reputable newspaper which not only will *publish* the opinions of those who disagree but will *re-examine* its own opinion in the light of what they *say*.

PROBLEM 25. Which of these two sentences do you suppose was the original one written by John Adams to Thomas Jefferson? What information would help you decide?

> (1) My thoughts and cares were nearly monopolized by the theory of our rights and wrongs, by measures for the defence of the country, and the means for governing ourselves.
>
> (2) The theory of our rights and wrongs, measures for the defence of the country, and the means for governing ourselves nearly monopolized my thoughts and cares.

PROBLEM 26. Why does the following passage have no passives in it? It is written by Frederick Turner, an American historian.

> The wilderness masters the colonist. It finds him a European in dress, industries, tools, modes of travel and thought. It takes him from the railroad car and puts him in the birch canoe. It strips off the garments of civilization and arrays him in the hunting shirt and the moccasin. It puts him in the log cabin of the Cherokee and the Iroquois and runs an Indian palisade around him. Before long, he has gone to planting Indian corn and ploughing with a sharp stick: he shouts the war-cry and takes the scalp in orthodox Indian fashion. In short, the frontier is at first too strong for the man. He must accept the conditions which it furnishes, or perish, and so he fits himself into the Indian clearings and follows the Indian trails. Little by little he overcomes the wilderness, but the outcome is not the old Europe. The fact is, that here is a new product that is American.

Rewrite this passage so that it is thoroughly passive: *The colonist is mastered by the wilderness. He is found by it a European . . .* What is the difference?

Transposed modifiers. A second topicalizing and stressing device is to shift a modifier from the end of a sentence to another position. Compare these two versions:

> Language must have consisted of single word signal cries uncombined into longer sequences in this early period of man's evolution for the most part.

> For the most part, in this early period of man's evolution, language must have consisted of single word signal cries uncombined into longer sequences.

The phrases *for the most part* and *in this early period of man's evolution* have been shifted to the beginning of the sentence not only because they orient a reader toward what is to follow but also to allow *single word signal cries . . .* to stand exposed in the stressed position. No syntactic anticlimax weakens the conclusion. Note too that the shift brings the phrase with a word relating it to the previous sentence; *in **this** early period of man's evolution,* closer to the beginning of its sentence, closer to the preceding sentence. We shall have more to say about this later.

It/Wh-/There. A third set of devices lets us shift toward the end of the sentence part of a clause, or even the whole clause, and thereby stresses it:

(1) a. That such an event occurred was *no surprise.*
b. It was no surprise that *such an event occurred.*

(2) a. Thomas Jefferson proposed *the first federally supported system of education.*
b. It was *Thomas Jefferson* who proposed the first federally . . .
c. What Thomas Jefferson did was *propose the first federally . . .*
d. What Thomas Jefferson proposed was *the first federally . . .*

(3) a. Several representatives were present to *discuss the first question.*
b. There were *several representatives present* to discuss the first question.

In each case, the emphasis is thrown on what follows the *it, there,* or introductory *who/what/*etc. Because the *there* sentences and the kind of *it* construction we have in (1)b effectively stress a whole clause by shifting it after the verb, such sentences typically occur first in a discourse:

> There are four reasons why you should know about Laetrile.
>
> It is no secret that American foreign policy has been bankrupt.

When sentences such as these occur inside of a discourse, they tend to slow the rhetorical pace because all they do is state a stressed rheme, with no clear theme in topic position.

Introductory shift. A fourth device lets us shift an introductory subject-verb inside its following clause, making the subject of that following clause a more clearly stated topic. Compare:

> We now know that the American Revolution was supported by no more than a third of the colonial population.
>
> The American Revolution, we now know, was supported by no more . . .

Topicalizing phrases. A fifth device is a set of fixed phrases that lets us announce a new topic, often one already mentioned or implied.

> As for *Europe,* nothing more can be said to explain the situation.
>
> In regard to these *results,* several points must be made.
>
> Turning to the problem of *abortion* now, we can immediately . . .

A more radical means of manipulating the position of elements in a sentence is to select different verbs which represent the same state of affairs but which allow us to switch subjects and objects. For example, in a sentence such as:

> The word *liberty* means different things to different people.

the topic is "the word *liberty*" and the stress is "different things to different people." We could reverse the topic and stress if we represented the semantic content behind "mean" with some other verb or phrase:

> Different people find different meanings in the word *liberty*.
>
> Different meanings of the word *liberty* occur to different people.
>
> Different people see in the word *liberty* different meanings.
>
> People understand the meaning of the word *liberty* differently.

Now certainly, if we studied these sentences at length and in detail, we could eventually discover fine nuances of different meanings. But whether the differences in the context of a discourse read at normal speed and normal attention would be sufficient to change the way we understand the sentences is a different sort of question and one extremely difficult to answer.

Now just as we can distinguish in the predicate of a sentence two parts, verbs and complements, so in a comment can we make some finer distinctions. In a simple sentence such as:

> Your wife is pregnant.

the topic is obviously enough the thematic information, *your wife,* and the comment is the rhematic information, *is pregnant.* But the crucial word in the comment is *pregnant.* The word *is* merely serves to get us from the topic to that crucial stressed word. Compare:

> Your wife appears to be that which we would describe in ordinary language as pregnant.

The topic and the stress are still the same as in the previous sentence. But now the comment includes words that serve only to delay getting to that crucial word, *pregnant.*

Because it does not add much to say that the comment is everything after *your wife,* we are going to subdivide the comment into two parts: the *stress,* that position at the end of the sentence that can most strongly emphasize the most crucial new information, and the *pivot,* everything between the topic and the stress.

Sometimes, the pivot is a single word:

> Your wife *is* pregnant.

Sometimes in wordy and indirect writing, it may consist of several words:

> Your wife *appears to be . . . as* pregnant.

Sometimes, the pivot is no more than the space between two words:

> You lose.

In cases such as this, the stress coincides with the whole comment.

We can distinguish styles by how pivots move us from topics to stresses, by whether the new information that should be stressed at the end of a sentence occurs there, or whether a sentence labors through verbiage in the pivot only to dribble off into anticlimax. Compare the original of the first part of Turner's passage on the American colonists with the revised version that follows it:

Original. The wilderness masters the colonist. It finds him a European in dress, industries, tools, modes of travel and thought. It takes him from the railroad car and puts him in the birch canoe. It strips off the garments of civilization and arrays him in the hunting shirt and the moccasin. It puts him in the log cabin of the Cherokee and the Iroquois and runs an Indian palisade around him.

Revision. The wilderness comes to exert a mastery over those who were in the position of being colonists. It finds him as someone who is a European in dress, industries, tools, modes of travel and thought. It takes him from the railroad car and puts him into something or other known as a birch canoe. It tends to serve to strip off the garments of civilization and makes a successful attempt at arraying him in the hunting shirt and moccasin. It has the effect of putting him in the log cabin of the Cherokee and the Iroquois and proceeds to run an Indian palisade around him.

Just as we were able to correlate position and meaning with subjects and agents, verbs and actions, complements and goals, so can we correlate topics with themes, and comments with rhemes. In fact, we can make a more significant correlation if we correlate all the levels:

Referential structure	Doer	Action	Receiver
Semantic structure	Agent	Action	Goal
Grammatical structure	Subject	Verb	Complement
Rhetorical structure	Topic	Pivot	Stress
Informational structure	Theme	Rheme	

It is by no means always the case that this is the preferred coincidence of these elements. But it does provide us with a base against which we can refer sentences. A very large component of verbal style and the structural cohesiveness of a discourse depends on how a writer or a speaker can manipulate these intersections. It is obvious how the rhetorical topic of a sentence depends on how we choose to manifest a relationship among these elements. Our ability to consistently topicalize the same or a related set of noun phrases can spell the difference between a coherent paragraph and an apparently disorganized one. (Look again at the Tocqueville paragraph in problem 21.)

But just as importantly, the subject of a sentence is so intrinsically associated with agency that making any noun phrase the subject of an active verb can invest that noun phrase with a semantic energy that makes it seem to be the source of the action. It allows us to attribute metaphorical animacy to inanimate and abstract entities:

> Every day confronts us with a new challenge.
>
> The decision doomed my plan.
>
> The dark forests intimidated us.

PROBLEM 27. Here are two paragraphs from Tocqueville, one a close translation, the other an adaptation. How do the functions of subject and agency contrast between the two versions? In which is the correspondence the most appropriate? What do you have to decide before you can answer that question?

(1) Before the Indians fled from the European's force, out of the wilderness in which they had found shelter, they needed few things. They made their own weapons, they drank the waters of the rivers, and they hunted animals for food and clothes.

Then the European introduced firearms, iron, and brandy to the indigenous population of North America; he taught the Indians to substitute his cloth for the barbarous clothes which had previously satisfied their native simplicity. Though the European gave the Indians new tastes, he did not teach them the arts to gratify them. The white man provided them with products from his industry. In return for these goods, the white man would accept from them only the rich furs which still abounded in the forest. From that time forward, hunting had to provide not only for the Indians' own needs, but also the frivolous passions of Europe. The forest animals no longer had to provide him only with food but also with the only things for which the white man would barter.

(2) Before the Europeans drove the Indians by force from the wilderness which previously had sheltered them, few needs inflicted themselves on them. Their weapons were the result of their own labors, the waters of the rivers provided them with drink and the animals of the forest their food and clothes.

Then the indigenous population of North America acquired firearms, iron and brandy from the European. They learned from him to substitute his cloth for the barbarous clothes which they had previously accepted in their native simplicity. Though the Indians acquired new tastes from the European, they did not learn his arts to gratify them. In return for these goods, the Indian was able to satisfy the white man only with the rich furs which still abounded in the forest. From that time forward, the Indian hunted not only to pro-

> vide for his own needs but also for the frivolous passions of Europe. He no longer hunted the forest animals only for food but also for the things which he could barter with the white man.

Both versions refer to the same state of affairs "out there." But in the first version (1) in the first paragraph, the Indian is the subject-topic-agent of sentences while in the second paragraph, the subject-topic-agent is the European. In the second version (2) the Indian is first the seeming "receiver" of actions, then the agent of his own actions. The rhetorical difference is considerable. In the first version, the Indian is first responsible for his own actions and then not. In the second, the Indian seems to be the object of the European's action and then the agent of his own.

PROBLEM 28. In the paragraph by Turner in problem 26, the colonist and the wilderness are alternately the topic-agents of their sentences. Revise the paragraph so that, as much as possible, the agent-goal relationship is reversed. That is, for the first sentence, we might revise *master* into *submit: The colonist must submit to the wilderness.* Which version is more appropriate? How do we decide questions such as this?

PROBLEM 29. Here is a passage from James Baldwin's essay, "A Stranger in the Village."

> **(1a)** The cathedral at Chartres, I have said, says something to the people of this village which it cannot say to me; **(1b)** but it is important to understand that this cathedral says something to me which it cannot say to them. **(2a)** Perhaps they are struck by the power of the spires, the glory of the windows; **(2b)** but they have known God, after all, longer than I have known him, and in a different way, **(2c)** and I am terrified by the slippery bottomless well to be found in the crypt, down which heretics were hurled to death, and by the obscene, inescapable gargoyles jutting out of the stone and seeming to say that God and the devil can never be divorced. **(3)** I doubt that the villagers think of the devil when they face a cathedral because they have never been identified with the devil. **(4)** But I must accept the status which myth, if nothing else, gives me in the West before I can hope to change the myth.

Answer these questions:

1. In sentences (1a) and (1b), why is the agent of the action the cathedral and not the people or Baldwin? That is, why not *The people of this village see in the cathedral something . . .* or *I cannot hear what the cathedral says to the people of this village . . .* ?
2. Why is sentence (2a) passive? What is the real world agency (the doer)?

3. Why is sentence (3) not in this form: *A cathedral never makes the villagers think of the devil because . . . ?*
4. Why is sentence (4) active? Why not *But I must accept the status which I derive from myth in the West . . . ?*

3. Verbal Nouns

3.1. Nominalizations

There is one stylistic device so central to these manipulations that we should devote a separate section to it. In English, we can turn a whole clause into a noun-like structure. We can "nominalize" it. We can nominalize a whole clause by adding a *that: That he failed surprised me*. We can transform a clause into a *for-to* construction: *For him to fail surprised me*. We can transform it into a gerund: *His failing surprised me*. And many verbs can be transformed into an abstract nominalization: *His failure surprised me*. Once these propositions have been transformed into noun-like constructions, a writer can maneuver them into various positions in a sentence, and with abstract nominalizations he can delete the underlying subjects and objects of the original verb:

> He surprised me when he failed.
>
> His failing was a surprise.
>
> The failure was a surprise.

It is no exaggeration to say that this particular grammatical structure, the abstract nominalization, has become centrally important in the style of much modern English prose. In conjunction with words borrowed from Latin and French, with the passive, and with those constructions that combine two or more general words where a single specific word would do, it has come to characterize what is known as bureaucratese, educationalese, medicalese—the worst kind of literate, the worst kind of super-literate writing in our society. It is the difference between:

> There is a need for the cessation of interdistrict vehicular transportation programs.

and:

We are not going to bus kids anymore.

An abstract noun is a nominalization if it may occur with its underlying subject and, if the underlying verb has one, its complement. If the complement is a direct object with the verb, it can follow the verbal noun only as a prepositional object:

Subject +	*Verb* +	*Direct Object*		*Subject* +	*Verbal Noun* +	*Prepositional Object*
Ned	discovered	the hole	→	Ned's	discovery	of the hole
They	attacked	the fort	→	Their	attack	on the fort

Other kinds of verbal complements tend to maintain the same form after verbal nouns:

Subject +	*Verb* +	*Complement*		*Subject* +	*Verbal Noun*	+ *Complement*
She	departed	from the city	→	Her	departure	from the city
Henry	failed	to leave	→	Henry's	failure	to leave

The subject of the underlying verb can appear in a variety of positions:

- As a possessive before a noun: the man's death
- In a prepositional phrase after: the departure of the train
misbehavior on the part of the students
- In a compound noun: student misbehavior
- In an adjective before the noun: a Polish invention

There are some possibilities for varied rhetorical structure with verbal nouns. The effect is more subtle than in sentences, but on the other hand there are some options open in the noun phrase not available in sentences. To begin with, verbal nouns allow more ellipsis than verbs: they always allow partial or total ellipsis of subjects and complements so that even just the action can be named (the departure, the misbehavior), and what is named is foregrounded at the expense of the rest. For another thing, there is a nominal version of the passive which allows a variety of possibilities for topical prominence or stress.

Sentences	*Noun Phrases*
The junta tortured Erica.	The junta's torture of Erica
	The junta's torture
	The torture

Erica was tortured by the junta.	Erica's torture by the junta The torture of Erica by the junta The torture by the junta of Erica
Erica was tortured.	Erica's torture

Noun compounds can accommodate objects and other kinds of complements.

They sell cars.	They make *car sales.*
They converse by telephone.	They make *telephone conversations.*
They loan money for the construction of buildings.	They make *building loans.*

And we can nominalize adjectives:

The boy was sick → the boy's sickness

The metal was warm → the warmth of the metal

The man is intelligent → the man's intelligence

PROBLEM 30. Make up your own subjects and objects and create nominal phrases like the preceding forms. Use these verbs and adjectives: *recognize, understand, deep, apply, restrict, intense, respond, decide, interfere, respect, hurt, fly, return, talk,* and *compel.*

PROBLEM 31. Rewrite these sentences into verbal form. For example, instead of "He gave a *description* of James Watt's *invention* of the steam engine," you could write "He *described* how James Watt *invented* the steam engine."

(1) He made a decision to leave.

(2) She had a feeling that I would make my departure.

(3) He gave a speech before the adjournment of the meeting.

(4) She did an investigation into the cause of the death.

(5) His performance of the music was characterized by sloppiness.

(6) His arrival was subsequent to my invitation.

(7) Her intention was the accomplishment of his graduation.

(8) His memorization of the facts needs our study.

(9) His specialization in Chinese is an indication of our failure.

(10) The insistence on the part of the navy as to its need for assistance came as a surprise.

PROBLEM 32. Transform these verbal sentences into a nominal style. Where you think that a more dishonest sentence would result from a deleted subject or object, delete it. For example:

Verbal: We need to continue to pollute the water because we do not have sufficient funds.

Nominal: A fund insufficiency has created a need for the continuation of water pollution.

(1) I recognized that the patient would never be conscious again, so I decided that I would disconnect the equipment that helped him to breathe. When I did that he died.

(2) Students who are unable to write good English should be failed by their teachers. Then the University should not register them.

(3) We are going to reduce how much money we spend on programs to keep poor people healthy because if we continue to tax people who have a lot of money, they will eventually refuse to pay their taxes.

(4) I am uncertain about whether we can rely on the devices that should prevent this atomic energy plant from dispersing radioactive particles if someone fails to realize that the core is getting too hot, but I estimate that we can risk it.

(5) We are going to employ fewer people because they cost us too much.

(6) You will have to wait a long time before any of us answer your question.

(7) You will have to pay more money if you want us to serve you because we are making less profit than before.

(8) This bureau will not inform you about what it has been doing. We have decided that the information should be confidential. If we released the information, we would not be able to act as freely as we do now.

There are a good many reasons why a writer rejects a verb

for the nominalization. The most obvious is when he cannot conveniently—or even possibly—select anything else if he is to say what he means. This next passage by Ernest Nagel is so abstract in its thought that it would be difficult, if not impossible, to rephrase it in a verbal version:

> However, although this *explication* as well as the one based on the personalistic *interpretation* of *probability* has a considerable *following,* neither has won general *acceptance* because each has features that many regard as grave *faults*. For example, according to most critics of personalistic *probability,* its chief *weakness* is that on this *interpretation, judgments* of *probability* rest ultimately upon the variable *idiosyncracies* of human beings, and that in *consequence,* no firm reasons can be given for *preferring statements* with high rather than low *probabilities* as *conclusions* of reliable *explanations* or as grounds for dependable *predictions*.

It is virtually impossible to write on a very general or abstract level without using nominalizations separated from their accidental subjects and objects. We ordinarily associate this kind of writing with advanced societies having the leisure to pursue philosophic thought. But those whom we call primitive peoples are not incapable of the same kind of linguistic choices. Franz Boas, an early twentieth-century linguist and anthropologist, reports this experience (my italics):

> It seems very questionable in how far the *restriction* of the *use* of certain grammatical forms can really be conceived as a *hindrance* in the *formulation* of generalized ideas. It seems much more likely that the *lack* of these forms is due to the *lack* of their *need* . . . Discourses on qualities without *connection* with the objects to which the qualities belong, or of the *activities* or states disconnected from the idea of the actor or the subject being in a certain state, will hardly occur in primitive *speech* . . . It happens that in languages in which the idea of *possession* is expressed by elements subordinated to nouns, all abstract terms appear always with possessive elements. It is, however, perfectly conceivable that an Indian trained in philosophic *thought* would proceed to free the underlying nominal forms from the possessive elements, and thus reach abstract forms strictly corresponding to the abstract forms of our modern languages. I have made this *experiment,* for instance, with the Kwakiutl language of Vancouver Island, in which no abstract term ever occurs without its possessive elements. After some *discussion,* I found it perfectly easy to develop the idea of the abstract term in the mind of the Indian, who will state that the word without a possessive pronoun gives a sense, although it is not used idiomatically. I succeeded, for instance, in this manner in *isolating* the terms for *love* and *pity* which ordinarily occur only in possessive forms, like *this love for him* or *my pity for you*.

PROBLEM 33. The nominalizations are in italics. Rewrite the first half of this excerpt in verbal style.

At the pole in opposition to a text with a high nominalization frequency distribution because of the impossibility of content expression in a verbal manner is the prose with a high nominal frequency distribution with no function other than that of the investment of a discourse with an impression of profundity and learning. Unfortunately, there is the probability of the success of this over failure due to the fact that nominal style associations are such that the elicitation of favorable responses based on past experience has a tendency toward interpersonal and intracultural reliability.

In other words, lots of nouns made out of Latinate verbs seem to impress some readers. That's why smart high school and college students learn to write like this:

> An extraordinary manifestation of the profundity of Shakespeare's conception of the function of the Fool in *King Lear* is in his removal from the action subsequent to Lear's entering into a state of insanity.

rather than like this:

> Shakespeare shows how profoundly he conceived the role of the Fool in *King Lear* when he removed him from the play after Lear became insane.

But it's not a style used by students alone. Even doctors have been accused of it:

> . . . it now appears that obligatory obfuscation is a firm tradition within the medical profession.
>
> Michael Crichton, M.D., New England Journal of Medicine

as well as lawyers:

> . . . lawyers and judges . . . are discovering that sometimes they cannot even understand each other.
>
> Tom Goldstein, *New York Times*.

Dr. Crichton had in mind language like this:

> In regard to the Custodis and Lincoff *operation,* there is the *necessity* for the *consideration* of the *mobility* of the retina after *detachment*. This *study* is a *report* of cases of retina *detachment* for the *determination* of the *occurrences* of periretinal fibrosis, its *effect* on retinal *mobility,* and *influence* on the *choice* of *operation*.

Now it is certainly not the case that all scientists, sociologists, and educators are trying to impress their colleagues with a pretentious style. It is clear, though, that a very large part of the scientific and professional writing in a heavily nominal style is unnecessary. A sentence such as:

> There was a successful determination in regard to the causes of the increase in criminal activity.

could be rewritten:

> We determined why crime increased.

with little or no loss in meaning and with considerable gain in understanding.

In cases such as this, what we have is a professional dialect that has almost become a prerequisite—or at least thought to be—that qualifies its user to be taken seriously. Those who have mastered it, who can use it in the accepted ways, are implicitly telling their readers that they are writers and researchers to be trusted, scholars who have been through the system and have been socialized into its values. There is no widespread sense of conscious deception but rather an acceptance of an unacknowledged standard, regardless of its intrinsic difficulty (as that sentence demonstrates).

3.2. The Historical Roots of Nominal Style

The source of this scholarly standard lies in the contact of English with other languages and in its subsequent historical evolution. After the Norman Invasion of 1066, most serious writing was done first in Latin, later in French. It was not until around the middle of the fourteenth century that England began slowly to emerge from under French domination and the English language began to be used again for serious purposes.

But in the meantime, for the more scholarly genres of writing, English writers had lost the habit of compounding a new word out of two old ones. In Anglo-Saxon England, before the Invasion, the English scholar borrowed some words from Latin, but when he needed a new word to express a new concept, he more often compounded a new one out of two words already in the language. Instead of borrowing *anxietas* (anxiety) from Latin, he put together *mod* (mind or spirit) and *cearo* (care or sorrow) to create *modcearo*. Even during the Conquest, the English continued to compound words for mundane, day-to-day concepts. We still do: *babysitter, doghouse, soap opera, splashdown, anchorman,* and so on. But for more learned discourses, we use words borrowed from Latin and French.

During the fifteenth and sixteenth centuries in particular, English writers translating foreign texts into English for the first time found that often, they did not have a native word to translate a French, Latin, or Greek one. So instead of going back to the native tradition of compounding, say, the verb *input* to translate the Latin *includere,* the English writer of the Renaissance just borrowed the Latin word as *include.* Because late Latin style was itself often nominal, the noun form of the word was often borrowed into English before the verb form. *Instruction,* for example, occurs in English about sixty-five years before the verb *instruct.* So it is partly because of the Norman Conquest that many of these Latinate nominalizations are in our more formal language in the first place. But another development also occurred.

By the nineteenth century, the prose style of scientific writing had begun to take on its current characteristics. Because much of the earliest and best scientific writing in the nineteenth century was in German, and because much German prose style was heavily nominal, writers of scientific discourses in English often tended to imitate the convolutions of German prose style. Moreover, as science attempted to become a more objective endeavor, relying on the impersonal observation of events and the inevitable and logical conclusions that such observations led to, scientific prose came to focus less on the experimenter and more on the conduct and results of the experiments. And because more and more research was conducted not by individual researchers but by groups of scientists, *I* became not only too subjective but too personal. The passive is one way to avoid *I. I* could write this sentence like this, or it could be written like this.

The depersonalization of language can be effected to an even greater extent by the combination of passivization and nominalization, resulting in the creation of sentences characterized by an absence of animate agency, thereby providing a heightening of the seeming objectivity of the representation of the conduct of an investigation by the deletion of the role of the source of the investigation. (Like that.)

When in this century, the social sciences began to develop as a field aspiring to the objectivity of the natural sciences, they developed the same style. And eventually, that style spread to become a kind of national educated standard in laboratories, classrooms, badly edited academic journals, government bureaus, and so on—an impersonal, Latinate, nominal, passive style whose mere presence now testifies that whatever it expresses aspires to profundity and reliability.

3.3 Some Affective Consequences of Nominal and Verbal Styles

In this essay, though, we are more interested in what lies between these two extremes: between a nominal style written by habit and a nominal style required by the content it expresses. We are interested in those moments when we can seem to choose a nominal or a verbal style, when we can choose to manifest even a phrase of ideational content in a nominal or verbal form. There are as many reasons as authors, audiences, subjects, and intentions. But some intentions are more likely to call for a nominal style than others.

One important intention, as we have seen, is to impress a reader with a learned and sententious tone.

Another is to make objective by deleting the accidental subjects and objects of verbs like *love, understand, feel, know,* and so on. But if we can delete to make general, we can also delete to make obscure, for a nominal style is perfectly suited to the speaker who wants to hide his own agency—or someone else's—behind an abstraction, who does not want to attribute agency to an action openly and directly. That sounds almost immoral. But it is more complicated than that.

There are those, to be sure, who nominalize lots of verbs to avoid responsibility for their actions. Several years ago, a freshly inaugurated governor of California was asked why he allowed a man to die in the gas chamber. He replied on national television:

> There was insufficient evidence on which to base a change of decision.

The two nominalizations, *change* and *decision,* are the key to unpacking the sentence. He could have answered:

> I did not see enough evidence to make me change my mind and decide to save the man's life.

Had he done that, he would have been admirably straightforward but at least in his own mind, we might presume, too blunt, too specific, too revealing of his responsibility for an action that was far from universally popular. So he nominalized two key verbs, deleted the agent, himself, and the man who went to the gas chamber.

PROBLEM 34. In the governor's original sentence, what is the topic? the pivot? the stress? How did he manage to avoid putting the negative directly next to *change?* Where is the negative in the sentence? Why is its placement crucial to the effect of the sentence? Where does it invest the responsibility for no change?

Obscuring who is doing what to whom perhaps more than any

other grammatical option characterizes bureaucratic prose. Because bureaucracies seem so often to expect us to serve them rather than to exert themselves to serve us, they must exercise their power in a way that prevents us from associating them with individual fallible people and instead make us believe that it is "agencies" as representatives of government which are insisting, for our own good, on our willing compliance with their desires. Here, for example, is part of a release from the National Highway Traffic Safety Administration directed to car manufacturers requesting information about the cost of safety devices:

> The NHTSA need current and correct information on the cost savings to motor vehicle buyers that will be achieved if one or more of the currently applicable motor vehicle safety standards are revoked in order to carry out its mission of maintaining standards that effectively meet the need for motor vehicle safety. Serious and continuing consideration must be given to the costs that may be saved by the revocation of existing requirements (as compared to their benefits), as well as the costs and benefits of adding new requirements.

This is the language of authority. An acronym (not people) needs information to carry out a "mission" of protecting—who? Only "safety" is mentioned. The only *people* specified are those who buy cars.

PROBLEM 35. The most dangerous kind of bureaucratic language, though, is not that which merely obscures the agent and the object from the reader, but which is written in a style that allows the writer himself to ignore who is doing and who is being done to. Revise this next passage, written in the mid-sixties by a political scientist who was advising our government on foreign policy:

> In the Congo, in Viet Nam, in the Dominican Republic, it is clear that *order* depends on somehow *compelling* newly mobilized strata to return to a measure of *passivity* and *defeatism* from which they have recently been aroused by the process of *modernization*. At least temporarily, the *maintenance* of *order* requires a *lowering* of *aspirations* and levels of political *activity*.

Most often, nominalization is a grammatical structure not consciously chosen but rather learned and used (or abused) as the accepted dialect of an educated caste—the dialect one finds in the academic journals, government directives, and business memos. It is a style in which the connection of ideas is expressed not by the syntactic backbone of the English sentence: [subject-noun-agent]—[verb-action]—[object-noun-goal], but by the sheer contiguity of words linked by prepositions; meaningless connecting verbs such as *make, have, be, do,* and so on; and by mere word order. The ideational structure is smeared across the surface of the sentence so that agents, actions, and their goals are disassociated from one another, relegated to prepositional phrases tacked on at the end of a sentence or to a phrase squeezed between meaningless function words. It is the style of those who assume that the connections between ideas that exist in their own minds will be apparent to anyone who reads a sequence of words that roughly corresponds to those ideas. And this is the kind of sentence that results:

> There is now no effective mechanism for *introducing* the *initiation* and *development* stages of *reporting requirements information* on existing *reporting* and *guidance* on how to minimize burden *associations* with new *requirements.*

There are a few other common ends to which nominalizations are put. For example, compare these two ways to end a sentence:

> You would have thought that men who passed their lives in the study of the great masters of literature would be sufficiently sensitive to the beauty of language to write
>
> (1) if not beautifully at least perspicuously.
>
> (2) if not beautifully at least with perspicuity.

The nominalization at the end of (2) requires an extra word, and it upsets the perfect parallelism of *beautifully—perspicuously.* But the nominalization also maintains the rhythm of the line: *ăt léast wĭth pérspĭcuitý* rather than ending with a series of very weakly stressed syllables: *ăt léast pĕrspícŭŏuslў.* And it provides a weight at the end of a sentence that the adverb cannot. *Perspicuity* is the stress and will be the local interest of the next few sentences. By nominalizing *perspicuous* into *perspicuity,* Somerset Maugham gives that concept a syntactic weight in the sentence commensurate with its stressed position and rhetorical importance. (As in that sentence.)

Here is another example, this one from Winston Churchill:

> . . . until in God's good time, the New World, with all its power and might, steps forth to the rescue and the liberation of the Old.

The two nominalizations at the end, *rescue* and *liberation,* are appropriate to the heavy matter. He could have written a less weighty:

> . . . until in God's good time, the New World, with all its power and might, steps forth to rescue and liberate the Old.

The conclusion of a sentence, the stress, calls for a syntactic and semantic weight equal to its rhetorical function.

So we have a number of possible reasons for choosing the nominalization over the verb. It can raise a passage to the level of a formal occasion. It can lend an air of profundity and intelligence even when the discourse itself lacks it. It allows the speaker to delete agency or object, or both, thereby obscuring who is doing what to whom, a syntactic option that allows us either to escape responsibility or raise our discourse to a level of philosophical generality. It may also be the only grammatical structure available for what the writer wants to say. In addition to these uses is another illustrated by this sentence, the topicalizing nominalization that refers to a series of preceding actions and summarizes them in a topic-noun phrase: *these uses*. This is one of the ways it allows us to express the relationship between complex ideas more concisely, and another is its key role in the stylistic device of *integration,* to which we will now turn.

4. Expansion and Architecture

Although the backbone of every sentence is the subject-verb-complement sequence, virtually every sentence we have examined is composed of more than just that central structure. Almost all are expanded, modified, elaborated on by peripheral structures, each with its own topic and comment, subject and verb, agent and action, each the product of a writer combining propositions into a single complex grammatical structure able to express a complex idea, a sentence such as the one you are now reading, one that could be segmented into several shorter sentences, sentences which have been modified so that they become part of one longer grammatical sentence.

PROBLEM 36. Break the previous two sentences down to their nuclear propositions. For example, *George and I left* can be broken into *George left* and *I left*. *I know that you left* could be reduced to *you left,* and *I know that*. *I tried to find out what you wanted* could be broken into *I tried something, You wanted something,* and *I found that out*. In some cases, the sentences you create will be awkward or incomplete, but that is because you are representing the propositions as fully realized sentences rather than as abstract relationships. Ignore the seeming awkwardness and the lack of perfect synonymy between the original and your nuclear propositions.

4.1 Expansion

When a sentence synthesizes several embedded or contained propositions, those contained propositions can be modified and connected one to another in three ways: *integration, subordination,* and *coordination.*

4.1.1 Integration

When we integrate propositions, one of them must be changed so that it can fill one of the two or three necessary structural slots in a clause.

> *Subject:* He left. [It] surprised me. → [That he left] surprised me.
>
> *Complement:* The truth is [this]. He left. → The truth is [that he left].
>
> *Verb:* He [makes strong] the wall. → He [strengthened] the wall.

Indeed, several propositions can integrate to fill the slots in an abstract structure that is only a series of three empty slots:

you are devoted	you make intense	I am resolved
your devotion	intensifies	my resolve
Subject	*Verb*	*Object*

We have already examined in some detail the most common way in which one sentence can be integrated with another: abstract nominalizations. And we have seen how revising nominalizations into fully specified propositions leads to a more verbal style, one more dependent on clausal subordination than on nominal integration:

> His realization of my loss was a surprise to me. (one clause)
>
> When he realized what I had lost, it surprised me. (three clauses)

Though abstract nominalizations are the most common kind of integrated structure, there are a few others. We can integrate *that*-clauses:

> He is old. I know it. → I know *that he is old.*

for-to constructions:

He did that. It surprised me. → *For him to do that* surprised me.

and *WH*-clauses:

He went somewhere. I know where. → I know *where he went.*

In all three cases, the integrated clause becomes a subject or object, topic or stress, seeming agent or goal. Probably more than any other grammatical process, integration characterizes mature expository prose. It allows us to make complex statements not just about things but about abstract concepts and their relationships.

4.1.2 Subordination: Periodic and Loose

When we subordinate one clause to another, the subordinated clause becomes dependent on some constitutive element of the main clause. The clause can be an adverbial clause dependent on the verb phrase:

George left. I left. → Because George left, I left.

or a relative clause dependent on a noun:

You met a boy. I know him. → I know the boy whom you met.

In both these sentences, the clauses depend on elements in the main clause. Subordination differs from integration in this way, that integration inserts a proposition into one of the necessary structural slots of a S-V-C structure, while subordination transforms a proposition so that it will qualify, modify, and remark on another structure. This is a purely formal description, of course, because virtually the same semantic content can be communicated through integration or subordination:

Because the war ended, everyone rejoiced.

The end of the war was a cause for everyone to rejoice.

And again, we can distinguish a verbal-clausal style from a nominal-phrasal one.

When a writer builds up a series of subordinate clauses or phrases before the grammatical subject or between the subject and verb, delaying the verb, his style is traditionally called *periodic* or *suspended.* It is a style that suggests a writer qualifying and refining the conditions of the statement in the main clause before he makes it. It is the style of the opening sentence of the Declaration of Independence that we presented in problem 10, beginning with a complex subordinate clause stating the conditions that pertain to what the main clause stresses: *to the separation.*

Subordinate Clause:	When in the course . . . entitle them,
Main Clause:	a decent respect . . . to the separation.

PROBLEM 37. Here are the next few sentences of the Declaration of Independence. Why is only the last periodic? (Slashes: /, indicate the boundaries of grammatical sentences; boldface indicates the main clause subject and verb.) What other segmentation is possible? What is the effect of breaking these sentences into shorter ones?

> **We hold** these truths to be self-evident, that all men are created equal, that they are endowed by their creator with certain unalienable Rights, that among these are Life, Liberty and the pursuit of Happiness. /That to secure these rights, Governments are instituted among Men, deriving their just powers from the consent of the governed./ That whenever any Form of Government becomes destructive to these ends, it is the Right of the People to alter or to abolish it, and to institute new Government, laying its foundation on such principles and organizing its powers in such form, as to them shall seem most likely to affect their Safety and Happiness./ **Prudence,** indeed, **will dictate** that Governments long established should not be changed for light and transient causes;/ and accordingly **all experience hath shewn** that mankind are more disposed to suffer, while evils are sufferable, than to right themselves by abolishing the forms to which they are accustomed./ But when a long train of abuses and usurpations, pursuing invariably the same Object evinces a design to reduce them under absolute Despotism, **it is** their right, **it is** their duty, to throw off such Government and to provide new Guards for their future security.

In the grandest style, several introductory clauses echoing one another in length, rhythm, and grammatical structure can build toward a grand conclusion:

> But if you think it profitable to turn man's intellectual and moral activity toward the necessities of physical life and use them to produce well-being,
> if you think that reason is more use to men than genius,
> if your object is not to create heroic virtues but rather tranquil habits,

if you would rather contemplate vices than crimes and prefer fewer transgressions at the cost of fewer splendid deeds,
if in place of a brilliant society you are content to live in one that is prosperous,
and finally
if in your view the main object of government is not to achieve the greatest strength or glory for the nation as a whole but to provide for every individual therein the utmost well-being, protecting him as far as possible from all afflictions,

then it is good to make conditions equal and to establish a democratic government.

Alexis de Tocqueville

PROBLEM 38. Construct a sentence on this model, using as subject matter either overpopulation or pollution. Now construct another on the same model using as subject matter a pet goldfish or brushing your teeth. What do you conclude? Describe the problem in terms of personae, scene, subject, and telos.

PROBLEM 39. Analyze examples from the prose of four or five modern writers to determine how many adverbial clauses of the kind we have been describing here occur in every grammatical (*not* orthographic) sentence. Such clauses can be sorted into groups based on their logical function:

Conditional: If, unless. *Temporal:* Before, when, while, as, after, until

Causal: Because, since *Concessional:* Although, though, even if, while

What are the most common kinds of clauses? Where do they ordinarily occur in a sentence? Do certain kinds ordinarily occur in a particular position?

A second kind of subordination is by means of relative clauses modifying noun phrases:

A man was in the house. I saw him.

→ I saw the man who was in the house.

Although these relative clauses typically serve only to modify the noun they are attached to, they can function semantically much as adverbial clauses do:

> People [who live in glass houses] should not throw stones.
> [If people live in glass houses,] they should not throw stones.
>
> Students [who do not study] often fail.
> [When students do not study,] they often fail.
>
> Countries [that cannot disagree peacefully] ultimately destroy each other.
> [Because some countries cannot disagree peacefully,] they ultimately destroy each other.

Every clause has its own topic and stress. But when a clause is located entirely inside a sentence, not set off by pauses, then the emphasis on the last stress of that buried clause can weaken to virtual nonexistence. In fact, this is one reason why some sentences seem to be an unbroken string of words going on and on without a rhythmic pause of any sort to relieve the flat tedium of almost equally stressed phrases that should be organized into shorter segments in order to provide some sense of pace that every sentence ought to have to be considered even slightly graceful by readers who have any desire to move through a sentence in a way that is not utterly without relief from the kind of tedium that results from sentences that read like the one you have now finished.

The fact that a long introductory noun clause which has in the subject position several internal modifying phrases and clauses has much the same periodic or suspended effect as a long adverbial clause which precedes an independent main clause is illustrated by this sentence. It requires the reader to process, store, and retain in his grammatical memory a good deal of grammatical information before he can complete the subject-verb structure:

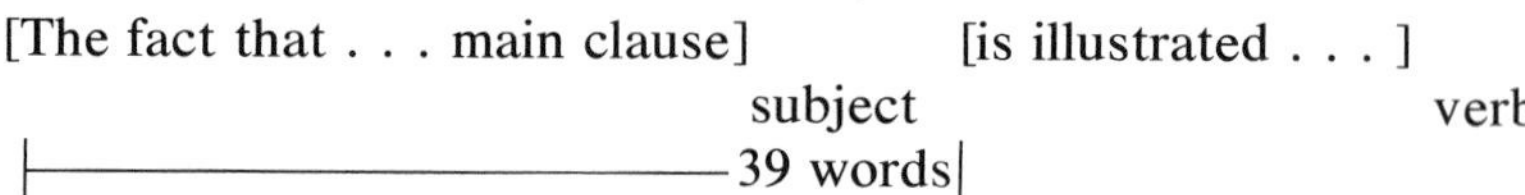

If the subject noun phrase in the main clause contains a subordinate clause with its own subject and verb structure, then we have to store not only the expectation of the verb to complete the subject of the main clause, but the expectation of the verb for the subject in the subordinate clause as well.

For example, consider this sentence:

The fact that work without satisfaction or reward leads to a life which is devoid of joy is known to all.

As the reader reads *The fact that work,* he knows he must store an expectation of a verb to go with *fact,* and that when he then reads *that work,* he knows too that he must store the expectation of another verb to go with *work.* As he completes *without satisfaction or reward* and gets to *leads,* he has found the verb to go with *work.* But he must retain the expectation of a verb to go with *fact.* As he moves through *to a life which is devoid of joy* and gets to *is known,* he takes out of storage the expectation of a verb to go with *fact* and can then piece together the meaning of the whole proposition. The more storage capacity a sentence requires or the longer any stored bit of grammatical information must be retained, the more periodic and suspended a style is and the more demanding it is on the reader.

PROBLEM 40. Which of these next three sentences requires the most storage? the least? Revise the one that requires the most so that it requires less storage. Revise one that requires less storage so that it requires more. What is the difference?

(1) Land being cheap in that country, from the vast forests still void of inhabitants, and not likely to be occupied in an age to come, insomuch that the propriety of an hundred acres of fertile soil full of wood may be obtained near the frontiers, in many places, for eight or ten guineas, hearty young labouring men, who understand the husbandry of corn and cattle, which is nearly the same in that country as in Europe, may easily establish them there.

Benjamin Franklin

(2) I was seated by the shore of a small pond, about a mile and a half south of the village of Concord and somewhat higher than it, in the midst of an extensive wood between that town and Lincoln, and about two miles south of that our only field known to fame, Concord Battle Ground; but I was so low in the woods that the opposite shore, half a mile off, like the rest, covered with wood, was my most distant horizon.

Henry David Thoreau

(3) There is a spider crawling along the matted floor of the room where I sit (not the one which has been so well allegorized in the admirable *Lines to a Spider,* but another of the same edifying breed); he runs with heedless, hurried haste, he hobbles awkwardly towards me, he stops—he sees the giant shadow before him, and, at a loss whether to retreat or proceed, meditates his huge foe—but as I do not start up and seize upon the straggling caitiff, as he would upon a hapless

> fly within his toils, he takes heart, and ventures on with mingled cunning, impudence, and fear.
>
> William Hazlitt

A more modern style is called *loose*. In no sense is it a pejorative term. Loose sentences require us to store little grammatical structure as we read them, because each construction immediately completes itself as the reader progresses through the sentence. The sentence you have just read is a good example. *Loose* links directly to *sentences*. *Sentences* links directly to *require; require* links directly to *us,* but forces us to briefly anticipate that a verb must follow; *to* indicates the verb to follow and links directly to *store; store* does not link directly to *little,* and so requires us to store for a moment the expectation of an object to come; *little* links directly to *grammatical structure,* however; and *grammatical* links directly to *structure,* completing the *store-structure* relationship, and so on.

Virtually every word represents a construction that is immediately completed or "closed" by the next word. At no time are we required to store the expectation of a completing structure for more than a word or two. In fact, since we ordinarily read not word-by-word but phrase-by-phrase, we probably do not have to store even that much, if the whole structures can be included and perceived in a single scan of the eyes as they flick back and forth across a sentence.

PROBLEM 41. Here is another version of that sentence. Why is it more "complex"?

> Sentences which, as we read them, because each structure as the reader progresses through the sentence completes itself, require us to store very little grammatical structure are loose.

Very long and loose sentences often suggest a mind at work, probing a subject, trying out an idea by putting it into words, letting the words take a sentence wherever they may lead it without the writer anticipating where the sentence will end, whether with an unexpected truth, or deceptively catching its syntactic breath, a breath that lets it move on again, adding member to member until it finally winds down to a welcome end.

That sentence was intended to represent what its structure suggested, a sentence that moves not quite aimlessly, but not toward an entirely anticipated end, either. If a loose style may seem to represent a probing, uncommitted mind, we should not assume that the movement of such a sentence is in fact always artless and unrevised. It may be. But it may also be the product of long and painful revision until it captures just the right nuance of a seemingly hesitant mind exploring an idea for the first time, catching in the act of writing that unexpected truth that lurks just out of the corner of the mind's eye.

Adverbial and relative clauses tacked on to the end of a sentence are one way to keep a sentence going, although too many of them suggest a writer who doesn't know where he is going because he hasn't thought out what he wants to say beyond the next phrase or two, which means just tacking on clause after clause, which is what I am doing right now.

More typical of a careful loose style are what we might call *loose modifiers*. Loose modifiers are sentence elements that expand on a noun phrase in a clause, but are attached to the end of the clause, adding some additional information (like that element):

sentence elements . . . , adding some additional information . . .

One common kind refers back to the subject. It may begin with an adjective phrase, a present participial phrase, a past participial phrase, or a noun phrase:

Adjective Phrase:	The arbitrators refused to continue the negotiations, *weary* of haggling over minor issues and *angry* that they had been misled. (Arbitrators were weary . . .)
Present Participial:	The words flow on without pause, *washing* away in a torrent of sincerity the questions he hoped to ignore. (Words wash . . .)
Past Participial:	A flurry of letters passed between them, *written* more to insult than to inform. (Letters were written . . .)
Noun Phrase:	The desire to smoke sprang at him without warning, *an irresistible beast* that clawed at his throat and tongue and lips. (The desire was a beast . . .)

This kind of modifier most often occurs in narrative, extending an action or explaining it, describing it, evaluating it in a way that makes it appear almost simultaneous with the action.

A somewhat more dramatic way to sustain a sentence combines the characteristics of loose modifiers and coordination. We might call them *resumptive modifiers* and *summative modifiers*. A resumptive modifier begins by repeating a key word that appeared earlier in the sentence, then continuing.

> Some elderly residents live in *apartments* subsidized by the government, *apartments* no young person would live in to save his life.
>
> Suppose the poor were given direct *grants, grants* in the form of cash, *grants* in the form of increased Social Security payments.
>
> It may be that housing has been *written off* as a national priority, *written off* because the young can afford whatever inflation brings, *written off* because the old have no power to threaten those who do not care.

If the repeated expression is a noun, the modifier is typically completed with a full or shortened relative clause, as in the first two examples. In the third example, the repeated expression is a verb; just as nouns are modified by relative clauses, so verbs and adjectives are modified by adverbial clauses, and the third example has two resumptive modifiers, each time with *written off* modified by an adverbial clause, first "because the young . . . ," and then "because the old. . . ."

The summative modifier is another kind of modifier that lets a writer extend the line of a sentence. It begins with a word that sums up a whole clause, then continues with a relative clause that describes that word or with some other construction.

> The American government has chosen not to develop the B-1 bomber or the neutron bomb, *decisions* which will haunt us for decades to come.
>
> In the past decade, our oil imports have continued to soar, *a result* of shortsightedness and indifference.
>
> The national political picture changed when George Wallace of Alabama withdrew from political life, *an event* which marked the end of an era.

In each of these cases, the summative word—*decisions, result, event*—sums up the previous clause and introduces a comment on it.

Both of these structures, summative modifiers and resumptive modifiers, characterize discursive prose more than narrative prose. Both allow a writer to catch his breath for a moment, then extend the line of the sentence in a way that avoids that stringy, straggling kind of sentence that seems to go on forever.

PROBLEM 42. Write a paragraph that illustrates each of these loose modifiers. Use the excerpt from Norman Mailer in Problem 11 as a model.

4.2 Architecture

4.2.1 Internal Architecture: Coordination and Balance

We shall devote a longer section to coordination because it is one of several distinctive grammatical patterns that characterize a "style" when those patterns occur so often in a text that a reader becomes conscious of them. (Others are abstract nominalizations, extended periodic introductory constructions, loose sentences with multiple clauses and free modifiers branching from the end of a sentence, and a discourse constituted of short, "curt" sentences.)

The simplest kind of coordination merely joins two clauses with one of seven coordinating conjunctions: *and, but, so, for, yet, or, nor.*

George went home, and I went to sleep.

Traditionally, this is called a compound sentence, but like this sentence it is structurally two grammatical sentences in a single orthographic sentence. The reader carries no grammatical baggage from one clause to the next. In a complex sentence:

George went home, because I went to sleep.

it is necessary to understand the grammatical dependence of the *because*-clause on the previous clause. And despite the occasional strictures of prescriptivists who do not know how the best writers actually write English, sentences frequently begin with coordinating conjunctions. (In fact, a good many paragraphs begin with *but.*)

Because these coordinating conjunctions have much the same semantic force as subordinating conjunctions, we can often translate a subordinate adverbial clause into a coordinate clause and vice versa:

Because he left, I stayed. ↔ He left, so I stayed.

Because he left, I stayed. ↔ I stayed, for he left.

If he doesn't stay, I leave. ↔ He stays or I leave.

As I danced, he sang. ↔ I danced and he sang.

The term *complex* in a complex sentence is often confused with *complex* meaning mature, profound, and so on, so some teachers value complex sentences with subordinate clauses more highly than compound sentences, and in some ways they are right, for a series of sentences joined with coordinating conjunctions can appear simple-minded, and they seem to run one after another without much careful synthesis, so it is generally not a good idea to join several successive clauses in such constructions, but sometimes a very casual tone calls for coordination rather than subordination.

PROBLEM 43. Rewrite the previous sentence, resegmenting and subordinating where appropriate.

PROBLEM 44. The King James version of the Bible is strongly *hypotactic,* composed of sentences joined to one another with conjunctions. (The opposite term is *paratactic,* without conjunctions.)

> *And* seeing the multitudes, he went up into a mountain,
> *and* when he was set his disciples came unto him.
> *And* he opened his mouth, and taught them, saying:
> Blessed are the poor in spirit,
> *for* theirs is the kingdom of heaven.

The text could have been translated like this:

> Seeing the multitudes, he went up into a mountain.
> When he was set, his disciples came unto him.
> Opening his mouth, he taught them, saying:
> Blessed are the poor in spirit,
> because theirs is the kingdom of heaven.

What is the difference? Revise Genesis 1: 1–10 in this way: Delete all conjunctions coordinating full clauses and replace them with subordinating conjunctions, where you can. What is the difference?

Parts of sentences can also be coordinated, of course:

Tom went home and Bill went home. → Tom and Bill went home.

When very short segments are coordinated, particularly more than two, we sometimes call the structure a *series:*

> In the 20th century, one -ism after another has inflicted itself on contemporary thought, existentialism, Marxism, capitalism, nihilism, socialism, conservatism, liberalism, agnosticism, transcendentalism, nationalism.

Two-part coordination has at least three sources. First, English prose has for the last six hundred years used *doublets* redundantly, almost as a verbal tic, as a way of emphasizing an idea. The doublets often consist of a native Anglo-Saxon word and a Romance word roughly synonymous with it:

> As hyt ys y-knowe houw meny maner people buth in this ylond, ther buth also of so meny people longages and tonges; notheles Walschmen and Scottes, that buth nowt y-melled with other nacions, holdeth wel ny here furste longage and speche, . . .
>
> John of Trevisa (1385)
>
> (As it is known how many manner [of] people be in this island, there be also of so many people languages and tongues; nonetheless, Welshmen and Scots that be not meddled with other nations, hold well nigh their first language and speech.)

Languages (Romance) and *tongues* (Anglo-Saxon), *language* (Romance) and *speech* (Anglo-Saxon) are for all practical purposes perfectly synonymous doublets.

The tradition of the learned Romance word and the plain Anglo-Saxon word (see Chapter 2, problems 25–28) still influences modern prose, though more often than not, the origins of the words are no longer so carefully distinguished. Here is a sampling of doublets from a single article that recently appeared in the sports pages of the *New York Times: bureaucratic and administrative problems, bickering and disagreements, problems and obstacles, bicker and argue, power and influence, belief and interest, cynicism and growing skepticism.* Others spring from the pen or typewriter almost of their own accord: *strength and power, wit and intelligence, love and adore, friend and companion, lovely and beautiful, sincere and honest, loose and faulty.* This is a habit and tradition so firmly and profoundly ingrained in English that we shall probably never expunge or banish it from our prose and speech.

When they are not merely redundant, paired coordinate members can exhaust the possibilities within the universe to which the discourse refers.

> The Equal Rights Amendment would benefit both men and women.

They may constitute logical antitheses:

> Success too often penalizes those who have earned it and rewards those who have not.

And, of course, the coordination may be merely representative:

> The pleasure of competition and the joy of victory cannot compensate the amateur athlete who must pay out of his own pocket his own money for food and lodging.

In this case, the compensations are more than the pleasure of competition and the joy of victory: health, testing one's own standards, and so on; and the expenses include more than food and lodging: transportation, equipment, and so on. But in both instances, the paired examples are sufficient.

Often, the paired coordinate construction communicates a sense of certainty and completeness:

> The time has come to realize that the interracial drama acted out on the American continent has not only created a new black man, it has created a new white man, too.
>
> James Baldwin

> We are at once instrument and end, discoverers and teachers, actors and observers. We understand, as we hope others understand, that in this there is a harmony between knowledge in the sense of science, that specialized and general knowledge which it is our purpose to uncover, and the community of man. We, like all men, are among those who bring a little light to the vast unending darkness of man's life and world. For us as for all men, change and eternity, specialization and unity, instrument and final purpose, community and individual man alone, complementary each to the other, both require and define our bonds and our freedom.
>
> J. Robert Oppenheimer

It is the style of a writer who confidently understands his position.

The first sentence in the Oppenheimer example also illustrates a three-member coordination. Three is a bit less dogmatic than two, perhaps a trifle more reasonable. Few phenomena in our experience fall neatly into dichotomous parts, few bifurcate into neatly opposed antitheses that exhaust the possible oppositions. Three implies a set that is open to additional members:

> I speak of the American in the singular, as if there were not millions of them, north and south, east and west, of both sexes, of all ages, and of various races, professions, and religions.
>
> George Santayana

The last sequence contains a triplet in a triplet:

of both sexes,
of all ages,
and of various races
professions
and religions.

Certainly, sex, age, and [race, professions, and religion] by no means exhaust the characteristics of Americans: Americans who come from different ethnic, geographical, and social origins; Americans of different political, philosophical, and educational backgrounds; Americans of different (you get the point). . . .

There are a few structural principles that ordinarily determine how these series are constructed. A very general one is that the length of the individual items in the series increases rather than decreases. Contrast these two versions of the "same" sentence:

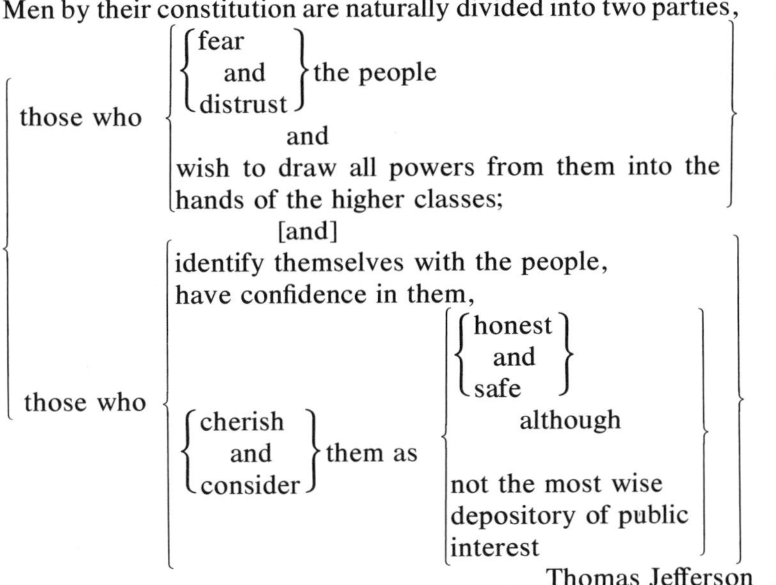

Men by their constitution are naturally divided into two parties, those who cherish and consider the people as not the most wise although the most honest and safe depository of public interest, have confidence in them, identify themselves with them; those who wish to draw all powers from the people into the hands of the higher classes and distrust and fear them.

A logical consequence of this general principle is the more specific one that series within series tend to spring from a member closer to the end of the series than to the beginning. Such series are more likely to resemble (a) than (b).

(a) Tyranny is tyranny,

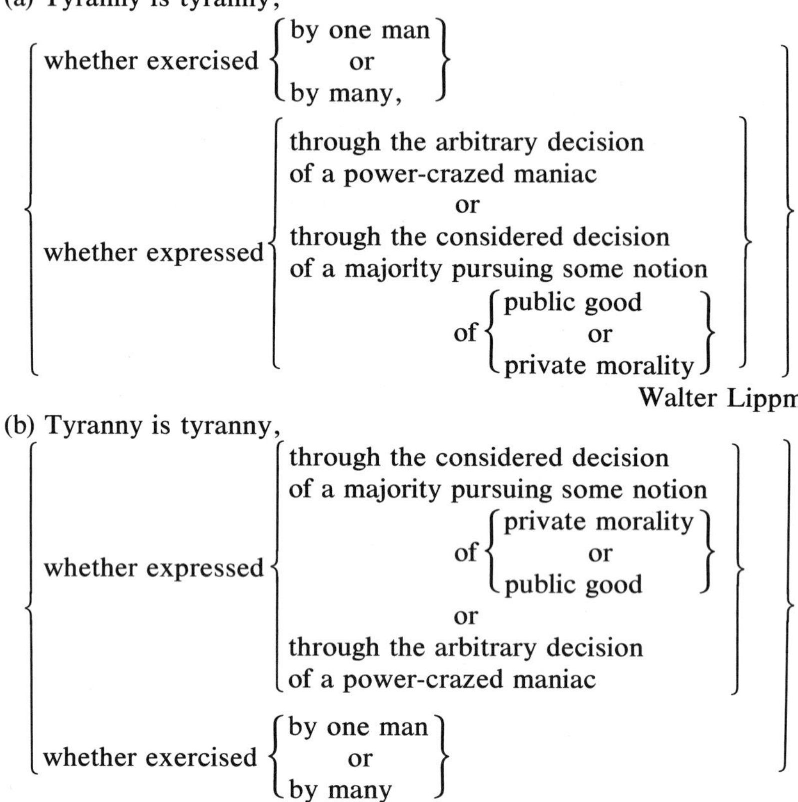

The rhythms of the two passages, again, are entirely different. The first sustains the rhythmic line, the second brings the reader down abruptly.

PROBLEM 45. Construct two sentences on the model of the one above, one increasing in coordinate complexity and length, the other decreasing in coordinate complexity and length.

Like loose modifiers and periodic structures, a coordinate series created out of stylistic habit or conscious intention may not just represent semantic content; it may also have channeled a writer's thought. If we commit ourselves to writing in this style, we do not merely represent already existing balanced and coordinate ideas in balanced and coordinate periods; we seek out balanced ideas; we create oppositions and invent parallels (as in this sentence) where they may not have otherwise existed, either on the page or in the imagination. Where a simple clause might serve a writer not addicted to balanced coordination:

> None of us can foretell his own fate in a mindless universe.

the writer who habitually constructs sentences with two or three coordinate members will almost unconsciously add an *either* so that as he creates one clause, another is called into existence after the *or:*

> None of us can forestall or even foretell either our own fate or the destiny of others in a universe born from a mindless protean fireball and expiring blindly in entropic silence.

It is this impulse that leads to empty parallels:

> Amateur sports are intended to provide an opportunity for people to compete and test themselves against one another, but the competitors and performers are being hampered and interfered with by a bureaucracy and an administration interested more in itself than in sports and athletics.

In many of the passages we have examined, the coordination is reinforced by parallel grammatical structures, and in some cases, by roughly equivalent length and phonological cadence:

That praises are without reason lavished on the dead
and
that the honors due only to excellence are paid to antiquity
is a complaint likely to be always continued by
by { those who, being able to add nothing to truth, hope for eminence from the heresies of paradox
or
those who, being forced by disappointment upon consolatory expedients, are willing }
to { hope from posterity what the present age refuses
and
flatter themselves that the regard which is yet denied by envy will be at last bestowed by time. }

Samuel Johnson

Praises lavished on the dead	=	honors paid to antiquity
those who, being able	=	those who, being forced
hope for eminence from the heresies of paradox	=	hope from posterity what the present age refuses

are only roughly parallel. Often, Dr. Johnson carries out the parallelism almost perfectly:

. . . and as this practice is a commodious subject {of raillery to the gay / and / of declamation to the serious}
it has been {ridiculed with all the pleasantry of wit / and / exaggerated with all the applications of rhetorick.}

Coordination is the simplest way to achieve syntactic and semantic balance and antithesis, but there are others. Among the more common is to balance a subordinate clause against a main clause:

{While China has conquered the problems of mass survival,
it has sacrificed the concept of individual freedom.}

Or a topic (or a part of it) can be balanced against a comment (or part of it):

{Most problems which theoretical critics find easy to describe
prove to be
social dilemmas which practical citizens find impossible to solve.}

Or the two parts of a comparison:

{The close sensitivity of a good friend is of more enduring value
than
the distant influence of a powerful benefactor.}

More complex parallels can be constructed out of sentence structures that have two or more noun phrases after the verb.

One should never give up {distant rewards of certain value
for
immediate pleasures of dubious worth.}

At too many colleges and universities, students concerned with vocational skills only take
{ practical courses
to obtain
saleable skills. }

Churches preoccupied with keeping a congregation regardless of moral cost have traded
{ the permanent truths proved by millennia of religious thought
for
the transient fads suggested by momentary enthusiasms. }

PROBLEM 46. Here are a number of two- and three-place frames. Create sentences that *balance* the X, Y, and Z structures, like those above. Some subject matters are suggested in parentheses.

(1) . . . demand X for Y (political favors)

(2) . . . build X on Y (plans for the future)

(3) . . . offer X for Y (the fruits of labor)

(4) . . . improve X with Y (the mind)

(5) . . . allow X to verb Y (raising children)

(6) . . . trade X for Y (personal integrity)

(7) . . . free X from Y (prejudice)

(8) . . . give X to Y for Z (loyalty)

(9) . . . sacrifice X for Y to Z (energy shortage)

(10) . . . preserve X from Y for Z (environment)

Because this kind of style lends itself perhaps too obviously to the clever balance and antithesis of a merely witty turn of phrase, the evident contrivance limits how often we can use it before we begin to sound only facile. When, like Dr. Johnson, we use it sentence after sentence, we impress our audience less with the good will of a human tentativeness than with the smug superiority of unqualified certainty.

4.2.2 External Architecture

This same kind of parallel internal architecture that organizes a single sentence can also structure the architecture of sentences in sequence:

(1) *Each of us knows* from his own life how much even a
{casual and limited} association of men goes beyond him
{in knowledge
in understanding
in humanity,
and
in power.}

(2) *Each of us,* {from {a friend or a book}
or
by concerting of the little we know with
what others know,}
has broken the iron circle of his frustration.

(3)a. {*Each of us has* {*asked* help
and
been given it,}
and
b. within our measure
each has offered it.}

(4) *Each of us knows* the great new freedom sensed almost as a miracle,
that men banded together for some finite purpose experience
from the power of their common effort.

(5) We are likely to remember the times of the last war,
where the common danger brought forth {in soldier
in worker
in {scientist and engineer}}
a host of new experiences {of {the power and the comfort} in even bleak undertakings
of {common, concerted, cooperative} life.}

(6)a. *Each of us knows* how much he has been transcended by
the group of which he has been part;

(6)b. *each of us has felt* the solace
{ of other men's knowledge to stay his own ignorance
of other men's wisdom to stay his folly
of other men's courage to answer { his doubts
or
his weakness. } }

J. Robert Oppenheimer

This is a passage whose coherence depends on the repeated *Each of us + Verb* structure. Any description of its style and rhetorical impact would have to allude to this dramatic sequence of parallel sentences (with their own internal series). Sentences (1), (3)a, (5), and (6)b reflect the principle of increasing length and complexity of a series, each containing series springing from the last element in its grammatical structure. Sentence (2) is a very rough mirror image of (1), with the early part of (2) continuing the complex series of the last part of (1). In (3), the series begins at the end of (3)a, with the second grammatical clause (3)b a simple grammatical sentence. (4) has no parallels at all, except for the very slight parallel between *for some finite purpose* and *of their common effort*. In the series as a whole, the last two sentences (5) and (6) are the most complex, with (6)b coming to rest after a regular cadence. Again, this is a style that suggests a writer that has considered his subject at length before he wrote about it.

5. Final Ordering

In our analysis of sentence structure at this final level of grammatical manifestation, there remains one last step in accounting for the *particular* form of a sentence. Once the grammatical functions of subject, verb, and object are specified; once the embedded propositions are integrated, coordinated, and subordinated; the grammatical structure of a sentence is relatively fixed. And yet enough flexibility remains to allow elements to occur in a variety of rhetorical positions without changing their grammatical functions:

Last night, a man walked into my room who said he was from Mars.

Last night, a man who said he was from Mars walked into my room.

A man who said he was from Mars walked into my room last night.

A man last night walked into my room who said he was from Mars.

Last night into my room walked a man who said he was from Mars.

In none of these variations do the underlying grammatical relationships among the elements differ. We will call this kind of transformation *repositioning*. Subjects, verbs, objects, modifying clauses and phrases—all retain their original grammatical functions. All that varies is their rhetorical function. Repositioning contrasts with those other ways in which the "same" proposition may be modified, including the passive:

I hit him. → He was hit by me.

the *wh*-displacement:

He stole the money. → What he stole was the money.
→ What he did was steal the money.

and the *it*-displacement:

He stole the money. → It was him who stole the money.
→ It was the money which he stole.

In each of these cases, the transformation results in new subject and verb relationships, new grammatical structures.

If for theoretical purposes we assume a basic underlying order at the level of grammatical manifestation of:

Sentence Adverbial—Subject—Verb—Complement—Adverbial Modifiers

we can better understand how word order can vary. We can vary the order by repositioning an element either to the left:

I spoke to a friend *yesterday*. → *Yesterday* I spoke to a friend.

or to the right:

Consequently, everyone has gone. → Everyone has gone, *consequently.*

Repositioning, left or right, occurs for one of two reasons: One is rooted in the structure of the discourse, the other in how we seem to prefer to process sentences cognitively. Those determined by the discourse allow us to manipulate topic and stress, and a third rhetorical function which we have not yet specifically discussed: *orienters.* When we topicalize, we most often reposition elements to the left, including objects:

Freedom of speech no tyranny can endure.

and prepositional phrases:

Of those great men who rose from obscurity, none rose so far as Lincoln.

About the causes of schizophrenia, very little is known.

We can also reposition to the right to let us topicalize what then stands revealed at the beginning of the sentence, using the device we have called *introductory shift:*

Most people believe that the Japanese attacked us without warning.

The Japanese, *most people believe,* attacked us without warning.

Most people believe is an element only commenting on, affirming the relative truth value of the proposition that follows. By shifting it to the right, *the Japanese* becomes the unequivocal topic-subject of the clause.

Just as we can topicalize elements by displacing them to the left, we can stress elements by displacing them to the right. In spoken short sentences, we often displace to the right relative clauses of striking semantic content originally in the subject noun phrase:

Do you know that a woman *who has a bone in her nose* is standing behind you?

Do you know that a woman is standing behind you *who has a bone in her nose?*

But just as we can shift an introductory element to the right to allow an otherwise buried noun phrase to emerge as the topic, so can we shift concluding adverbial elements to the left, to allow an otherwise buried phrase to emerge as the stress:

> One can observe a frightening lack of fixed values *everywhere today.*
>
> *Everywhere today,* one can observe a frightening lack of fixed values.

In these last two examples, the most striking information now concludes the sentence, in the stressed position: The relative clause telling us that the lady has a bone in her nose has been shifted to the right; *everywhere today* has been shifted to the left.

In some cases, shifting an adverbial from the end of a clause to its beginning performs a double function. It allows an element that would not otherwise have done so to conclude a clause and thereby become stressed; but it also moves an element that *orients* the reader toward the clause it now introduces:

> *In the 17th century,* the doctrine of the motion of the earth was condemned by a Catholic tribunal. *A hundred years ago* the extension of time demanded by geological science distressed religious people, Protestant and Catholic. And *today* the doctrine of evolution is an equal stumbling-block.
>
> Alfred North Whitehead

Compare:

> The doctrine of the motion of the earth was condemned by a Catholic tribunal *in the 17th century.* The extension of time demanded by geological science distressed religious people, Protestant and Catholic, *a hundred years ago.* And the doctrine of evolution is an equal stumbling-block *today.*

Ordinarily, the adverbial segments that set the time and place of the event referred to in the main part of the clause occur at the beginning of a sentence, not in their grammatically defined "normal" position, after the verb and complement. An adverbial segment will occur there only if something about it is so special that it requires the stress of a final position:

> The last government in the Western world to possess all the attributes of aristocracy in working condition took office *in England in June of 1895.*

> Great Britain was at the zenith of empire *when the Conservatives won the General Election of that year,* and the Cabinet they formed was her superb and resplendent image . . .
>
> Barbara Tuchman

Compare:

> *In England in June of 1895,* the last government in the Western world to possess all the attributes of aristocracy in working condition took office. *When the Conservatives won the General Election of that year,* Great Britain was at the zenith of empire, and the Cabinet they formed was her superb and resplendent image . . .

In the original, the place and time are stressed because it is a crucially important place and time. The next sentence topicalizes it: *Great Britain,* and stresses the time when the Conservatives won the general election of that year, leading to the topic of the next clause: the cabinet they formed. Compare this sentence:

> On May 29, 1974 he [Kissinger] was well into his thirty-second day in the Middle East and had endured a month of grueling shuttles between Damascus and Jerusalem, seeking disengagement of the Israeli and Syrian forces in the Golan heights.
>
> Bob Woodward and Carl Bernstein

In the context of the narrative of President Nixon's last months in office, May 29, 1974 has no particular significance, and so occurs merely as an orienter, setting the date of the event that follows. Contrast this:

> We have been together ever since we came to Washington in 1969 as part of this great adventure, on January 20 of that year, and we shall leave together only when we have completed our service, and we shall leave heads high on January 20, 1977.
>
> Richard Nixon

January 20, 1977 is important enough to stress at the end of the sentence, for it was that day he expected to transfer power to the new President.

Often, these orienting elements coincide with the topic of a sentence. For example, in this next sentence, *In a narrative* is a kind of adverbial of location, but it also functions to introduce the topic of the sentence. The sentence exists to comment on narrative sentences:

In a narrative, it is usually important to know the time and location of an action before the action is described.

Contrast:

It is usually important to know the time and location of an action before the action is described in a narrative.

In order to understand the context of the proposition, one must know that it pertains to narrative. If *in a narrative* occurs at the end, it is necessary to reintegrate the semantic content of the sentence, to reinterpret it in the context of *narrative*. In fact, we can discover that *narrative* is also the topic of the sentence if we paraphrase:

As for narrative, it is usually important to know . . .

In regard to narrative, it is usually important to know . . .

A narrative requires us to know the time and place of its action . . .

A second principle of positioning rises out of the way we cognitively process syntactic units. It is a principle related very generally to that of increasing length in coordinate structures. The principle is this: Sequences of moveable syntactic units should, in general, increase rather than decrease in length. Compare these sentences:

(1)a. . . . his attendants placed *before them* a huge pile of coats, shirts, and hunting-knives . . .

Francis Parkman

b. . . . his attendants placed a huge pile of coats, shirts, and hunting knives *before them* . . .

(2)a. They . . . strove *earnestly* to keep *alive and potent in their increasingly restless sons* a notion of honor distinctly bearing the aristocratic impress, and not altogether without success.

W. J. Cash

b. They strove to keep a notion of honor distinctly bearing the aristocratic impress *alive and potent in their increasingly restless sons earnestly*, and not altogether without success.

(3)a. What seemed *to one auditor* the expression of clear religious faith seemed *to another hearer* the uncontrolled expression of the formal words the General had loved and learned.

Douglas Southall Freeman

b. What seemed the expression of clear religious faith *to one auditor* seemed the uncontrolled expression of the formal words the General had loved and learned *to another hearer.*

In (1)a, (2)a, and (3)a, the shorter segment occurs before the longer segment, even though it means interrupting the normal order of the verb and its complement. Now this also has the result of stressing the longer structure, a structure that by its very length is usually more complex and therefore semantically more forceful. The principle of processing the shorter element before the longer, even if it means postponing the longer, appears to be so strong that we can predict with a good deal of accuracy that in sentences such as the one you are now reading, a relatively long object clause [predict . . . that] is more likely to occur after *with a good deal of accuracy* than before.

PROBLEM 47. The following sentences are in "normal" syntactic order. But because they are sentences in isolation from any syntactic context or intention that would tell us what semantic component of the sentence should be topicalized, stressed, or converted into an orienter, we have no way to decide whether their "normal" grammatical order is their appropriate rhetorical order. Rewrite these sentences, rearranging the bracketed elements so that they sound more like sentences you would be likely to find in print. Then select three or four and write a preceding or following sentence that would justify your rhetorical ordering. For example, given:

> Organizations such as the PTA have begun to protest the renewal of broadcasting licenses [vigorously] [because TV violence has reached levels unacceptable to large numbers of viewers] [in recent years].

we could reorder it into the following:

> Because in recent years TV violence has reached levels unacceptable to large numbers of viewers, organizations such as the PTA have begun to vigorously protest the renewal of broadcasting licenses. They have appeared at renewal hearings across the country to demand that stations clean up their programming and reduce the bloody . . .

(1) The answers we give to moral questions depend on practical consequences [in practice].

(2) Great art asserts itself on the spirit of its time [eventually] [regardless of transient tastes].

(3) Everything can be reduced to numbers that specify the nature of things [neatly] [by the rigors of calculus] [in theory].

(4) We can create organizations of molecules which can be called life [by scientific means] [in a test tube] [now].

(5) The miracle of spring signifies the fact that nature never gets bored with doing what it has done a million times [before] [one more time] [to me].

(6) Statistical techniques relying on the substantial use of computer technology are absolutely necessary [for the study of large groups of random individuals].

(7) Sentimental scenes of picnics and bathers were considered to be high art [equal to the Dutch and Italian masters] [in seriousness] [by some critics].

(8) The urge to sweep the streets clean of those who would prey on their innocent neighbors [with bombs and machine guns] lies [in the dark soul of urban man].

(9) Actions designed to improve the lot of lower-class indigents [by middle-class moralists] seem condescending [to those groups] [in ways that would be insulting] [if their roles were reversed] [invariably].

(10) Young people rehearse the lines and movements of their current heroes and heroines [in their imaginations] [every Friday and Saturday night] [in movie houses across America].

(11) There can be no ambiguity [about the sanctity of life] [for those who profess to be Christians] [in their heart of hearts].

(12) The Federal Administration would acquire more and more power to determine the course of our daily existence [in an entirely nonmalevolent way] [except for the Constitution].

(13) One must consider the risk of psychoses that may linger for an indefinite period of time [alongside the heightened powers of perception that LSD produces] [very carefully].

(14) Physicists continue to chase that smallest particle which promises to be the ultimate building-block of existence [into the contracting soul of nature] [in spite of so many who doubt the ultimate order of nature].

(15) Pornographers often include a reference or two to contemporary social problems [to justify their claim that their product provides some redeeming social value] [to avoid accusations of merely pandering to prurient interests].

6. A Note on a Logical Hierarchy: Adjusting the Model

The order in which we have discussed the various aspects of style has been dictated more by pedagogical convenience than by logical or theoretical necessity. The order, you may recall, was this:

1. Segmentation.
2. Lexicalization.
3. Manifestation.
   a. Grammatical structure: subject-verb-complement.
   b. Semantic structure: agent-action-goal.
   c. Rhetorical structure: topic-pivot-stress.
   d. Expansion: integration, subordination, coordination.
   e. External architecture.
   f. Final ordering.

We discussed segmentation first because it is the easiest to understand. In manifestation, we discussed grammatical structure first because it is the most familiar and so the easiest to describe. Final ordering seems to be only minor adjustments in word order, and so we discussed it last.

But the order of these elements in an adequate theoretical model that would account for the logical relationships among these components would have to be a bit different. Because external architecture—unifying a series of sentences by means of parallel structure—shares in problems of form, large chunks of meaning have first to be identified in order to be segmented into parallel sentential units.

At the level of the individual sentence, the first theoretical level of structuring would have to be the assignment of rheme and theme to topic-pivot-stress relationships among the elements, even before the grammatical relationships among the propositional structures were defined. That is, given a set of relationships that we might represent (in words, by unfortunate necessity) like this:

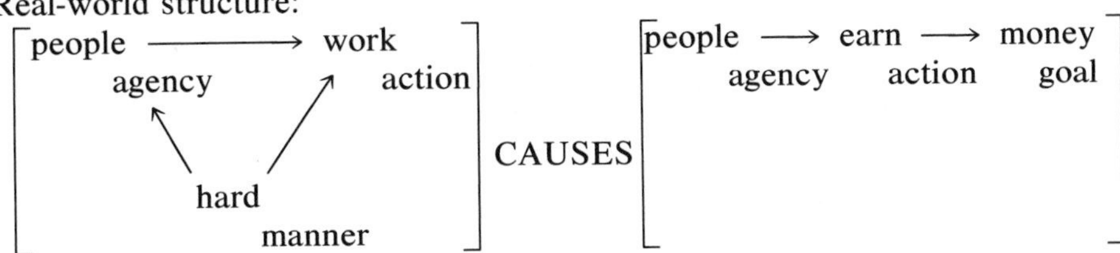

we would have to decide even at this point what we expected to topicalize and what we expected to stress, because the various options of coordination, subordination, and integration will result in different orders of elements. And those orders of elements *must* be established on the basis of the telos and form of the speech event.

Coordination:	Some people work hard, and so they earn money. Some people earn money, for they work hard.
Subordination:	People who work hard earn money. If people work hard, they earn money.
Integration:	Hard workers are money earners. Working hard results in earning money.

And of course, it is at this level too that the topic-stress relationships will at least partly determine—or at least interact with—decisions about agent-action-goal relationships, that sense of dynamic relationship that obtains among sentence elements. We can vary it depending on what we want to topicalize and stress but also on what we want to invest with agentive energy:

Money comes from hard work.

People can get money if they work hard.

Hard work earns money for people.

Earning money requires hard work.

Working hard will earn people money.

Now on the one hand, it would appear that all of this would determine how these units of meaning are finally lexicalized, how they are put into words that would let us represent these relationships of logic, semantics, and rhetoric in an appropriate grammatical structure. But it is equally true that not all orders are possible because no language has an infinitely large lexicon that lets its speakers arrange elements in any order. There is no convenient way in English, for example, to arrange elements in this order:

work hard—money—people—earn

So our model will have to provide some kind of filtering device that will check whether an order called for by problems of rhetoric and semantics can be lexicalized in a particular way in a particular language.

The last stage in the model, then, is the grammatical manifestation. Once the topic-stress relationships have been defined, once the propositional relationships have been defined, once the semantic energy of agency-action has been defined, then some appropriate grammatical structuring can be assigned to the sequence. And again, we need another filtering device that will check whether an order called for by all these considerations is possible in a given language.

Schematically, the entire sequence might be laid out as shown in Figure 5.1 on the following page.

7. Metadiscourse

Before we conclude with a longer analysis of a text, one in which we will try to pull together all the levels of analysis and explanation that we have discussed so far, there is one more level of structure in a sentence that is important in our description of style. Every text, regardless of its ideational content, is produced by one of the personae in the speech event, the speaker or writer. As I write each of these sentences, I am the agent of their composition, but for the most part, my authorial agency overtly intrudes into the discourse rather infrequently.

Sometimes, the author speaks in the first person and refers directly to the discourse as he constructs it, sometimes including even the audience as a specifically mentioned *you:*

> I would now like to turn your attention to the subject of women. I submit to you that this is a difficult question. It is not my intention to dwell upon this subject at too great a length, but it is a question which we all know has vexed the male gender for centuries and centuries.

In sentences such as these, the author is conducting his discourse on two levels. First, he is mentioning the content of his *primary discourse:*

> . . . women . . . vexed the male gender for centuries and centuries.

But this primary discourse is embedded in *metadiscourse,* discourse about discourse, words and phrases and clauses—even sentences—that refer not to the subject "out there" but to the act of discoursing, to the speech event that the discourse and its reader create. Most of this passage is metadiscourse:

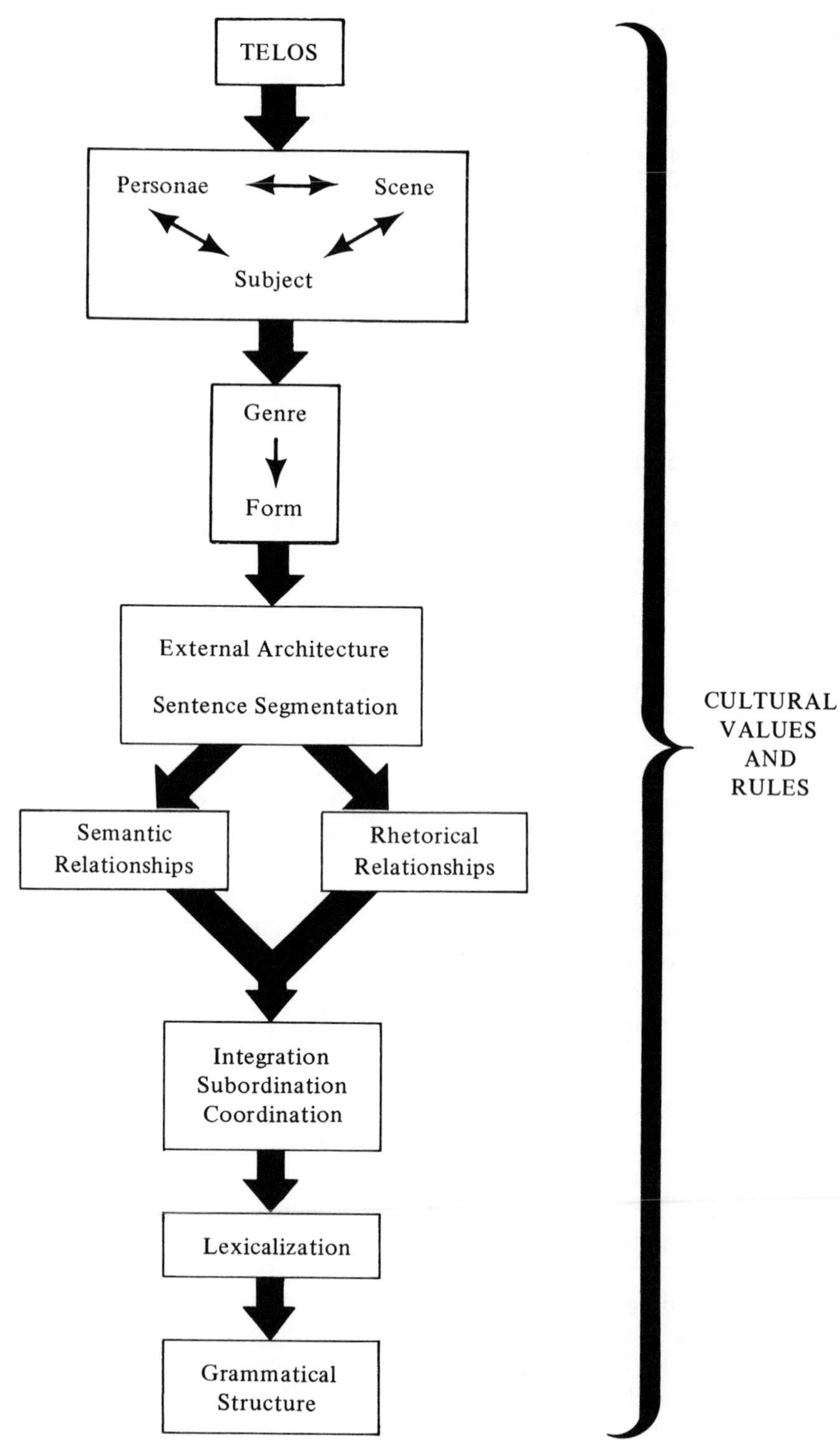

Figure 5.1. *A Speech Event.*

> I would now like to turn your attention to the subject of . . . I submit to you that this is a difficult question. It is not my intention to dwell upon this subject at too great a length, but it is a question which we all know . . .

None of this refers to the subject of his discourse but only to the process of discoursing.

Many writers stay out of their text almost entirely, relying on shorter discourse signals such as those that indicate cause: *therefore, consequently, as a result, so, for,* and so on; or contrast: *on the other hand, instead, though, but, however,* and so on; or the continuation of the discourse: *indeed, moreover, in fact, in any event, at least, and, also, too, neither, second, then, next.*

An even less obvious presence is felt in words that comment on the probability of the proposition expressed in a sentence: *probably, possibly, undoubtedly, certainly, surely, seemingly, apparently, clearly; it would seem that, it appears that, it is obvious that, it could be that.* Other words express an attitude toward an event: *It is fortunate that, inevitably, it is odd that, interestingly,* etc.

Styles differ to the degree the author makes himself overtly present in the text and refers to the discourse itself. In the *Federalist Papers,* for example, those essays by Alexander Hamilton, John Jay, and John Madison supporting the Constitution, discourse about discourse is very prevalent. Almost one out of every three or four paragraphs begins with some reference to the state of the argument, to the reader's understanding of it, to the author's understanding of his own argument:

> It may be objected to this . . .
>
> But however little this objection may be countenanced . . .
>
> It may not be amiss in this place concisely to remark . . .
>
> This simpler train of inquiry furnishes us . . .
>
> When we pass from the works of nature . . .
>
> There are other considerations, of less importance, perhaps . . .

This is the style of rational men arguing, debating, discussing with other rational men the great questions of a new form of government. On the other hand, excessive metadiscourse can become mechanical and obtrusive, drawing too much attention to the process of discoursing.

PROBLEM 48. Here is a paragraph from Henry David Thoreau. Rewrite it to remove all reference, implied or direct, to the author or to the reader. What is the effect?

> However mean your life is, meet it and live it; do not shun it and call it hard names. It is not so bad as you are. It looks poorest when you are richest. The fault-finder will find faults even in paradise. Love your life, poor as it is. You may perhaps have some pleasant, thrilling, glorious hours, even in the poor-house. The setting sun is reflected from the windows of the alms-house as brightly as from the rich man's abode; the snow melts before its door as early in the spring. I do not see but a quiet mind may live as contentedly there, and have as cheering thoughts, as in a palace. The town's poor seem to me often to live the most independent lives of any. Maybe they are simply great enough to receive without misgiving. Most think that they are above being supported by the town; but it oftener happens that they are not above supporting themselves by dishonest means, which should be more disreputable. Cultivate poverty like a garden herb, like sage. Do not trouble yourself much to get new things, whether clothes or friends. Turn the old; return to them. Things do not change; we change. Sell your clothes and keep your thoughts. God will see that you do not want society.

PROBLEM 49. The following is a passage from Ezra Pound. It lacks almost entirely any reference to the audience, the author, or the discourse itself. Revise it so that the presence of the author is much more directly felt in the passage. What is the difference?

> Literature does not exist in a vacuum. Writers as such have a definite social function exactly proportioned to their ability as writers. This is their main use. All other uses are relative and temporary, and can be estimated only in relation to the views of the particular estimator.
>
> Partisans of particular ideas may value writers who agree with them more than writers who do not, they may, and often do, value bad writers of their own party or religion more than good writers of another party or church.
>
> But there is one basis susceptible of estimation and independent of all questions of viewpoint.
>
> Good writers are those who keep the language efficient. That is to say, keep it accurate, keep it clear. It doesn't matter whether the good writer wants to be useful, or whether the bad writer wants to do harm.
>
> Language is the main means of human communication. If an animal's nervous system does not transmit sensations and stimuli, the animal atrophies.
>
> If a nation's literature declines, the nation atrophies and decays.

PROBLEM 50. Here is part of Article I, Section 2 of the Constitution.

Revise it so that the author and the audience are clearly present throughout. What is the difference?

> Representatives and direct taxes shall be apportioned among the several States which may be included within this Union, according to their respective numbers, which shall be determined by adding to the whole number of free persons, including those bound to service for a term of years, and excluding Indians not taxed, three-fifths of all other persons. The actual enumeration shall be made within three years after the first meeting of the Congress of the United States, and within every subsequent term of ten years, in such manner as they shall by law direct. The number of representatives shall not exceed one for every thirty thousand but each State shall have at least one representative; and until such enumeration shall be made, the State of New Hampshire shall be entitled to choose three, Massachusetts eight, Rhode Island and Providence Plantations one, Connecticut five, New York six, New Jersey four, Pennsylvania eight, Delaware one, Maryland six, Virginia ten, North Carolina five, South Carolina five, and Georgia three.
>
> When vacancies happen in the representation from any State the executive authority thereof shall issue writs of election to fill such vacancies.

PROBLEM 51. Select a definition from a dictionary and a piece of the phone book to revise so that the author and the audience are clearly evident in the text. What is the problem?

PROBLEM 52. Here is a list of types of texts. Why do some allow more easily than others the presence of an author and an audience? cookbook, encyclopedia, guidebook, history, home repair manual, mathematics textbook, weights and measures conversion table, parts catalogue for automobiles, newspaper, street guide, and joke book.

8. A Demonstration

Having examined some of the most salient features of English which lend themselves to particular stylistic effects, we ought now to demonstrate how all these features come together in a single text, transformed by the telos of the event, manifesting that telos in their particular forms. The text is Lincoln's Second Inaugural Address, one of the great speeches in American history. We have already glanced at the style of the opening paragraph (Problem 22), at the way Lincoln subordinates himself as a persona in the event to the event itself. Lincoln does this, we might recall, by nominalizing the key verbs: *appear, address, state, declare, hope,* and *predict;* and deleting their underlying agent—himself. He further subordinates himself to the event by making sentences (3) and (6) passive (*could be presented, is ventured*) and deleting himself again.

In order to demonstrate how we might explain a text in the ways we have discussed, we will use our model of a speech event and the various levels of analysis we have described in this chapter.

(1) At this second appearing to take the oath of the presidential office, there is less occasion for an extended address than there was at the first. **(2)** Then a statement, somewhat in detail, of a course to be pursued, seemed fitting and proper. **(3)** Now, at the expiration of four years, during which public declarations have been constantly called forth on every point and phase of the great contest which still absorbs the attention, and engrosses the energies of the nation, little that is new could be presented. **(4)** The progress of our arms, upon which all else chiefly depends, is as well known to the public as to myself; **(5)** and it is, I trust, reasonably satisfactory and encouraging to all. **(6)** With high hope for the future, no prediction in regard to it is ventured.

(7) On the occasion corresponding to this four years ago, all thoughts were anxiously directed to an impending civil war. **(8)** All dreaded it—**(9)** all sought to avert it. **(10)** While the inaugural address was being delivered from this place, devoted altogether to *saving* the Union without war, insurgent agents were in the city seeking to *destroy* it without war—seeking to dissolve the Union, and divide effects, by negotiation. **(11)** Both parties deprecated war, **(12)** but one of them would *make* war rather than let the nation survive; **(13)** and the other would *accept* war rather than let it perish. **(14)** And the war came.

(15) One-eighth of the whole population were colored slaves, not distributed generally over the Union, but localized in the Southern part of it. **(16)** These slaves constituted a peculiar and powerful interest. **(17)** All knew that this interest was, somehow, the cause of the war. **(18)** To strengthen, perpetuate, and extend this interest was the object for which the insurgents would rend the Union, even by war; while the government claimed no right to do more than restrict the territorial enlargement of it. **(19)** Neither party expected for the war the magnitude, or the duration, which it has already attained. **(20)** Neither anticipated that the cause of the conflict might cease with, or even before, the conflict itself should cease. **(21)** Each looked for an easier triumph, and a result less fundamental and astounding. **(22)** Both read the same Bible, and pray to the same God; **(23)** and each invokes His aid against the other. **(24)** It may seem strange that any men should dare to ask a just God's assistance in wringing their bread from the sweat of other men's faces, **(25)** but let us judge not that we be not judged. **(26)** The prayers of both could not be answered; **(27)** that of neither has been answered fully. **(28)** The Almighty has His own purposes. **(29)** "Woe unto the world because of offenses! **(30)** for it must needs be that offenses come; **(31)** but woe to that man by whom the offense cometh!" **(32)** If we shall suppose that American slavery is one of those offenses which, in the providence of God, must needs come, but which, having continued through His appointed time, He now wills to remove, and that He gives to both North and South this terrible war, as the woe due to those by whom the offense came, shall we discern therein any departure from those divine attributes which the believers in a Living God always ascribe to Him? **(33)** Fondly do we hope—fervently do we pray—that this mighty scourge of war may speedily pass away. **(34)** Yet, if God wills that it continue, until all the wealth piled by the bondman's two hundred and fifty years of unrequited toil shall be sunk, and until every drop of blood drawn with the lash shall be paid by another drawn with the sword, as was said three thousand years ago, so still it must be said "the judgments of the Lord are true and righteous altogether."

(35) With malice toward none; with charity for all; with firmness in the right, as God gives us to see the right, let us strive on to finish the work we are in; to bind up the nation's wounds; to care for him who shall have borne the battle, and for his widow, and his orphan—to do all which may achieve and cherish a just, and lasting peace, among ourselves, and with all nations.

8.1 The Telos of the Speech Event

Lincoln had a problem: the Civil War was drawing to its end with the North victorious and the South destroyed. But the costs of the war were so terrible that there grew in the North a thirst for retribution, on account of both the war and the slavery that many perceived to be its ultimate cause. Any additional punishment, Lincoln believed, would widen and make permanent the already devastating division between the North and the South.

At the same time, though, it was clear that in some simple and obvious sense, the South was responsible—that slavery was the cause of the secession, that hundreds of thousands had died to preserve the Union against the Southern separation. Lincoln could not deny that the immediate agency of the secession was the South, but neither could he intensify the virulent hatred in the North. He had to find a way to acknowledge that while the North did not start the war, neither was it the South's sole responsibility. He had to find a way to make his listeners soften their demands for retribution without seeming to excuse the South for what it had done. Most importantly, he had to find a way to reunify the North and the South into a single Union, to change the perception of a North divided against a South to a perception of a single shared experience.

He solved the problem by acknowledging in the most general way that there were indeed insurgents who sought to rend the Union and that the consequences of their actions led to a war far more terrible and costly than either side had contemplated. He then tried to argue that a Christian nation must finally acknowledge in all such terrible and awesome events the hand of God working His mysterious ways, that the North and South together were in the eyes of God working out His providence. Once he established the idea that God was ultimately responsible for the actions immediately carried out by the North and South, then any particular retribution against the South might be deflected and the two sides reunited.

8.2 Personae, Scenes, and Subjects

8.2.1 The Personae

Lincoln as American President is the principal persona, of course, but because his intention is to assign to God ultimate responsibility for the events of the last several decades, making himself highly visible in the speech would have made his own agency too prominent. If God is to be made ultimately responsible, then other agents ought not to be highlighted. The other persona, the audience, included both the North and the South. He can afford to alienate neither, so his best tactic is to avoid bringing any person in particular into the speech.

8.2.2 The Scene and Subject

The scene is the Inauguration, in Washington, in the North, so Lincoln is required to be more rather than less formal. The opening paragraph, with its high frequency of nominalizations, the quotations from the Bible, the balance and parallelism of the last sentence, the slightly archaic diction toward the end—all contribute to a formal tone. Moreover, because of the scene, which is also the putative subject, Inauguration, Lincoln must make some reference to that event, acknowledging its purpose while at the same time using the occasion to say what he wants to say about the approaching end of the war.

8.3 Genre and Form

8.3.1 Genre

By convention, Lincoln must deliver a speech.

8.3.2 Form

Lincoln first acknowledges the occasion for the speech, the Inauguration; then quite in keeping with the larger scene, the imminent end of the war, he reviews past and present events, including a disarming acknowledgement that insurgent agents were afoot in the Capital four years before. Then in a series of statements intended to identify the North and the South as sharing in the same series of events, he points out that neither side was ready for what happened, that neither side has had its prayers answered. The introduction of the Bible and prayers allows Lincoln to introduce the question of God's judgment and providence. This finally allows him, in sentence (32), to assign ultimate responsibility for the war and for slavery to the agency of God, however obscure His ways are in visiting on the North along with the South the terrible conflict. It is a move that unifies the two sides in God's plan and which allows Lincoln to hope for a unified future. From that point he is able to move to his peroration about binding up wounds and unifying the nation.

8.4 The Linguistic Texture

8.4.1 Segmentation

The segmentation of all the sentences would require an analysis more detailed than we can provide here, but we might examine those sentences that are unusually long or unusually short. The shortest sentences form two groups:

(8) All dreaded it— **(9)** all sought to avert it.
(11) Both parties deprecated war.
(14) And the war came.

(26) The prayers of both could not be answered; **(27)** that of neither has been answered fully. **(28)** The Almighty has His own purposes.

Short sentences demand attention. They often seem to express absolute truths. No qualifications. No modifications. Just simple straightforward truths. In the speech, three of the shortest grammatical sentences emphasize that even though no one wanted the war, the war—quite on its own, apparently—came anyway. Their curt certainty asserts the seeming inevitability of the war, despite the best efforts of the parties involved to avoid it.

The other three shortest sentences constitute a sequence. After introducing the Bible as one of a series of experiences shared by North and South alike, Lincoln continues the religious theme, asserting in short, sententious clauses that neither side seems to have been entirely favored by God, and that despite the fact that the North would seem to deserve divine favor, God in His mysterious purposes visited great suffering on both. This last short, crisp assertion of a universal truth introduces both the Biblical quotation from Matthew 7:1. and the longest sentence, sentence (32), in which Lincoln justifies the ways of God to Northern men.

The longest sentence is sentence (32), the key sentence in Lincoln's argument. Seventy-eight words long, it expresses the position on which he will stand or fall. The last sentence, of seventy-five words, is the most self-consciously constructed sentence, with multiple balanced coordinate clauses and coordinations within coordinations, an appropriately elegant and rotund peroration to a majestically formal speech. The sentence just before it, (34), is the third longest and is almost as self-conscious in its rhetorical swelling in preparation for the conclusion. In these three sentences, length seems to reflect the rhetorical demands placed on them. Lincoln could have broken them into shorter clauses, but we would have lost the complex internal balance of the last two and perhaps would have changed the longest and most crucial in ways that would have been fatal to his argument.

8.4.2 Lexicalization

Perhaps the most striking feature about the lexicalization is in the way Lincoln mentions only once, in sentence (32), the South or Southerners by name. The closest he comes elsewhere is in sentence (15), when he observes that slaves were localized in "the Southern part of" the Union. In all other cases, the agency of verbs is named by the most general of words: *all, both parties, one of them, the other, neither party, neither, each, both, men, those*. He calls Southerners insurgent agents and insurgents, but never Southerners, slaveholders, or rebels. The reasons would seem self-evident: the telos of the speech is to downplay factionalism, identification of the South as the source of the war. And so in stating who was doing what to whom, he merely refers to them as *parties* or with pronouns. More importantly, he refers to the North and Northerners in the same way, insisting through these general and identical words that both share the same responsibilities, the same concerns, the same past, and the same future.

In fact, the diction is throughout very general. God is named as one of the few specific agents, and in (35) he names

> . . . him who shall have borne the battle, and for his widow, and his orphan . . .

as three specific goals. The only other specific language is in sentence (24), a sentence difficult to explain. The phrase:

> . . . wringing their bread from the sweat of other men's faces . . .

is so explicit as to be almost inflammatory. We might legitimately wonder whether Lincoln may not have made a rhetorical mistake in stating this so explicitly. In the context of its introductory phrase:

> It may seem strange that any men should dare to ask a just God's assistance in . . .

and the almost sanctimonious conclusion in (25):

> . . . let us judge not that we be not judged.

the intensity of the phrase stands out dramatically and perhaps inappropriately.

On the other hand, the explicitness of the next-to-last sentence:

> . . . bondman's two hundred and fifty years of unrequited toil . . .
>
> . . . every drop of blood drawn with the lash shall be paid by another drawn with the sword . . .

is entirely appropriate. Lincoln is moving into his peroration, again justifying the bloodshed attributable to the South by turning back to God:

> . . . the judgments of the Lord are true and righteous . . .

8.4.3 Manifestation

Describing the manifestation of each abstract proposition would take several pages, so we shall concentrate on only those sentences most salient to Lincoln's telos. We have already discussed the opening paragraph in which Lincoln appears deliberately to withdraw himself from the scene. Had he chosen a verbal style, with himself as the agent of the verbs *appear, address, state, declare, present, hope, predict, venture,* he would have opened his speech by specifically assigning responsibility for specific actions. But this he wants to avoid, so that when he reaches sentence (32), he can assign responsibility in a more dramatically isolated way. Moreover, the Union is about to be reasserted in the quadrennial ceremony that marks every President's term in office and the democratic transfer of power. The re-establishment of the Union is only a few weeks away, so it is appropriate that Lincoln topicalize not himself, but the elements of that national renewal.

In the second paragraph, agency is made manifest, but as we saw, in so general a way that the listeners' passions are not immediately aroused by such words as *South, Confederacy, Dixie, Rebel,* and so on. And again, Lincoln subordinates himself in the passive:

> . . . the inaugural address was being delivered from this place, devoted altogether . . .

In sentences (12) and (13), Lincoln implicitly makes the North and South the agents without naming them, and topicalizes them in the subject-agent position:

> . . . one of them would make war rather than let the nation survive . . .
>
> . . . the other would accept war rather than let it perish.

(though he clearly assigns more consciously active agency to the first, *make war,* than to the second, *accept war*).

It is in the next short sentence (14) that Lincoln performs his first rhetorical sleight-of-hand:

> And the war came.

Lincoln does not say, for all the reasons we have suggested:

> And the South began the war.

Instead, he topicalizes war and makes it the seeming agent of its own coming, stressing the inevitable seeming action, *came.* It is the first step away from . . . *one of them would make war* . . . and toward attributing the war to God. He continues the indirection in the next three sentences. The generality of sentence (15) avoids the more specific:

> Southerners enslaved one out of every eight Americans.

Then in sentence (16):

> These slaves constituted a peculiar and powerful interest.

Lincoln makes the slaves into an abstraction, an interest derived from something like:

the next clause that parallels . . . *that American slavery* . . . , Lincoln specifically assigns to God the remote agency even of the war. In this clause too he mentions both North and South by name, not to distinguish them but to link them as the objects of God's punishment, for he goes on to attribute to both North and South their responsibility for the offense. But at the very end of that clause, he draws back from stating overtly that they offended God, but that it was "by" them that the offense "came." Lincoln has completed the transition of responsibility:

> The war came.
>
> . . . the cause of the conflict might cease . . .
>
> . . . the conflict itself should cease . . .
>
> . . . offenses . . . must needs come . . .

as opposed to:

> . . . He now wills to remove . . .
>
> . . . He gives to both North and South . . .

Sentences (33) and (34) continue the pattern. First, Lincoln again makes the war its own agency:

> . . . this mighty scourge of war may speedily pass away . . .

but then in a reversal makes God the explicit agency again:

> . . . if God wills that it continue . . .

By this time, the audience, if Lincoln has succeeded, is ready to accept God's ultimate responsibility for the war, even for the blood and sacrifice that it has cost. In a final Biblical quotation, he reasserts the ultimate righteousness of God and his judgments.

The last sentence is appropriately low key but syntactically elegant. We can best appreciate its full rhetorical complexity if we lay the sentence out schematically, as on the following page. The sentence follows the principle of increasing length and complexity in successive coordinate members until it reaches the last (*to do all* . . .), in which multiple coordinations within a multiple coordination bring the sentence to a close on an appropriately resonant note.

> Southerners interested themselves in slaves.

Of course, the nominalization in (16) lacks its underlying agent. In (17), it is this abstraction *interest* that then becomes the cause of the war—not the verbally direct *caused the war,* but the nominal and more indirect, *was the cause of the war.* Now recall the progression:

> . . . one of them would make war
>
> . . . the war came
>
> this interest was . . . the cause of the war

In the next sentence, Lincoln does not specify Southerners as those who would strengthen, perpetuate, and extend this interest, and rend the Union but rather the more general *insurgents.* But just as importantly, neither did he say that they wanted to enslave more slaves, but more abstractly, wanted to strengthen, perpetuate, and extend this interest.

Paragraph two and these first four sentences in paragraph three constitute the transitional sections of Lincoln's speech: a brief history, a noninflammatory justification for the war, but a subtle moving away from the war being started by the South and toward postulating a more impersonal source of the war.

Sentences (19–27) continue his move toward sentence (32), in which Lincoln will introduce God as the real agent in the affair. He links both North and South into a single experience by making general words the topic-agent-subjects of their clauses: *Neither expected* . . . , *neither anticipated* . . . , *each looked*. . . . In the process, he again refers in the most general way to the substance of the conflict:

> . . . the cause of the conflict might cease with, or even before, the conflict itself should cease.

Note again that the active:

> Southerners enslave slaves

has been transformed into the abstract *slavery,* and that abstract slavery has been identified as *the cause,* another abstraction. And now, like the war, the cause also has its own seeming activity independent of any human agent:

> . . . the cause of the conflict might cease . . .

just as the conflict itself can of itself cease, just as in sentence (14), the war can of itself come.

And again, it is not difficult for us to understand why these sentences should have the form they do. Lincoln is disengaging the South from sole responsibility for the war preparatory to assigning it to God. But at the same time he must, in rehearsing the history of the previous four years, acknowledge that another party engaged in the war. To ignore that fact would have been ludicrous. He manages to accomplish both rhetorical tasks by generalizations and nominalizations, by attributing independent agency to abstractions, by topicalizing *interest, cause,* and *conflict* by making them subjects of their own verbs.

Because sentence (32) is so complex and so crucial, let us first lay it out schematically:

If we shall suppose:
that American slavery is one of those offenses
which, in the providence of God, must needs come
but
which, having continued through His appointed time,
He now wills to remove
and
that He gives to both { North and South } this terrible war
as the woe due to those
by whom the offense came,
shall we discern therein any departure from those divine attributes
which the believers in a Living God
always ascribe to Him?

First, let's consider the metadiscourse that frames the propositions and lends an air of self-evident truth to them, the *If we shall suppose* and *shall we discern therein*. By framing the proposition in the metadiscourse question whose only answer can be a metadiscourse *no,* Lincoln draws the other persona in the speech event, his audience, into the event. When they tacitly answer *no,* they necessarily subscribe to the proposition expressed in the conditional *if*-clause—the proposition which is at the heart of Lincoln's argument.

The seeming semantic structure of the first contained clause does not correspond to its real-world semantic structure, at least as a Christian would understand it. If we rephrase the propositions into

their most explicitly revealing verbal form, we can better understand what Lincoln was up to:

> American slavery was one of those offenses which, in the providence of God, must needs come . . .
>
> God provides that Americans enslave slaves; this offends [______]

In Lincoln's sentence, the real agency and originating action is buried in the pivot of the clause: *the providence of God;* the seeming agency of the action is *slavery,* named as a nominalization, *offense,* a nominalization which like the war (14) and the cause and conflict (20) acts on its own: *offenses . . . must needs come,* a structure which leaves the verb in the stressed position of the clause. The underlying agency and goal of *slavery* have both been deleted. Only the adjective *American* remains to suggest a general agent.

More interestingly, the goal of the underlying action, *offend,* has also been deleted. Presumably, it is God whom slavery offends, but we cannot be sure. Indeed, in the experience of the sentence, we *must* not be sure, because if God is the goal of *offend,* then a too obvious theological paradox arises: God provides that Americans must enslave Blacks but enslaving Blacks offends God. Lincoln avoids this by burying in the pivot God's ultimate agency and by stressing *must needs come,* emphasizing the seeming inevitability of the offense. This syntactic maneuver allows Lincoln to cover an offense with a theological blanket, but not too obviously.

In the next clause, Lincoln performs an even more clever maneuver.

> . . . having continued through His appointed time, He now wills to remove [it] . . .

opens with an ambiguous modifier. *Having continued* can mean either:

> The offense has continued through the time God appointed for it.

or:

> God has continued the offense through the time He appointed for it.

This flicker of uncertainty is perhaps the best transition to the main clause, which now, overtly and specifically, transfers to God the complete responsibility for not starting slavery but for stopping it, and in

With malice toward none;
with charity for all;
with firmness in the right
as God gives us to see the right,
let us strive on
to finish the work we are in;
to bind up the nation's wounds;
to care for him who shall have borne the battle
and
for his widow
and
his orphan
to do all which may achieve
and
cherish a just
and
lasting peace
among ourselves
and
with all nations.

8.4.4 *Internal and External Architecture*

The last sentence in the speech is the most complex, but only a bit less so than the penultimate sentence:

. . . if God wills that it continue,
until all the wealth piled by the bondman's two hundred and fifty years of unrequited toil shall be sunk,
and
until every drop of blood drawn with the lash shall be paid by another drawn with the sword,
as was said three thousand years ago,
so
still it must be said
"the judgments of the Lord are true and righteous altogether."

Only paragraph two balances part against part in the same complex way. The external balance of sentences (8) and (9) is obvious; so is it in sentences (11), (12), and (13).

The internal architecture of sentence (10) is just a bit awkward, perhaps:

While
{ the inaugural address was being delivered from this place,
devoted altogether to saving the Union without war, }
insurgent agents were in the city
{ seeking to destroy it without war—
seeking to { dissolve the Union
and
divide effects } by negotiation. }

In contrast, the first paragraph is almost entirely lacking in any rhetorical play. Only *absorbs the attention and engrosses the energies* has a ring to it. But then, as we have seen, the opening of this speech is—perhaps must be, if it is to succeed—low key and unselfconscious.

8.4.5 Final Ordering

By now, the reasons for opening sentences (32) and (34) with their subordinate clauses are self evident: the suspended, periodic style allows Lincoln to build to a conclusion, a conclusion that stresses the primacy of God in matters of ultimate judgment.

In several sentences, Lincoln has opened with an orienter:

(1) At this second appearing . . .

(2) Then . . .

(3) Now, at the expiration of four years, during which . . .

(7) On the occasion corresponding to this four years ago . . .

(10) While the inaugural address was being delivered from this place . . .

But once he has finished with the history of recent events, he turns from narrative to analysis.

8.4.6 Metadiscourse

In a sense, the whole first paragraph is given over to metadiscourse, as is much of the second. But then as we pointed out, the occasion of the speech, the scene and its telos, are also the subject of the speech. Once past that opening, though, metadiscourse virtually disappears. *All knew* in sentence (17) emphasizes the truth of what follows it. In sentence (24), *It may seem strange that . . .* glances toward the beliefs of his audience. Only in sentence (32), that most crucial of sentences, does Lincoln rely on metadiscourse as part of his argument: *If we shall suppose . . . shall we discern therein . . . ?* But again, metadiscourse calls attention to the speaker, to his act of discoursing, to his control over the way an audience understands what it is hearing, and Lincoln seems intent on withdrawing himself from the speech almost entirely. Only a modest *I trust* in (5) explicitly mentions the first person of the speech.

The speech is not a perfect one, but it is a great one. Even the heavy indirectness of the opening paragraph, understood in light of the telos of the speech and how it determines the structure of the whole, is appropriate. The same style in another context would be ludicrous:

> At this second appearing to take a test in this class, there is less occasion for an extended address than there was at the first. Then a statement, somewhat in detail, of a course to be pursued, seemed fitting and proper. Now, at the expiration of ten weeks, during which class discussion has been constantly called forth on every point and phase of the great subject which still absorbs the attention and engrosses the energies of the students, little that is new could be presented. The progress of our studies, upon which all else chiefly depends, is as well known to the class as to myself; and it is, I trust, reasonably satisfactory and encouraging to all. With high hope for the future, no prediction in regard to it is ventured.

9. A Final Word on the Meaning of "Style"

It has surely occurred to some of you that defining style as the way a writer consistently chooses to express the meaning of his propositions is meaningless—at least if by choose we mean what a writer is free and unconstrained to put down on a page. If we assume that a text manifests at its different levels the individual telos of the speech event that the text is part of, then strictly speaking, we cannot say that a writer chooses. The selection and arrangement of words in sentences is determined by the telos of the work. They can be in no other form than that which they are in; otherwise, they manifest a different text with a necessarily different telos. Thus choice, as a component of style, disappears.

There are a number of ways to respond to such an argument.

First, we know that some writers habitually write in some structures rather than others. Walter Lippmann wrote in a balanced and coordinate style; Ezra Pound often wrote in a curt and sententious style. Norman Mailer is a master of the loose style. Even though they may have written what they wrote because they could not have said what they had to say otherwise, we can still compare one author with another in terms of the linguistic features they habitually employ. The terms "choose" or "select" are useful fictions in these kinds of comparisons, because we know that such writers often consciously—or at least at a very shallow level of the subconscious—choose to write in one style rather than another. Dr. Johnson, whose nominal, Latinate, balanced, and antithetical style virtually defined the limits of that kind of writing, once said of a play:

> It has not wit enough to keep it sweet.

then caught himself and recast that Anglo-Saxon verbal sentence into a Latinate nominal one:

> It has not vitality enough to preserve it from putrefaction.

On the one hand, we could argue that he "had" to "choose" to revise that sentence to say exactly what he wanted to say, in which case it makes no sense to say "had to choose." There is no choice where there is necessity. But at some level, Johnson along with many other writers must have felt himself genuinely choosing.

Can the same be said when we contrast one period of a writer's work with another, or even one section of a writer's text with another? Lincoln must at some level of consciousness have "chosen" to construct his most elegant sentence structure at the end of his speech. Yet its telos "demanded" it. It is here that the concept of choice becomes most difficult to defend. But perhaps the simplest argument is also the best. Just as we "choose" to do what we are obliged to do if we are to succeed in our task, so a writer, consciously or subconsciously, also chooses to arrange his text in the way that will lead to its success. Even though constrained, we choose.

That explanation, however, deals with the problem only from the point of view of the author. How is style experienced from the point of view of the reader? Do we not as readers experience an indeterminacy of sentence structure because we can never know what the organizing intention, the telos of the text, will finally be until we have finished the text? We may be guided through the text by a developing hypothesis about how we are to understand what we are reading, but at any given moment, we cannot know what the next sentence will bring, whether we will have to modify our understanding of the text, whether some feature of style will serve a very different function than one it has already served, whether a new feature of style will impose itself on our experience. From the point of view of our imperfect experience, every new sentence is strange territory capable of contradicting whatever expectations we have set up on the basis of previous sentences. A text written in a very verbal or very nominal, a very periodic or very loose, a very balanced or a very straightforward kind of style may lead a reader to expect that kind of style in every subsequent sentence, until one appears that contradicts the developing regularity. And we experience that surprise as a choice, both in terms of the background of the regularity the writer created and the deviation from that background. So style can be *experienced* as choice.

It is only from the point of view of the critic of style, of the explicator who understands the totality of the text—its telos, its personae, its scene, its subject matter, its genre, its form, its grammatical and lexical manifestation—that style disappears into the determinacy of the whole. If we understand utterly Lincoln's Second Inaugural Address and believe that the telos that organizes it is perfectly realized by the text, then every sentence becomes like the dial of a watch. If the watch is to perform its function, it must have its inner workings in the form that intention requires. From the point of view of the explicator of the watch, no alternative wheels, no alternative organizations, no alternative relationships are possible. The watch is determined in its form.

So if we want to talk about style as choice, we must take care to stipulate from what point of view we are speaking. In one sense, this is no different from the way physicists talk about light. Sometimes, they say, you have to talk about light as particles. And sometimes, you have to talk about it as waves. In the same way, sometimes we can talk about style as choice. And sometimes not. It all depends on what we want to say.

I wish I could end this chapter by assuring you that if you have mastered everything you have read, then you have mastered the art of analyzing and describing style. But if I did that, those of you who have read *very* carefully would instantly reply that no set of rules or inventory of features, no matter how exhaustive, can ever lead to such an analysis or description. You would reply that because every text is a unique text with its own unique telos and because any analysis and description of a text requires that we articulate that telos before we can understand any of the stylistic features, no set of rules of interpretation that begins with the identification of features can possibly be more than a handy but incomplete guide toward what might be relevant in analyzing or explaining any given text.

No analysis or explanation of style can precede a sensitive and discriminating reading of a text and an articulate understanding of how that text determines our experience of it. We might analyze various features of the text so that we might better understand it. We might modify what we think we experienced on the basis of that better understanding. But ultimately, our explanation of a text rests on our understanding of how we as readers relate to it. And there are no handy rules for achieving that.

Suggestions for Further Reading

A number of journals devote themselves largely to matters of style: *Style, Language and Style, Poetica, Journal of Literary Semantics, PTL. The Annual Bibliography* published by the Modern Language Association has an extensive listing under style.

A bibliography of works on style written before 1968 is contained in Bailey, Richard and Burton, Dolores M., eds. *English Stylistics: A Bibliography.* Cambridge, Mass.: M.I.T. Press, 1968. Two collections of essays are particularly useful: Sebeok, Thomas, ed. *Style in Language.* Cambridge, Mass.: M.I.T. Press, 1960, an example of very early work in style in a number of areas; a collection of recent essays is in Fowler, Roger, ed.: *Style and Structure in Literature.* Ithaca, N.Y.: Cornell University Press, 1975. Two linguistic introductions to matters of style are Hendricks, William. *Grammars of Style and Styles of Grammar.* Amsterdam: Elsevier, 1976; Enkvist, Nils. *Linguistic Stylistics.* The Hague: Mouton, 1973. One can refer to the bibliographies in these works for additional references.

The excerpt on page 127 from *The Armies of the Night,* by Norman Mailer, is reprinted by arrangement with The New American Library, Inc. The excerpt from "A Stranger in the Village," on page 153, is from *Notes of a Native Son,* by James Baldwin, published by Beacon Press. The passage by Ernest Nagel on page 158 is from his book *The Structure of Science,* published by The Hackett Publishing Co., Inc.

Sociolinguistic Variables

Chapter 6

A Researcher's Guide to the Sociolinguistic Variable (ING)

Benji Wald and Timothy Shopen

Benji Wald was born in New York City and has taught courses in linguistic variation and dialectology at UCLA. He has worked on dialect variation in English in urban centers of the U.S. and Great Britain, and in Swahili in Tanzania and Kenya. His current interests focus on the linguistic and social aspects of multilingualism in English and Spanish in the United States, and in Swahili and various other languages in East Africa.

Introduction

This chapter and the next are for readers who would like to do sociolinguistic research. They are also for those who might like to know something of the interplay between data and theory in this kind of investigation, even if for the moment they only want to see how others do it.

To readers of English, the sociolinguistic variable (ING) is familiar in the spellings *-ing* and, in the representations of casual speech, *-in'*. It is one of our most widespread variables. Most, if not all, speakers display it (even if they do not want to own up to it), saying *talking* and *nothing* on some occasions and *talkin'* and *nothin'* on others. The *-ing* variant probably originated in the Old English *-unge* ending that turned verbs into verbal nouns. Many historians of the language speculate that our modern present participle verb ending, *-ing* as in *he is hunting,* evolved out of the verbal noun ending. Earlier patterns such as *he was on huntunge* (he was on hunting) weakened to *he was a-hunting,* which then weakened further to *he was hunting*. Whatever its origin, patterns like *he's hunting* occur in London by the fourteenth century and in northern England and Scotland by the sixteenth century.[1]

The *-in'* variant is probably a newcomer. Although Wylde cites spellings such as *holdyn* (holding) and *drynkyn* (drinking) from the Norfolk Guild records as evidence for its existence since at least the late fourteenth century,[2] the *-in'* never gained wide adherence until the eighteenth century, at least if we can trust the way the ending was spelled.

Many historians of the language believe that this *-in'* ending evolved out of the *-ing* ending, as speakers pronounced the ending more toward the front of the mouth, finally behind the teeth. Other historians have suggested that it may have evolved from a much older form. Old English had something like the present participle ending, *-ing,* but it was spelled *-inde* or *-ende*. They speculate that our modern *-in* ending is actually a remnant of *-inde,* the *-d* having been absorbed into the *-n*. This would argue that *-ing* evolved from *-unge* and *-in'* from *-inde*. Barring discovery of a good deal more evidence for either position, the question will continue to be debated.

In any event, up to the eighteenth century, there is little evidence in the written records that the *-in*' pronunciation challenged *-ing*, but then there appears testimony both to the presence of *-in'* in the pronunciation of 'good' speakers, and its alternation with *-ing*. Johnson in his 1764 *Pronouncing and Spelling Dictionary* says that *g* is "quiescent in the termination *ing* as in *reading*, *writing,* etc., which may also be sounded," and Walker in his 1791 *Pronouncing Dictionary* says "Our best speakers do not invariably [sic] pronounce the participle *ing* so as to rhyme with *sing, king* and *ring*." In what we might see now as an attempt to make peace between antagonists by dividing the contested territory, Walker advocates the *-in*' pronounciation on some verbs and *-ing* on others, *-in*' when the verb already ends in *ing* and *-ing* elsewhere. Wyld quotes from an 1801 work of Walker's:

> Our best speakers universally pronounce *singin, bringin, flingin* . . .What a trifling omission is *g* after *n*. Trifling as it is, it savours too much of vulgarity to omit *-g* in any words except the *-ing* type. *Writing, reading, speaking* are certainly preferable to *writin, readin, speakin* wherever the language has the least degree of solemnity.

1. Otto Jespersen, *A Modern English Grammar* (London: George Allen & Unwin Ltd., 1961, Copenhagen: Ejnar Munksgaard). vol. 6, section 21.9, pp. 377–79. Fernand Mossé, *Esquisse d'une Histoire de la Langue Anglaise* (Lyon: IAC, 1947), p. 62.
2. Henry Cecil Wyld, *A History of Modern Colloquial English* (Oxford: Basil Blackwell, 1953), p. 289 ff.

Wyld then makes the memorable comment, "Walker is here trying to run with the hare and hunt with the hounds."[3]

-In' gained ground in the British Isles during the nineteenth century. In 1905, speaking of regional (nonstandard) dialects, Joseph Wright wrote "Final unstressed *η* has generally become *n* in all dialects, *evenin(g), farthin(g), mornin(g), sendin(g),* and similarly in all present participles and verbal nouns in *-ing*."[4] But perhaps *-in'* had already reached its summit and had begun its retreat by the time Walker wrote. In 1909 Otto Jespersen, in Volume 1 of his great *Modern English Grammar,* referred to *-in'* as "this formerly fashionable pronunciation" (see footnote 3). Jespersen said "The aristocracy and 'horsy' people generally, are said to favor [in], which is certainly less frequent among ladies," but in 1954 Alan S. C. Ross reported that while *-in'* in verbal forms such as *huntin', shootin',* and *fishin'* had undoubtedly been an upper-class indicator in Great Britain at one time, it then survived among only a few very elderly upper-class speakers.[5]

We find (ING) in our own social stereotypes and while their accuracy is not guaranteed, such stereotypes can demonstrate the values a community places on variant kinds of behavior. A good place to find them is in literature, especially comic strips. Hank Ketcham represents the preadolescent Dennis (the Menace) as always using *-in'*, and his mother as always using *-ing*. The implication is that Dennis's use of *-in'* is "boyish" and socially immature. His sister Margaret's use of *-ing* is in character with her stereotype as a precocious little girl. Another instance is the invariant use of *-in'* by Reg Smythe's cockney characters, Andy Capp and his wife, with *-in'* as a part of a popular image of the British working class; outside Britain, the presence of *-in'* in this comic strip seems readily understood as symbolizing a lack of education and/or low job prestige.

---

3. Jespersen, *A Modern English Grammar,* vol. 1 (first published 1909), section 13.11, p. 356 ff., Wyld, *A History of Modern Colloquial English.* After citing Walker's prescription for when to use *-in'* and *-ing,* Jespersen points out that likewise Batchelor, *Orthoepical Analysis* 1809 admits [in] after [ŋ], saying "as it prevents a monotonous sound." Jespersen says that in other cases Batchelor looks upon it as vulgar. Jespersen says "Several rimes show this formerly fashionable pronunciation [-in]," and he cites *flirting:curtain* and *willing:villain* from Garrick's *"Prologue"* to the *School for Scandal* in 1777 as well as others from Wordsworth, Byron, Shelley, and Tennyson. Both Jespersen and Wyld note inverse pronunciations with [iŋ] for [in] such as *linning* for *linen, ribbing* for *ribbon, chicking* for *chicken,* and *kitching* for *kitchen.*

4. Joseph Wright, *The English Dialect Grammar* (Oxford: Henry Frowde, 1905), section 274, p. 224.

5. Jespersen, *A Modern English Grammar.* Alan S. C. Ross, "Linguistic Class-Indicators in Present-Day English," in *Bulletin de la Société Néophilologique de Helsinki* 55 Jahrang (Amsterdam: Swets and Zeitlinger N.V., 1968).

The (ING) variable occupies a notable position in sociolinguistic studies: it was the first to be studied quantitatively in speech. In a study published in 1958, Fischer observed that preadolescent schoolchildren in a small New England town used both *-ing* and *-in'*, but that females tended to use *-ing* more often than males; in addition, a "model" boy (well-behaved, school-oriented) used *-ing* more often than a "typical" boy, and changed the frequency of *-ing* to accord with different social situations. This frequency was highest in a test situation comparable to formal classroom recitation: the boy used *-ing* thirty-eight times and *-in'* once; on the other hand, in answers to questions read by the investigator from a questionnaire, he used *-ing* thirty-three times and *-in'* thirty-five times, and in a more relaxed interview the count was twenty-four for *-ing* and forty-one for *-in'*. Fischer also noted that for markedly "formal" words, he tended to use *-ing* and for markedly "informal" ones *-in'*. This same boy used *-ing* in *criticizing, correcting, reading,* visiting, and *interesting,* but *-in'* in *punchin', flubbin', swimmin', chewin'* and *hittin'*, while for some common verbs such as *play, go* and *do,* he alternated between *-ing* and *-in'*.[6]

Fischer's main observations have been replicated in studies elsewhere, all confirming that (ING) is sensitive to situations, the stylistic properties of words, and the social identity of speakers.

The authors have both conducted research on (ING) with introductory sociolinguistics classes, first Wald in Los Angeles and then Shopen in Canberra, Australia.[7] The comparison of our results shows how linguistic variables can provide a useful index to social structures in different communities. In particular, our results with (ING) imply that Canberra is more conservative than Los Angeles in respect to the status and behavior of women. This kind of research is an excellent teaching instrument. It requires a minimum of apparatus (ears, pencil, and paper), and we suspect that it would be a feasible and revealing project for students in virtually any English-speaking community in the world.

In this chapter, we will first consider some concepts fundamental to the notion of (ING) as a sociolinguistic variable, and then we will proceed to the research project. In our conclusion, we will discuss the significance of the fact that *-ing* and *-in'* are both well entrenched and have long been in competition, a conflict many speakers may actually have encouraged.

6. J. L. Fischer, "Social Influences in the Choice of a Linguistic Variant," *Word* 14(1958):47–56.

7. T. Shopen, "Research on the Variable (ING) in Canberra, Australia," *Talanya* 5 (1978):42–52.

1. Sociolinguistic Variables

1.1 Linguistic Norms

A linguistic norm is any linguistic feature that occurs regularly in the speech of more than one speaker in a community. It can be phonological, morphological, lexical, or syntactic. The spellings *-ing* and *-in'* represent two distinct linguistic norms; their decisive characteristics are phonological, but their choice is sensitive to several aspects of morphology and the lexicon.

In most dialects of English, the *-ing* norm is pronounced [iŋ], and its most important characteristic is the *velarity* of the final nasal, i.e. that the place of contact for the tongue is *velar*. We articulate velar consonants by raising the back of the tongue to the velum (soft palate), as in [ŋ], [k], or [g]. The *-in'* norm is pronounced in a variety of ways, all of which amount to closing the air stream through the mouth farther forward than for *-ing*, usually with an *alveolar* closure, with the tongue touching the gum ridge just behind the upper teeth, as in [n], [t], or [d]. The nasal may either stand by itself as a syllable, as in [kətn̩] for *cuttin'*, or follow a reduced central vowel, as in [rābən] for *robbin'*. There is also more extreme reduction, as in *some'm* [səmˀm] for *something,* with a glottal stop [ˀ] between two [m] sounds. We will refer to the *-ing* norm as G, a reminder of its velarity, and the *-in'* norm, in all its reduced variants, as N.[8]

Norm	*Traditional Orthography*	*Phonetic Notation*	*Distinctive Feature*
G	*-ing*	[iŋ]	Velar
N	*-in'*	[ən], etc.	Reduction, usually alveolar

8. Of the 1660 instances of (ING) in the Canberra study, 16 pronunciations were reported as [iŋk]. We had -INK on the research form along with -ING and -IN and were prepared to count it as a third norm, but so few instances of it were reported that we felt no valid judgments were possible on its social distribution or stylistic value and included the 16 in the total for -ING, 1332. These 16 were produced by three women and four men, 14 in the words *something, nothing,* and *anything,* and the remaining 2 in *hoping* and *going*. -INK would appear worth studying in its own right in Australia, if only because non-linguists find it noteworthy and report it. This pronunciation is also reported for native speakers in the British Isles. Wyld, writing in 1920 declared "Among very vulgar speakers —not in London alone—we sometimes hear *nothink* for *nothing* at the present time......"

1.2 Linguistic Variables

A linguistic variable is any linguistic unit realized by more than one norm. The test for a variable is that one norm can be substituted for another without any change in *meaning* (without any change in the semantic representation for utterances). One can, for example, say "He's working" with the pronunciation [wərkiŋ], and that sentence will mean the same as if one had said "He's workin'," with [wərkən]: it would in that sense be the same sentence. Since this would be true wherever this verb form was used, [wərkiŋ] and [wərkən] are variable realizations for the same word. Identical variation occurs in the articulation of many English words spelled *-ing*. In the range of pronunciations, what speakers regard as crucial is the presence or absence of *velarity*. From this we abstract the notion of the G and N norms and the (ING) variable.

Much work on linguistic variables depends on the unifying notion "same truth value"; that is, we justify including G and N in the same variable because we note "He's working" is true if and only if "He's workin'" is true. But only statements can be said to be true or false, and we are equally interested in other kinds of speech acts, including questions, commands, greetings, and insults: questions such as "Where are you going?", commands such as "Start walking!", greetings such as "Good morning," and insults such as "You blooming idiot!" We should also add 'performative' sentences, a special kind of statement that itself performs an action and does not have truth value, such as "I now declare this meeting closed." All these can have the relevant kind of variation, and can be studied appropriately under the notion 'same meaning.'

Now we should give careful scrutiny to the linguistic contexts that favor the variation of the (ING) variable. Note that G and N are interchangeable in *eating* and *something,* but not in *singer, sing,* or *Peking,* in which the syllable ending in *ing* is stressed. In these words a G pronunciation is invariant, so we cannot say they have the (ING) variable. It is essential to *exclude* contexts in which only one norm occurs. Thus we exclude:

(1) Contexts which are not completely unstressed. The word *thing,* made up of one stressed syllable, allows only the G norm. Compare *something, nothing,* and *anything* where *thing* occurs unstressed and allows both the G and N pronunciations. The word *Peking* illustrates that the syllable in question must be completely unstressed to accommodate the variation of (ING). Either syllable of *Peking* may receive primary stress, but even when the primary stress falls on the first syllable, the second one receives a reduced stress. The part of the

word spelled *ing* is never fully unstressed, and we can infer that it is because of this that it is pronounced with just the G norm. Interestingly, there is an older variant *Pekin,* not in current use but found in the adjective *Pekinese*.

We also exclude:

(2) De facto invariance. This is any case which might appear to have the variation of (ING), but which was invariant in actual use with either the G or the N norm 100 percent of the time. One such case might be *gonna* [gənə] or *goin' ta* [gəntə] as pronunciation of the future auxiliary verb, as in "gonna leave." In some communities people never say things like "going to leave," or "going to eat" with a G pronunciation for the "going"; they always give one of the reduced pronunciations. This was the situation in Los Angeles and so Wald excluded this expression from his research. In Canberra, Shopen found some variation in the everyday use of this expression and so included it in his research. It favored the reduced pronunciation, but because there were some unreduced pronunciations, it was a part of variable behavior, and he counted the *gonna* and *goin' ta* pronunciations as N, the *going to* pronunciations as G.

There are other linguistic factors that are a part of variable behavior but show a *tendency* to influence the variable. Verbs tend to allow N more than nouns: for instance, *runnin'* is more likely than *ceilin'*. As Fischer pointed out, everyday words of frequent use are more tolerant of N than learned specialized words: for example, *talkin'* is far more likely than *communicatin'*. Consider if one of these is easier to say than the other:

He's givin' $10 to the Red Cross.

He's donatin' $10 to the Red Cross.

Compare the stylistically neutral verb *moving* with the word derived from it in "That was a very moving speech" or "The prayer was even more moving than the sermon." This *moving* is an adjective. Its form is identical to the verb, but its meaning is narrowed to just one, the one in "The poem moved us" and not in "They moved the refrigerator." Because it has a 'lofty' stylistic value, we tend to use it to describe art works, ceremonies, or love scenes more than motor repairs, auctions, or hockey matches. N turns out to be a good test against formality, elegance, and loftiness. The reader can confirm this by trying the following sentences with an N pronunciation each time:

We're movin' out on Saturday.

He composed a movin' epitaph for the slain hero.

John and Bill are movin' the table over to our house.

The concerto for flute and harp was especially movin'.

The comfort or discomfort one feels in consciously pronouncing N here reflects the different tendencies for N in everyday usage. Though the adjective will have an occasional N, the N/G ratio will be higher for the verb than the adjective. The adverb *movingly,* derived from the adjective, appears even more high-flown and resistant to N (try "It was a movin'ly delivered address"). How much the verb accommodates N seems surely to depend on its particular usage or meaning: instead of the sentences above, try N on the verb in "Her new symphony is moving the audience to tears." Ultimately, it is the full message of the speech act and intention of the speaker that most influences the style, the choice of words, and the choice of variant norms for their pronunciation. Even with its common meaning, the verb *moving* will be less likely to carry N if it is involved in a 'lofty' message; but just because it carries that common meaning, it will often be involved in the kind of speech event where N is tolerated and indeed encouraged. Such observations are important because they tell us about factors inherent to individual words that influence variation and linguistic change. Little detailed research of this sort has been done on (ING) in present-day English.

Bona fide cases of (ING) occur only in unstressed syllables. Such syllables with (ING) are almost always *word final;* words such as *movingly* and *interestingly* are infrequent exceptions.[9] An unstressed syllable occurs only in words more than one syllable long, and words of one syllable are always stressed, e.g., *thing, ring, wing, king;* these words are never pronounced with N, and so do not express the (ING) variable. We can sum up: whenever G occurs in an unstressed syllable, you can expect N to occur at least sometimes; look for this variation at the end of words of two or more syllables. N is most likely to occur in everyday words and in some parts of speech more than others—especially in verbs such as *laughing, running, cooking, putting, studying, listening, borrowing, bothering,* and *establishing*. The next most likely hosts for N are the three pronouns *something, nothing,* and *anything*. Then there are nouns and adjectives that usually but not

9. We suspect that the *-ly* suffix tends to resist N stylistically in all its occurrences. While we believe N *can* occur here, for instance, *borin'ly* for *boringly* in "He always makes his stories too long and he tells them borin'ly," it is not a place where much variation will occur. Quite apart from that, there is great advantage in the method of research if you set out to look for (ING) only at the ends of words. It is easier to hear. It is a small compromise that we made in our research projects, and it did much to make the observations more feasible.

always derive from verbs, nouns such as *morning, railing, ceiling, writing, mining, boxing,* and *traveling,* and adjectives such as *boring, tiring, interesting,* and *exciting.*

One can find (ING) in virtually any English-speaking community, but its particular manifestation can vary. We have noted the different status of *going to,* a part of the variable in Canberra but not in Los Angeles; and in Canberra there is an -INK pronunciation, particularly in the words *something, nothing,* and *anything,* that appears to have a life of its own (see footnote 8). Researchers in other communities should be prepared to recognize special local features and take them into account in their research design.

1.3 Sociolinguistic Variables

A sociolinguistic variable is a linguistic variable sensitive to social context. We know we have a sociolinguistic variable when some feature of a social group or social situation allows us to predict which norms will be used from a variable. This is a phenomenon that gives us insight into both language and social structure.

Our task is to understand the linguistic inventories available to a conversation and how speakers choose among the variable norms. To do this, we look for the social characteristics that influence language behavior, characteristics of speakers and listeners, and situations and topics, as well as historical factors that might explain changes in linguistic standards—whatever motivates people toward opposing linguistic variants.[10]

10. To illuminate the theory and substance of sociolinguistic variables in a way ideal for students at the early stages of an introductory course on language and culture, sociolinguistics, English grammar or style, we recommend a research project we learned about from the anthropologist Joel Sherzer. In situations where you have heard perfectly well what your interlocutors have said, ask them to repeat (''Huh?'' ''What's that?'' ''Would you say that again?''). If there is a difference between the initial utterance and the repetition, jot down as soon as possible the two versions, and brief notes on the social identity of the people involved in the speech event, their relationship to each other, the setting, the subject of the conversation, the apparent intention of the speaker, and anything else that might help explain the variation. When researchers have each recorded variation from a minimum of say twenty speakers, they write a report organizing their data and discussing the main tendencies. The teacher in turn gives a lecture based on all the observations by the class, using their data to illustrate concepts such as ''variable, standard, stylistic level, hypercorrection, presupposition,'' etc. and pointing out the speech variation in the community that appears to have the greatest social significance.

When someone asks them to repeat something, speakers usually think there may have been something defective about the way they said it the first time. From this we have found two main tendencies: they can think the first version may have lacked *clarity*—presupposed too much common knowledge, or was inaccurate or too subtle—and they add more information, change to what they deem more accurate terms, or make a stronger statement. But at least as often they think they may have lacked *etiquette,* and then they shift to norms they consider more formal or more standard.

Consider the use of two languages in the same community. This is a choice between two sets of norms organized into distinct linguistic systems. There are communities where teenagers talk to each other in one language and to their parents in another. The topics they communicate about in the two languages vary; nevertheless, the great majority of meanings they express in one language they could express in the other, and that means that when they discuss most topics they can choose which language to use. The choices they make portend much for the future of the communities. In a report on a Puerto-Rican community in New York City in the early 1970s, Wolfram describes how adolescents speak to their parents in Spanish but to their friends in English, even in some cases where the parents understand English and the peers Spanish. He notes that social forces operate so strongly that many parents insist on the use of Spanish, while peers may ridicule its use and demand English.[11] Similarly, Swahili is commonly used by Miji Kenda youth in urban coastal Kenya, but they report that their elders require them to use the home language, or risk being accused of disrespect or lack of ability in their cultural heritage.[12]

Bilingual systems that divide generations tend to be unstable. The language more prestigious among the young usually gains ground as that generation grows older, while the language favored by their parents fades away. In other situations two languages, or two varieties of the same language, may be used in complementary social situations. In this case, the opposition tends to be more stable: the young may not command the same range of expressive forms as their parents, but they grow into them because they need them to fully participate in their culture. In the situation Ferguson calls *diglossia,* two varieties of a language, labelled "high" and "low," are used in complementary social situations.[13] Most norms are shared by the two varieties of the language, while smaller differences set them apart. The high variety of Greek (Katharevousa) refers to "water" as *idhór,* while the low variety (Dhimotiki) uses *néro.* The choice is a sensitive index to social situations. Katharevousa tends to be used on public, sometimes ceremonial occasions such as addresses through the mass media, while Dhimotiki tends to be used for private or intimate occasions such as conversations among friends.

Brown and Gilman discuss the variables to the second-person

11. W. Wolfram, *Sociolinguistic Aspects of Assimilation: Puerto Rican English in New York City* (Washington, D.C.: Center for Applied Linguistics, 1974).
12. B. Wald, "Bilingualism," in B. Siegel, ed., *Annual Review of Anthropology,* 3 (1974): 301–21.
13. C.A. Ferguson, "Diglossia," *Word* 15:325–50.

singular ("you" said to one person) in French, Italian, and German.[14] They conclude that the choice between the T and V forms (e.g., *tu* and *vous* in French) is predictable according to the relative status of the speakers, particularly whether they are equal or unequal in power and/or solidarity. Ervin-Tripp has done a similar study on terms of address in English asking under what circumstances a person is addressed by his first name, or by a title such as "mister" or "doctor."[15]

Sociolinguistic research usually uses well-recognized labels for participants in conversations, identifying speakers and listeners by sex, age, ethnic background, and socioeconomic status. Advances in sociolinguistics depend greatly on general social theory and its ability to offer an empirically supported and well-articulated view of the structure of society, one of the important sources of empirical support being linguistic data. But the linguistic data itself can also suggest lines of demarcation for social categories that might have been previously unsuspected. A study done by an undergraduate student at the Australian National University found an opposition between adult men under fifty on the one hand, and another group that consisted of both adult women and men fifty and over. The study concerned expressions for time. The men under fifty consistently used expressions for time that revealed a clock-governed perspective, while the other group used expressions that revealed a more intuitive and clock-free notion of time. This gives us a basis for saying that men fifty and over belong to a distinct social category from men under fifty, one which is likely to involve additional cultural traits besides time expressions, and one sharing at least some characteristics with adult women.[16]

As a phonological variable (ING) occurs in the pronunciation of many words and so pervades conversations in a wide range of social situations. It is sensitive to social groups and social situations, but as with many variables, we cannot make *absolute* predictions about which norm will be used in a given utterance. It has *inherent* variability that is embedded in the social context.

It is in this light that the notion of *relative frequency* has taken on such importance. In his study of English spoken in New York City, Labov demonstrated that the higher the socioeconomic class of the speaker, the more frequent the use of G. He showed further that differ-

14. R. Brown and J. Gilman, "The Pronouns of Power and Solidarity," in T. A. Sebeok, ed., *Style in Language* (Cambridge, Mass.: The MIT Press, 1960), pp. 253–76. Reprinted in P. P. Giglioli, *Language and Social Context* (Baltimore: Penguin Books, 1972), pp. 252–82.

15. S. Ervin-Tripp, "On Sociolinguistic Rules: Alternation and Co-occurrence," in J. J. Gumperz and D. Hymes, eds., *Directions in Sociolinguistics* (New York: Holt, Rinehart and Winston, 1972), pp. 213–50.

16. A. Hazelwood, "Have You Got the Time?" Department of Linguistics, SGS, Australian National University, 1976.

ent speakers in a community used different absolute frequencies of G but varied their frequency *in the same direction* according to the social situation: G was favored in spontaneous but guarded speech to a stranger-interviewer and less favored the more the speaker was involved in what he was saying.[17] These findings recurred in Trudgill's study of members of the Norwich community in the East Anglia area of England.[18]

In his work on sociolinguistic variation, Labov has contributed much to the theory of linguistic change, particularly on the workings of *linguistic change in progress*. Linguists have not always admitted that one could observe linguistic change in progress. In 1885 Schuchardt published a number of astute observations on sound change, arguing, as we would, that sound change spreads gradually through a language and through its community of speakers, with some vocabulary and some social contexts accommodating the new norms more than others. But his views were in direct opposition to those of a then more influential group, the *Junggrammatiker* (Neogrammarians), who held that sound changes were imperceptible, mechanical, and exceptionless.[19]

Even in 1933 the great Leonard Bloomfield wrote, "The process of linguistic change has never been directly observed; we shall see that such observation, with our present facilities, is inconceivable." He viewed sound change as a gradual replacement, by small steps, of certain phonetic features over others.[20] In his presidential address to the Linguistics Society of America in 1964, Charles F. Hockett expressed similar views.[21]

But recent work has demonstrated that sound change *can* be perceived in progress, with competing variants existing side by side in the same community, sometimes in the behavior of individual speakers. However little they can describe the variants, speakers often hear the differences, and the social values they place on opposing variants is a major influence on sound change. In the following chapter we will describe change taking place in the pronunciation of vowels in Los

---

17. William Labov, *The Social Stratification of English in New York City* (Washington, D.C.: Center for Applied Linguistics, 1966). See also Labov, *Sociolinguistic Patterns* (Philadelphia: University of Pennsylvania Press, 1972).
18. P. Trudgill, "The Social Stratification of English in Norwich:" (Cambridge Cambridge University Press, 1974).
19. Schuchardt's essay can be found in the original German and in English translation along with relevant essays by Wilbur and Vennemann, in T. Vennemann and T. H. Wilbur, *Schuchardt, the Neogrammarians, and the Transformational Theory of Phonological Change,* Linguistische Forschungen, Band 26 (Frankfurt: Athenäum Verlag, 1972).
20. L. Bloomfield, *Language* (New York: Holt, Rinehart and Winston, 1933), p. 347.
21. C. F. Hockett, "Sound Change," *Language,* 41, no. 2 (1965): 185–204.

Angeles, where the direction of change is discovered by comparing successive age groups. Chapter 7 of the companion volume, *Standards and Dialects in English,* offers some observations on sound change in progress in New York City.

It may be that someday the opposition in (ING) will resolve itself. We can imagine a situation where the new norm has triumphed, while the few scattered G pronunciations that remain are viewed as quaint vestiges of the past. Spelling reformers might then demand that the modern character of the language be recognized and give us *nothin, negotiatin, talkin,* and *communicatin.* But we cannot know how or when—or even whether—the opposition will end. Both norms have had ups and downs; right now, G and N each have well-entrenched positions; in this sense (ING) is a stable variable.

Linguistic change has three phases: (1) a new norm appears, (2) the new and the old norm compete, and, if the change goes through, (3) the new norm displaces the old. (ING) is in a prolonged and stable phase (2). It provides a good opportunity to learn about this aspect of language because the variation (the competition) is so widespread in the speech of most native speakers. It is a typical situation: speakers tend to accord prestige to the older norm and view it as the only "correct" one (though N carried prestige among sections of the British aristocracy when the process of change might have been completed, but wasn't). Speakers tend to view the new norm as more casual and more intimate; some words accommodate it more easily than others. Some social gatherings welcome it while others resist it; speakers control the formality of their language as they play out different social roles.

2. Research on (ING)

2.1 The People and the Categories

The researchers who cooperated in our studies were students in introductory sociolinguistics classes, and we defined our projects so as to be feasible for them, people with good energy and motivation but no previous experience in sociolinguistic research. In Los Angeles, the population studied consisted entirely of speakers residing in and usually native to Los Angeles, generally of middle-class status, and in contact with the students through work, family, or friendship. In Canberra, the population studied consisted entirely of native speakers of Australian

English, most often *not* born in Canberra (Canberra being a community even younger than Los Angeles), but otherwise with a social definition similar to the one in Los Angeles.

An individual or group of any size could carry out research of the sort we describe here, and provided it is done with reasonable care, it is bound to be to good advantage. The size of the "sample" to be studied is of only relative importance. Small projects can help design later investigations of larger scale; their reliability can be checked by replicated studies. Social structure may be so uniform that basic patterns emerge out of a small study. The first study of (ING) by Fischer had a small sample population but found sexual differentiation and sensitivity to situations that agreed to a striking degree with the larger studies by Labov and Trudgill in other communities (Trudgill's on the other side of the Atlantic Ocean).

Don't wait to do a study large enough for statistical reliability, but if that is possible, so much the better. The number thirty is a good guide. If you are comparing men and women speakers, get data on at least thirty of each; if you are studying the effect of speaker and addressee sex in conversations among friends, then get counts of (ING) in at least thirty of each of the four kinds of conversations that are relevant: a man talking to a man friend, a man talking to a woman friend, a woman talking to a man friend and a woman talking to a woman friend.

We recommend the categories *man* and *woman* as a primary focus of study. It is an easy difference to identify, and it is likely to lead to interesting results anyplace. Previous linguistic research, including work on (ING), and factors other than language all lead us to expect sex to be important whenever status and degrees of formality are important, which is to say almost always.

Our research plan requires a population you can listen to, without intruding, in at least two conversations for each speaker with different addressees and that will let you interview them later. You are going to observe their use of (ING) in several conversations without telling them what you are doing; only afterwards will you explain the project and ask for an interview. You ought to be reasonably sure they will not mind being an object of study. If someone objects, discard the notes, make your apologies, and go on to someone else.

According to our research plan, you identify each speaker and addressee in a conversation by sex and then identify a relationship between them. If you do not know the relationship, you can ask afterwards. For our research we chose three categories, *friend, family,* and *other.*

Categorize each conversation with just one of these labels. In

Social Relationship	*Typically Includes*
Friend	boyfriend, girlfriend, co-worker, fellow student, etc.
Family	all kin, including by marriage
Other	boss, customer, salesperson, teacher, stranger, etc.

particular, if the speaker and addressee are *family,* then categorize them as such along with whatever else you know about them, and then for those who are not *family* decide whether the relationship is *friend* or not. For people who are neither *family* nor *friend,* you put down *other.* Ask these interview questions:

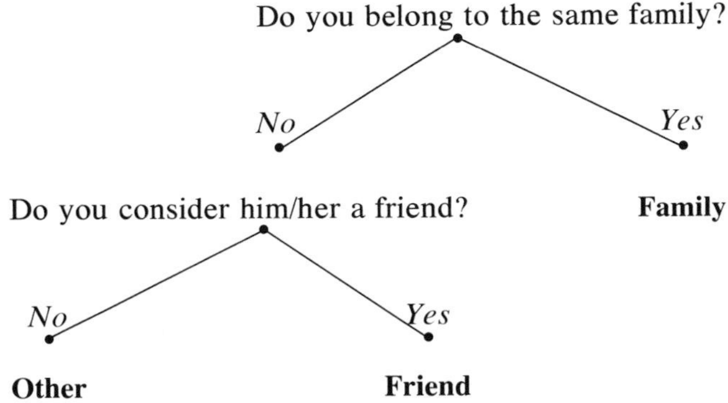

In a more extensive study more types of relationships could be distinguished, and one might want to apply more than one to a conversation, also recognizing different relationships for the same people in different situations. There is such a thing as a boss who is also a friend, and both *boss* and *friend* might be relevant categories, but it might also matter whether the speakers are conversing at their place of work in front of other employees or sharing a meal alone together after hours.

Using our three categories for relationships, you want to discover how the addressees affect the behavior of the speakers, with as little influence from you as possible. You should be like the proverbial fly on the wall.

You are going to be studying people you know or are in contact with fairly regularly. You will not be doing a comprehensive study of your community, but rather a *pilot study,* a preliminary investigation the conclusions from which can be hypotheses for later research.

2.2 Gathering Data

You will be studying individual speakers and then comparing them according to social categories. Organize the study of each speaker in two parts, "Observations of Language Use," and "Interview." You do the interview *after* you have made all your observations of language use. It will be best to run off a form for each speaker, one that everyone cooperating on the project can use, with space to record observations on as many conversations as possible, as well as the results of the interview. You will correlate the G/N counts for particular speakers with their answers to interview questions (see Figure 6.1).

In the first part of the study, you are going to listen while a person talks to someone else. Count ten *consecutive* instances of the (ING) variable as we have defined it (unstressed *-ing* at the end of a word) and keep a running tally in your mind with the ratio of G to N pronunciations, e.g., "1–0, 2–0, 2–1, 3–1, 4–1, 5–1, 5–2, 5–3, 6–3, 7–3." You might find it difficult at first, but everyone reports being able to do it after only a little practice. It is important that the count be consecutive to guard against the possibility of a biased selection in which you might have picked one norm and ignored the other.

Note down your tally, together with your description of the situation, including the sex of the speaker, M(ale) or F(emale); the sex of the addressee, m(ale) or f(emale); and the relationship between the speaker and addressee, FR(iend), FAM(ily) or O(ther). We suggest making the counts when you are not the addressee because it is too difficult to both count (ING) and maintain a natural role in the conversation. Repeat this procedure with the same speaker and at least one other addressee. Take care the person does not know what you have been listening for until after you have finished this part of the study. Then do the interview.

Explain the purpose of your study. If necessary ask the person you are interviewing about his or her relationship with the addressee. Then ask three questions.

First ask a question about their preference for one of the (ING) norms: you can lead off with "Which pronunciation sounds better, *somethING* or *somethIN'?*" and then if you think it will help your speakers understand, elaborate with the variant pronunciations of other words such as *working, swimming, nothing,* and *morning*. Then add "Or have you no preference?" Indicate the answer as -ING, -IN,

Figure 6.1. (opposite) ***Completed Research Form of a Sort to Be Used with Each Speaker Studied. A group of researchers all use copies of the same form and compile them later for analysis. Here the researcher made observations on a speaker in two conversations (it could have been more), and then did the interview.***

Researcher M. Morgan Speaker No. 27

Sex of speaker:
M(ALE) or F(EMALE) F

LANGUAGE USE

Conversation	1	2		
Date	Oct 10	Oct 12		
Sex of Addressee m(ale) or f(emale)	m	f		
Relationship FR(IEND), FAM(ILY) or O(THER)	FR	FR		
Variable Data (n/10): -ING	8	9		
-IN	2	1		

INTERVIEW

1. *Preference*
   Which pronunciation sounds better *somethING* or *somethIN*"? – Or have you no preference (n.p.)? Consider *working, swimming, nothing, morning,* etc. (Answer: -ING, -IN or n.p.) -ING

2. *Self-Report*
   Which pronunciation do you use when you talk, -ING, -IN or both? -ING "Unless I was tired and made a mistake"

3. *Stereotype*
   What kind of people say -IN frequently? "Poorly educated people, people who don't care about the language, the kind with no ambition, no desire to better themselves."

or n.p. (no preference). Note down that preference without distinction for the particular reasons. When one norm gets a preponderance of preferences, you have a basis for saying it is the prestige norm, or the *standard*.

The next question is "Which pronunciation do you use when you talk?" There are three possible answers, -ING, -IN, or BOTH. The most accurate answer for most people would be "both," but some will favor -ING because they are not aware that they vary their pronunciation. But they can also answer -ING because they interpret the question to mean "Which pronunciation is most typical of your speech?" In this case -ING would be accurate for most speakers. Try to get people to interpret -ING as meaning *only* -ING. The answer to this question is the speaker's *self-report*.

Finally, ask "What kind of people say -IN frequently?" A few speakers dislike this question because they may feel it demands they reveal a personal prejudice. Try to get the person to give a *personal* opinion: this question is intended to get an index of the attitudes of speakers. If they report what is said by others, what "people say," you should ask them whether they agree. See our discussion in Section 2.3.2 for how we have categorized the answers to this question.

Repeat this procedure with as many speakers as you can. The goal is to get data on as many speakers and as many different speaker-addressee combinations as possible, and that makes working in a group a big advantage. In an introductory course each student could set out to study at least two speakers, each one in at least two conversations with different addressees.

2.3 The Canberra Study

2.3.1 Observations of Language Use:

We will use the Canberra study for illustration.[22] The most important social distinction that emerged in the study was the one between men and women in their roles as both speakers and listeners; next most important was the distinction for men speakers between the relationship *friend,* as opposed to *family* and *other*. The results will be pre-

22. We will make several references to some statistical tests familar to anyone with background in statistics. Readers with no background in statistics who would like to use such tests to check the validity of their findings should seek help, and in most places it should not be hard to find. If you compile your data neatly, there will usually be knowledgeable people around who would then be glad to give you help on the statistics.

sented in a way to highlight these oppositions.

In the Canberra study forty-seven male speakers were observed in one hundred conversations, and thirty-three female speakers in sixty-six conversations, a total of 166 conversations. With 10 consecutive instances of (ING) having been observed in each, we have a total of 1660 observed instances of (ING). Of these 1660, 328 were N, or 1.98 N per 10 instances of (ING). The N per 10 (ING) for male and female speakers is as follows:

Male	2.44
Female	1.56

The standard deviations were M 2.04 and F 1.64. The variances of the two samples (the standard deviations squared) are 'same' by a significant margin, and therefore the means can be meaningfully compared. By a standard test, the difference between the two means is large enough to make the possibility of error only 3.2 percent. See Figure 6.2 for the distribution of G and N pronunciations among male and female speakers.

Only in conversations between *friends* does the difference between M and F speakers become apparent, and as it happened, the great majority of conversations observed fell into this category. The sample collected on conversations between friends is quite large enough for the results to be statistically significant; the results from *family* or *other* conversations are based on a comparatively small sample and should be regarded as only suggestive. Table 6.1 reveals the opposition between *friend* and the other two relations for M speakers, the similarity between M and F speakers for the other two relation categories, and the similarity in the style level (the N/G ratio) for F speakers in all relation categories.

On the basis of these figures, we can see that only M speakers

Table 6.1. ***Male and Female Speakers: Frequency of -IN per Relation Category in Canberra, Australia***

	Relation	*Instances of (ING)*	*Occurrences of -IN*	*-IN % of Total*
Male Speakers	Friend	760	200	26
	Family	130	18	14
	Other	110	15	14
Female Speakers	Friend	470	68	14
	Family	130	19	15
	Other	60	8	13

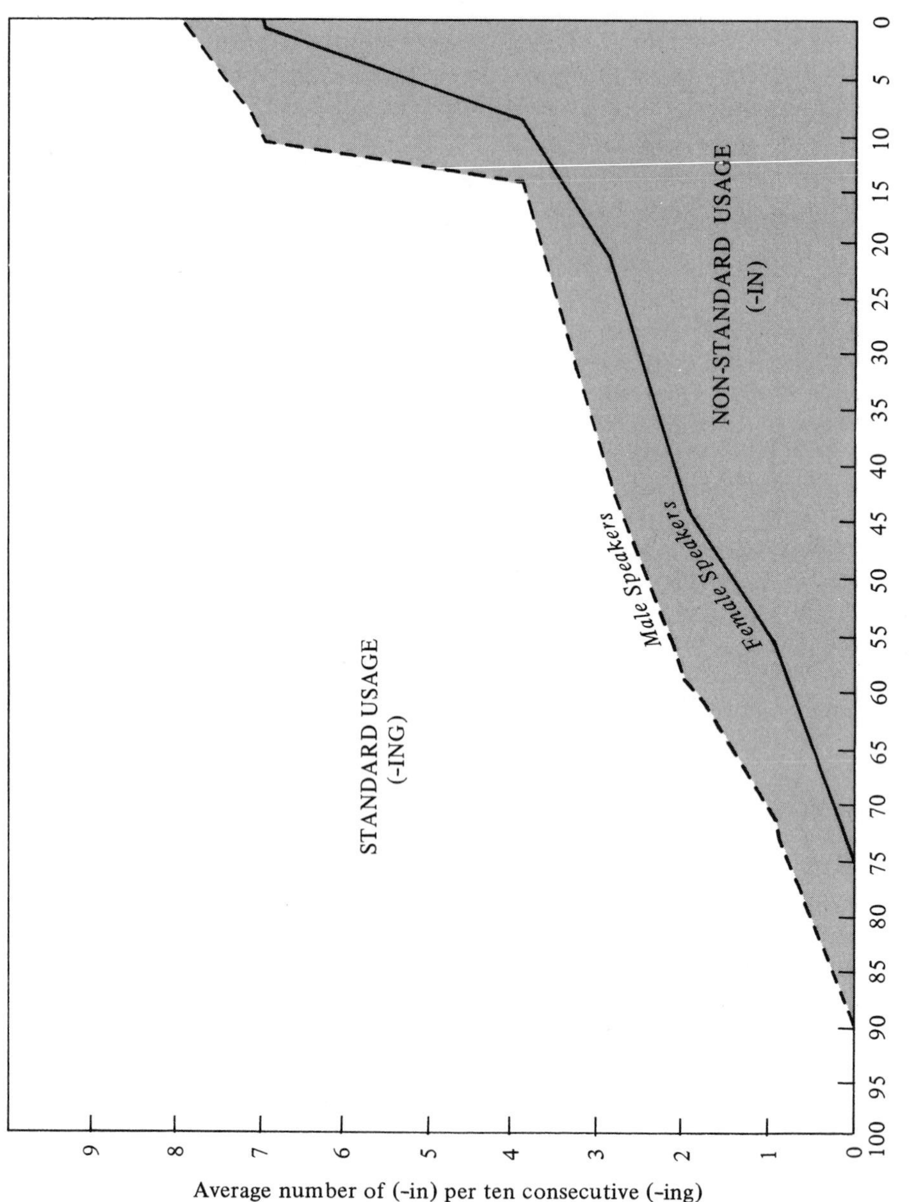

Figure 6.2. ***Nonstandard Usage of the (ING) Variable Among Men and Women Speakers in Canberra, Australia. In 100 conversations with men speakers and 66 with women speakers, a total of 166 conversations, each conversation with a count of 10 consecutive instances of (ING), a total of 1660 instances of (ING).***

shift their style significantly according to their relation to the addressee. They shift to a significantly higher percentage of N when talking to friends as opposed to non-friends. However, both the men and women in the Canberra study shift their style in another way, and here the women more than the men. If their addressee is male, both men and women use more N; if the addressee is female, both men and women use less N. The extent of the style-shifting is similar in absolute terms: in conversations between friends (the relation category where we have the most data), men speaking to men produced on average 2.90 N per 10 consecutive (ING), men speaking to women produced 2.29 N, a difference of .61; women speaking to men produced 1.88 N per 10 consecutive (ING), women speaking to women 1.20 N, a difference of .68. The absolute indices of style-shifting according to the sex of the addressee then are .61 for men speakers and .68 for women speakers. When we look at the matter in relative terms, we can see that the women shift their style more than men. Where men reduce their N by 21 percent when talking to women friends, women reduce theirs by 36 percent. Alternatively, we can say that when talking to men friends as opposed to women friends, women *increase* their N by 57 percent; the comparable figure for men is only 27 percent.

We have ranged the figures in Table 6.2 with the number of N per 10 (ING) going from highest to lowest. Men-to-men are at the top and women-to-women at the bottom. The differences between adjacent pairs on this scale was only suggestive statistically, but the

Table 6.2. ***Style Shifting and Absolute Frequency of -IN Forms in Conversations Between Friends in Canberra, Australia***

	Average Number of -IN per 10 (ING)	*Style Shifting Depending on the Sex of the Addressee (a–b)*
Men Speaking		
(a) To men friends (M-m-FR) 420 (ING), 122 -IN	2.90	
		.61 (27% of 2.29)
(b) To women friends (M-f-FR) 340 (ING), 78 -IN	2.29	
Women speaking		
(a) To men friends (F-m-FR) 170 (ING), 32 -IN	1.88	
		.68 (57% of 1.20)
(b) To women friends (F-f-FR) 300 (ING), 36 -IN	1.20	

of potentially distinctive social relationships that we should be wary of small undifferentiated samples. Another likely place to look for further differentiation relevant to speech behavior is within the category *family*. We might expect differences based on the relative *generations* of speaker and addressee within the same family (peer vs. parent-child vs. child-parent, etc.), and again between members of different families (it might turn out that peers speak to each other in the same style whether they belong to the same family or not, but that between members of different generations family membership is decisive, and so on).

Despite their limitations, our three categories proved useful for a research project of this scale. We have results that provide support for a compelling perspective on women and their status. Together all our generalizations are consistent with the view that of the two sexes women are both more constrained by, and more aware of, the conservative forces in our culture. There are fewer situations in which they vary their style, and fewer in which they speak in a relatively nonstandard, and we will argue, intimate way. (They can be intimate with men, but not so much with members of their own sex!) They use less nonstandard forms in absolute terms, but on the other hand in the social situations we have found where they do shift style, they show a greater range of style-shifting than men do, and we can explain this by saying that they have a greater awareness of the stylistic affect of the style-shifting.

2.3.2 Interviews

As in Los Angeles, the Canberra researchers conducted interviews with each speaker after they had observed him or her, usually in several conversations. Researchers asked speakers which variant sounded better, which pronunciation they thought they used, and stereotypes of the kind of people they thought used frequent nonstandard pronunciations of (ING). The G pronunciation emerged unquestionably as the standard, and N as a nonstandard variant. In their judgments about language usage, women emerged as more conservative than men, just as they did in their speech behavior. Because of additional evidence obtained after the data was compiled for Table 6.3, the sample considered for the interview was somewhat larger, 52 men (an increase of five) and 36 women (an increase of three).

In answer to the question about which pronunciation they preferred, *somethING* or *somethIN'*, 94 percent of the women said they believed G sounded better than N, as opposed to 82 percent of the men. Fourteen percent (7) of the men had no preference; only one woman (3 percent) gave that response. Two men (4 percent) and one woman (3 percent) said N sounded better.

There were discrepancies between self-report and actual performance, but they do not appear significant. When asked what pronunciation they used, 33 of 52 men (63 percent) said G, and only 15 (29 percent) reported both G and N. In fact all those reporting both *did* use both forms in the counts, but only 6 of the 33 reporting G used *only* G. However, the question may have been interpreted to mean "Which variant is most *characteristic* of your speech?"—in which case G would have been the appropriate answer.

Four men gave a self-report of N, and these men were indeed high N speakers, with counts of 9/20, 13/20, 8/10, and 3/10 respectively. No one produced only N.

A similar pattern emerged for women. Twenty-five (69 percent) gave self-reports of G when in fact just 6 of those used only G. Ten (28 percent) reported that they used both G and N, and in fact did so. One (3 percent) reported N, and she was a high N speaker, with 15/20. Table 6.4 summarizes the results of the interview.

The stereotypes ("What kind of people say -IN frequently?") provide some of the most interesting results, but also some of the most difficult to categorize. We imposed a three-way distinction to the answers, "personally negative," "socially lower," and "neutral."

Personally negative. These are stereotypes that denigrate the personal character of the N speakers. The most common comments referred to education, "not educated properly, uneducated," or "less educated." These expressions occurred seventeen times. The word "lazy" was used eleven times and "careless" six. The expression "Ockers" was used twice: this is an Australian term for Australian-style boorish and uncouth behavior. Other negative expressions occur-

Table 6.4. ***Beliefs and Self-Reports of Men and Women Speakers***

	All Speakers (88)		*Male (52)*		*Female (36)*	
Preference ("Which pronunciation sounds better?")						
-ING	77	(87%)	43	(82%)	34	(94%)
No Preference	8	(10%)	7	(14%)	1	(3%)
-IN	3	(3%)	2	(4%)	1	(3%)
Self-Report ("Which pronunciation do you use?")						
-ING	58	(66%)	33	(63%)	25	(69%)
Both	25	(28%)	15	(29%)	10	(28%)
-IN	5	(6%)	4	(8%)	1	(3%)

ring once each were "less aware," "drunk," "sloppy," "lousy," "slack," and "not thinking." Almost half of the answers by our eighty-eight interviewees fell into the "personally negative" category.

Socially lower. These stereotypes say nothing about the intelligence, education, alertness, etc., of speakers, but rather are a comment on "lower" social origin. The most common expressions were "working class, lower class," and "blue collar." About 27 percent of the answers placed users of N in a social class lower than that of the respondents (who were middle class).

Neutral. These responses carried no obvious sense of "better" or "worse." It is a matter of inference that the expression "working class" means "socially lower," and in the world view of some people, "working class" is surely a neutral expression. Hence our distinction between "socially lower" and "neutral" is not reliable or valid in all cases. We grouped under the "neutral" category answers such as "Everyone tends to say -IN some of the time" (seven such responses), "It depends on the origin or environment one comes from" (two responses), and "average Australian" (two responses). We classed 23 percent of the answers as neutral. Two percent (two people) held no opinion.

Table 6.5 compares men and women speakers for their answers to the stereotype question. There is further suggestion here that women are more conservative in their judgments about the (ING) norms than men. And with both men and women speakers we see how strongly the community accords prestige to the G norm. What is left unsaid is why people feel motivated to use the N norm as well, for indeed it cannot be just the inherent variability of (ING) that accounts for the presence of N. The consistent tendencies for all speakers to produce more N in some social situations rather than others is proof that N has social motivation. Bringing to bear our general understanding of society we can interpret the language behavior and attitudes we have discovered. It can give us insight into social phenomena popularly referred to as "friendship," "women's place," "mateship" (an Australian term for males in group companionship), "polite behavior," "family upbringing," and the like.

Table 6.5. ***Stereotypes of -IN Speakers Given by Men and Women***

	All Speakers (88)	*Male (52)*	*Female (36)*
Personally negative	42 (48%)	23 (44%)	19 (53%)
Socially lower	24 (27%)	13 (25%)	11 (31%)
Neutral	20 (23%)	14 (27%)	6 (17%)
No opinion	2 (2%)	2 (4%)	–

2.4 Extensions

2.4.1 Comparing Communities

The Canberra study was patterned after one in Los Angeles. Canberra emerges from the study as the more linguistically conservative community, especially in regard to women. The linguistic structures in the two communities are identical, G and N. Speakers use them differently enough to imply differences in social structure. G was unquestionably the prestige norm in Los Angeles, N the nonstandard norm. Los Angeles speakers produced more N overall, 2.48 per 10 (ING), as opposed to the 1.98 in Canberra. Speakers of both sexes used more N talking to *friend* and *family* than to *other,* with similar frequencies of N for *friend* and *family*. But men used more N, and had a notably wider range of styles than women. With one exception, all speakers used less N speaking to women than to men. The one exception is important: In conversations among friends, Los Angeles women used more N speaking to women than to men. Recall that in Canberra, speech to women was always more conservative, even among women friends. It should be obvious how revealing similar research projects could be in other English-speaking communities.

2.4.2 The Los Angeles Family (ING) Study

The research design presented here can be expanded in two ways: one with respect to social structure, and the other with respect to the speech acts themselves.

Besides sex, one could easily control for the age of speakers and addressees: We could guess age by appearance, to the nearest number divisible by five, 20, 25, 30, 35, etc., or we could ask. While the criteria for sex and age are unequivocal, important social categories such as ethnic group and socioeconomic class are much more difficult to identify. Because they are so important, it is a challenge to define them in distinct, nonoverlapping, and reliable ways. Sociologists can give guidelines on how to gather and interpret information here. Socioeconomic class is typically identified on the basis of education, occupation, and income—information that must be obtained in interviews. As a somewhat rougher and more feasible method, one can do counts on (ING) in different *places* known to be frequented by people of distinct social groups, for example, among people in places of work with contrasting social status: factories vs. jewelry stores, banks vs. garages.

To understand (ING) better in relation to the internal structure of speech acts, we can control for several features, some of which require recording the speech acts to be studied. A number of things are of interest, from the specific words on which the G and N occur to topics and the styles in which they are discussed.

In Los Angeles we carried out a reasonably feasible project, one that can be done again without tape recorders, and one that expands the research design both for social structure and the internal workings of speech acts. We investigated the use of (ING) among family members, controlling for generational as well as sexual differences. In addition, we controlled for the effect of *style* on (ING) by getting counts from at least two conversations for each pair of interlocutors studied, a "joking" conversation (a humorous one accompanied by good-natured smiles and laughter), and an "arguing" one (one where the predominant tone is one of disagreement, as can happen when people discuss politics, the death penalty, and other moral issues). In principle, one could find the same topic discussed in both a joking and an arguing style, but in practice joking is usually about small, personal things, and arguing about big issues.

Researchers sought to observe the same pair of family members conversing on at least two occasions that could be characterized as "joking" and "arguing." In each of these conversations, researchers made a count of *twenty* consecutive (ING) *for each interlocutor,* two counts of twenty in each conversation. The results were then compared for the influence of sex, generation, and style. The sample consisted of members of twelve middle-class families falling into two generations, a younger generation, under thirty (the age of most of the researchers and their siblings), and a generation over forty—as it turned out in all cases, the parents of the younger generation. For most of these families, the period of observation was the Thanksgiving holiday on which families share a traditional dinner.

The study of different generations produced interesting results. The older generation had the more standard usage, 24 percent N as opposed to 33 percent N for the younger generation. Both the younger and the older generation, especially female speakers, had more G and less N speaking across generations than to the same generation. An interesting difference in style shifting between the generations was that the younger generation used more G and less N when speaking across sex than to the same sex; the older generation had the same frequencies of G and N for both across sex and to the same sex.

The result of "joking" vs. "arguing" was as might be expected. Eleven of the twelve families used more G and less N when arguing than when joking. Table 6.6 shows the average frequency of N for all families by sex of the speaker. One can see style shifting by speakers of both sexes but a familiar pattern of contrast between the sexes. Male speakers use more N than female speakers, and, most notably, the male speakers have by far the wider shift between the two styles.

Table 6.6. ***The Effect of the Styles "Joking" and "Arguing" on the Percentage of -IN Pronunciations for Male and Female Speakers in Twelve Los Angeles Families (with 64 conversations in the joking style with male speakers and 51 with female speakers; 65 conversations in the arguing style with male speakers and 51 with female speakers)***

The Percentage of -IN from Total Occurrences of (ING)		
Speaker	*Joking Style*	*Arguing Style*
Male	46	24
Female	28	21

Conclusion: The Usefulness of Sociolinguistic Variables

It is significant that G and N have coexisted for so long without one driving out the other. It has been suggested that N would have taken over by now had it not been for the conservative force of the spelling *-ing*.[23] We should keep in mind that while spelling is indeed a conservative force, spelling norms have been overcome by change before. We have evidence of this in spellings that have been retained in spite of sounds that have disappeared or changed, for example, the silent *l* of *half, talk, salve, calm,* and *should,* pronounced until early modern English; the *k* of *knee,* and *know,* lost in the seventeenth century; the *w* of *two, who, sword, wring, wreck, answer,* and *toward;* the *b* of *climb, comb, dumb, bomb,* and *womb;* the *gh* (from old [x]) of *through, daughter, high, dough, right, sight,* and *eight;* the *p* of *cupboard;* the *t* of *Christmas;* the *d* of *handsome;* and the *g* of *gnaw* and of many words like *sing*. The spelling *gn* is retained in words such as *sign, design, deign, reign,* and *champagne* borrowed from French. English speakers used to give this *gn* the French palatal articulation (just as for the *n* in the middle of *onion),* but now it has an alveolar pronunciation so the *reign* sounds just like *rain*. Last but not least there is the *r* at the end of syllables, standard pronunciation until the seventeenth century, but now absent for many speakers in the British Isles and for as many as a third of the speakers in North America, so that *farther* and *father* sound the same.[24] N could have displaced G entirely in spite of the spelling. That it came as close as it did at one point is evidence for this.

23. See also M. L. Samuels, "Linguistic Evolution," *Cambridge Studies in Linguistics* 5 (London and New York: Cambridge University Press, 1972).

24. For sound change and spelling, see Jespersen, *A Modern English Grammar,* vol. 1, and H. Kurath, *A Phonology and Prosody of Modern English* (Ann Arbor, Mich.: University of Michigan Press, 1971).

N could also have retreated and disappeared—more needs to be said.

The longevity of the opposition between G and N is a sign of their usefulness. (ING) has endured in spite of the impulse language users have to resolve variable conflict and tidy up their language, their need for a standard in the form and meaning of each linguistic unit to which all members of their community can refer. Such a standard makes communication possible, and it is the stuff of group identity. But while people need a tidy, standardized language, they also appear to tolerate *some* variation to add to their expressive power.

Quite apart from the literal meaning of the utterance "He's working," it adds an extra social dimension to have both G and N available as possible pronunciations. If the speaker said G, it could have been N; and if N, it could have been G. Listeners can and will make social interpretations of the choice. The interpretations depend on a calculus of time, place, topic, and personae. But above all nowadays, N appears to convey or solicit a feeling of intimacy and G one of respect. We live in a culture with elaborate status distinctions. We tend to measure almost everything in terms of status, alternately signaling respect ("I give you respect," "I give respect to what I am talking about," "I want respect from you") or intimacy ("I am together with you: no status distinctions come between us," "I am close to what I am talking about," "I want you to be close to me"). We reveal this in our style of behavior as much as in what we explicitly say.

So there is more to the variation of speech sounds than sound change in progress. It is relevant that sound changes take different lengths of time to complete themselves, and that there can even be variables such as (ING), which for the moment appear to be stable. The opposition in (ING) could have led to definitive sound change, but community after community gave N vs. G a social interpretation, found it useful, nurtured it, and made it part of their culture. Just so, each time the process of linguistic change completes itself, we are seeing the propensity of communities for a single standard; but each time we see the process prolonged, we are seeing evidence for the social usefulness of variation.

Thanks to Mike Heany for aid on the statistics in this chapter and to Mike, Frank Anshen, David Bradley, Bob Dixon, John Haviland, and Anna Wierzbicka for helpful comments.

Suggestions for Further Reading

Readers wishing to read further on the topic of sociolinguistic variables would do well to begin with the classic work introducing sociological techniques into urban dialectology:

Labov, William. *The Social Stratification of English in New York City.* Arlington, Va.: Center for Applied Linguistics, 1966.

Many of the findings in this work, together with a development of and refinement of the sociolinguistic issues are presented in:

———. 1972. *Sociolinguistic Patterns.* Philadelphia: University of Pennsylvania Press.

We also recommend:

———. 1972. *Language in the Inner City.* Philadelphia: University of Pennsylvania Press.

Here are the findings of the survey by Labov and coworkers of Black and Puerto-Rican speakers in New York City with discussion of Black English speech communities elsewhere. Finally, for an application of Labov's techniques to the large British urban community of Norwich:

Trudgill, Peter. *Social Differentiation of English in Norwich.* Cambridge. Cambridge University Press, 1974.

Chapter 7

English in Los Angeles: Searching for a Speech Community

Benji Wald

1. Established Speech Communities

In this chapter, we will see Los Angeles as a *developing* speech community. We have found that from generation to generation the speech standards of L.A. are becoming more homogeneous, a fact that tells us something about the city as a community, as people living together with a common sense of identity. To the extent that L.A. is a community, we can expect to see agreement in the standards not only for speech behavior, but for many kinds of behavior. And it is the standards for behavior that are decisive, more than any particular degree of homogeneity or diversity in behavior itself. We quote William Labov, who stresses the notion of 'norm' in the sense of an evaluative standard:[1]

> . . . The speech community is not defined by any marked agreement in the use of language elements, so much as by participation in a set of shared norms; these norms may be observed in overt types of evaluative behavior, and by the uniformity of abstract patterns of variation which are invariant in respect to particular levels of usage.
>
> In fact, it seems plausible to define a speech community as a group of speakers who share a set of social attitudes towards language. In New York City, those raised out of town in their formative years show none of the regular pattern of subjective reactions characteristic of natives where a New York City variable such as the vowel of *lost* is concerned . . .

1. William Labov, *Sociolinguistic Patterns* (Philadelphia: University of Pennsylvania Press, 1972), pp. 120–21, p. 248, fn. 40.

A group of people can exhibit great linguistic diversity and yet still be a speech community; conversely, people can have relative homogeneity in their language and not constitute a speech community. The common denominators in speech communities are the social bonds that reveal themselves by a sense of linguistic identity and common *attitudes* toward language. Halliday, McIntosh, and Strevens illustrate this point: [2]

> . . . The language community is a group of people who regard themselves as using the same language. In this sense there is a language community 'the Chinese,' since they regard themselves as speaking 'Chinese,' and not Pekingese, Cantonese and so on. There is no language community 'the Scandinavians'; Norwegians speak Norwegian, Danes Danish and Swedes Swedish, and these are not regarded as dialects of the 'Scandinavian language,' even though they are by and large all mutually intelligible. . . .

We see how people in speech communities share evaluative behavior when we compare the way speakers of British and American English judge selected features of language. Consider *syllable final* [r]. In words such as *cart, car, fourteen, dear,* etc., some speakers strongly pronounce the [r] and some do not. Most American speakers judge the *r*-ful variant to be "correct," i.e. preferred in public and careful speech, while most British speakers prefer the *r*-less variant. These preferences, moreover, correspond not only to the way most British and American speakers speak but to how they say they tell each other apart. On the basis of this [r] and many other characteristics, Great Britain and the United States form two distinct speech communities. Part of the common knowledge of the English-speaking world is that there are different groups of dialects that belong to British and American English. Both have smaller speech communities whose speech correlates with geographical, socioeconomic, and ethnic differences. The differences in dialects between neighboring communities are usu-

2. M.A.K. Halliday, Angus McIntosh, and Peter Strevens, *The Linguistic Sciences and Language Teaching* (London: Longmans, 1964), passage here reprinted in J.A. Fishman, *Readings in the Sociology of Language* (The Hague: Mouton, 1968), p. 140. The Chinese language is made up of a number of dialects that are mutually incomprehensible and might be called distinct languages were it not for the cohesive nature of the Chinese speech community. For an introduction to this speech community see Charles N. Li and Sandra Thompson, "Chinese: Dialect Variations and Language Reform," in *Languages and Their Status,* ed. Timothy Shopen (Cambridge, Mass.: Winthrop Publishers, 1979), pp. 294–335. For a description of a stable speech community with an extraordinary amount of multilingualism, see the chapter in the same volume by John Haiman, "Hua: A Papuan Language of New Guinea," pp. 34–89. Two other chapters in the volume describe the rapid homogenization of language in large urban societies where local languages are being replaced by a dominant lingua franca.

ally unknown to those from far away. But the differences are readily recognized by the local people themselves and are used in the same kinds of evaluative judgments that larger communities make.

We may begin our search for speech communities with *dialect stereotypes.* These have a *target* and an *audience:* the audience is the group that believes in the stereotype, while the target is the group that the audience stereotypes. British stereotypes of American English include the way Americans are thought to pronounce the *t*'s in words such as *writer* and *latter* as a voiced tap sounding like the *d* in *rider* and *ladder.* Many Americans pronounce the pairs of words *writer:rider* and *latter:ladder* as *homonyms,* i.e., so that they sound the same. The stereotype reveals as much about the language of the audience (the British) as it does about that of the target (the Americans), because it suggests that British speakers do distinguish *t*'s and *d*'s in such pairs as *writer:rider* and *latter:ladder* and many other words with stress on the vowel preceding the *t* or *d.* We can hear this is so for most British speakers. Most Americans do not pronounce *t*'s and *d*'s differently in this context; nor do they perceive their voiced, tapped *t*'s to be a dialect stereotype.

Where language contact is intense and personal and the target believes a stereotype accurate, *self-stereotype* can occur. For example, speakers of the rural Swahili dialect Vumba are conscious of the fact that they use *r,* where their urban neighbors to the north in Mombasa use other sounds, especially *t,* as in *rere rwaa* for *lete twaa* "bring (it) take (it)." On the other hand, while Mombasan Swahili speakers are aware that the Vumba use *r* where they use *t,* they do not think of themselves as using *t* for Vumba *r.* For them, *t* is not part of a self-stereotype.

A useful research technique is to elicit dialect stereotypes (Do people in X talk differently from people around here? Can you think of any examples of how they speak? Can you imitate them?) or self-stereotypes (Do you speak differently from the people in X?, etc.). Stereotypes of others are more common than self-stereotypes and often reveal more about the audience than the target.

A word of caution: long-established communities in the United States have been the target of widespread stereotypes, but the stereotypes are not always entirely accurate. A common stereotype of New York English, for example, has the sound *oi* [əy] as the vowel of *bird* and *word.* But this sound is rare among speakers under fifty; it was a common New York pronunciation at the turn of the century and the stereotype has been preserved perhaps because of its entertainment value. On the other hand, this pronunciation is commonplace today in Charleston, South Carolina, and New Orleans, Louisiana. Boston is stereotyped as having an *ah* vowel sound in *park, car,* etc., without the *r* sound. In fact, this is so not only for Boston, but for all of coastal New England. The moral is that stereotypes provide leads that are worth following up, but they must always be checked for accuracy.

Almost all speech communities feel they are distinctive from their neighbors. Most studies in the United States have dealt with communities that have a sense of their linguistic distinctiveness, such as New York or Boston. Many natives of those cities think they can—and often do—identify others as insiders or outsiders on the basis of speech alone.

2. Los Angeles As a Developing Speech Community

While linguistic homogeneity in stable situations is a relative matter, patterns of change are not. Rapid homogenization of language is often a sign that communities are knitting themselves together. The most dramatic example is that of creole languages. A linguistically diverse people find themselves in need of a common language and so create one, usually at the expense of their older languages. Such a language is called a *pidgin*. When a new generation adopts the pidgin as a first language it is called a *creole,* and rapidly homogenizes across speakers when compared with the pidgin spoken by their parents.[3] Something similar can happen when people speaking diverse varieties of a single language want a common identity.

Since World War II, Los Angeles has grown so fast that except for the youngest generation, the immigrants outnumber the native-born. Researchers randomly selecting speakers in public places were hard put to find native Angelenos over thirty.

At present, Angelenos do not exhibit the social consciousness of a speech community. They don't have stereotypes for speech elsewhere in California, and others do not have stereotypes of them. They do not have self-stereotypes. They cannot distinguish a San Franciscan from an Angeleno, even though their two cities have different speech. We have played tapes for Angelenos with L.A. speakers mixed together with speakers from Detroit, and they cannot identify who is from L.A.

Yet we have found dialect features of Angeleno speakers that distinguish them from the rest of the United States, and a pattern of change towards linguistic homogeneity that we will argue shows L.A. to be a developing speech community. Not surprisingly, our research demonstrates that geographical proximity has made the language of

3. See Terry Crowley and Bruce Rigsby, "Cape York Creole," in Shopen, *Languages and Their Status;* and Derek Bickerton and Carol Odo, *Variation in Hawaiian English,* Vol. 1-2. (Honolulu: University of Hawaii, 1966–67).

Angelenos more homogeneous. Geographical proximity is a physical dimension and we believe there must be a social explanation for the change as well. First, the growing homogeneity we have studied is in terms not of speech itself, but in terms of a kind of evaluative behavior (more about that in a moment). Second, there is evidence of everyone moving not towards some undifferentiated statistical mean, but towards the norms of one particular ethnic group, the Anglos. Angelenos not only live close to one another, but they are aware of each other, and from among great diversity are choosing a common linguistic standard. This is evidence that social bonds are being formed and that there is a growing sense of common identity. Our findings are especially noteworthy when we consider the varied geographical origins of Angelenos. It is as if together they are searching for a speech community.

We will narrate here how we acquired evidence for this view of Los Angeles as a developing speech community. The researchers were undergraduates with little or no prior training in linguistics. Our theory and method can be used to seek out and describe other speech communities. We have added two appendices with specific instructions to aid those wishing to organize research projects similar to ours.

3. Self-Reports of Vowel Mergers in Los Angeles

3.1 English Vowels

Because we are concerned with Los Angeles as a *geographically* localized community, we have concentrated on phonological variables. All linguistic behavior is relevant to sociolinguistic research, but for discovering a speech community, the most accessible and best understood aspect of speech is phonology. This is most true for English-speaking geographical communities, less for socioeconomic dialects. The latter tend to have some syntactic differences, as in the *multiple negation* ("They don't tell me nothing") stereotyped for lower classes. Multiple negation cuts across a number of geographical dialects and a variety of pronunciations. In this study we are interested in a standard of pronunciation that is spreading across socioeconomic groupings.

Among phonological variables in English, vowel sounds most distinctly mark geographical speech communities. English has a large inventory of distinct vowels that vary considerably in number and quality from one geographical area to another. A prime stereotype of Southern American speech is the pronunciation represented orthographically as *ah,* e.g., with "ride" as *rahd*. This is generally [āᵊ] (with just a slight upglide) where most other Americans have a fully upglided dipthong [āy]. Then "ride" can be only subtly different from "rod" [rād] with [ā]. In words such as *rod, hot, cot,* and *on,* where they generally have the vowel [ā], Americans are struck by the British (standard) pronunciation with [ɒ], which can sound to Americans like their lower, stressed [ə] in *cut, but,* and *lunch.* Americans are also struck by the standard British "broad a" pronunciations in words like *aunt, glass,* and *bath.* Here Americans use [æ], the same vowel they and the British produce in *hat,* but the British "broad a" is close to the American [ā] of *hot.*

Of course, stereotypes of vowel sounds can be imprecise, because most people lack the technical vocabulary to describe the vowels. Nor do they know the geographical areas to which the stereotypes apply or the details as to how they apply. Most speakers in the coastal American South above Georgia use the sound [āᵊ] *(ah)* in words like *ride* and *nine* ending in voiced consonants, but the diphthong [əy] *(oi)* before voiceless consonants, as in *right* and *twice.* The American stereotypes of British English apply largely to the standard language of the mass media and of highly educated British people. Northern British English is like American English (except for Eastern New England) in not using a "broad a" for words like *aunt,* with [ænt] (as in *ant*) instead of [ānt].

There is no common standard one can refer to for vowel sounds in the United States: British standards do not apply, and there is no single standard within the U.S. either. In American dictionaries, one can find two pronunciations listed for the same word, e.g. *dog* as [dɔ̄g] with the vowel most Americans use for *hawk,* and as [dāg] with the vowel of *hock.* That is a case where pronunciation varies between two *phonemes* (two contrastive sound units). There are many more cases where educated speakers in different parts of the country (who, everyone would agree, speak "correctly") use the same phoneme, but with notably different phonetic forms. In these cases, dictionaries often state correctly what phonemes are standard usage, but they cannot describe exactly what they sound like. In still other instances, standard pronunciation in various localities goes unrecognized or unrecorded in even its phonemic structure.

Consider the "*r*-less" dialects, spoken by as much as a third of the population of the United States—the absence, or near absence, of *r* at the end of syllables, as in many dialects of the British Isles. Dialects that have given up the *r* in that position have developed a new set of vowel phonemes which, in most cases, distinguish pairs such as *bun:burn,* but with some mergers, as when *father:farther* are pronounced identically. It is a situation too complicated for dictionary makers. If one wanted to know how *r*-less speakers in the United

States pronounce words such as *burn, bird, park, cork, fear, poor,* etc., he or she would probably do better to look in a British dictionary than in an American one. American dictionaries list only the pronunciation with the *r*.

The complexities described so far concern the differences that distinguish speech communities. But complicating even this is the fact that speakers within the same community realize vowels in different ways. It is a marvel that people succeed in communicating with each other, but they do. Where meaning is important, people can focus on just those sound differences that distinguish one unit of meaning from another. But there are other kinds of variation that can be just as important, other pronunciation differences that have stylistic effect or that mark social identity. People notice this kind of variation as well. These three elements—meaning, style, and social identity—are all aspects of speech sounds that are relevant to the notion of 'speech community.' A community can have its own conventions for any or all of these.

3.2 Vowel Mergers

The fluctuating nature of English vowels provides researchers with formidable challenges. If we wish to characterize the phonetic quality of a vowel phoneme in a community, we must make painstaking acoustic measurements of many individual pronunciations and then describe statistically what must be a large mass of heterogeneous data. If the goal is to describe style or define social identity, we must correlate a number of extra-linguistic factors with acoustic measurements. Such studies can be of great value, but few readers will have the time, training, or equipment to undertake them.

We have taken a complementary approach here, one requiring less technical expertise. We focus on the function of vowels in distinguishing meaning and record people's self-reports about vowel *mergers*. Vowel mergers are the disappearance of contrast between vowel phonemes, as when the words *pin* and *pen* come to sound the same. Our data is on self-reports—on what people *say* is their pronunciation and not on the pronunciations themselves. This is evaluative behavior. In asking people to give yes or no answers about what they do, one is asking them to judge what is *normal* for them.

Consider a vowel merger the only evidence for which now lies in spelling. In Early Modern English (EME), a standard dialect of England circa 1550–1750, there was a merger of short vowels before *r* in closed syllables that resulted in rhymes such as *bird:word*. The result appears to be so uniform in the United States that although speakers from various parts of the country pronounce these words differently from one another (some with the *r* sound still there and some not, for example), they all rhyme *bird* and *word* and many other words like them.

On the other hand, some other mergers have occurred recently in only some parts of the country. They are important, because they distinguish speech communities from each other. For example, in communities as diverse as those in Eastern New England, Western Pennsylvania, and much of the Southwest, speakers have merged a class of words that includes *cot* and *hock* on the one hand, and a class of words with *caught* and *hawk* on the other. Whatever the phonetic norms in these communities, *cot* sounds the same as *caught,* and *hock* sounds the same as *hawk.* It is useful to know that the vowel in words like *cot* descends from EME "short o" [o], as reflected in the spelling *o,* in *cot, hock, Don,* and *collar,* etc. In most parts of the United States, Early Modern English [o] has become [ā]. The vowel in words like *caught* comes from EME "long open o," which was pronounced much as it is today in most of the United States, [ɔ̄]. The spellings for this vowel include *aw (dawn, law, hawk); au (pause, launch, caught); a* before *l (fall, wall, caller);* and *o* before the voiceless fricative sounds [f], [θ], and [s] *(off, cloth, loss).*

Here are some other vowel mergers. The merger of EME "short a" [æ], "short e" [e], and "long a" [ēy] before [r] in some dialects has led to the homonymy of words such as *marry, merry,* and *Mary. Marry* used to have the vowel sound [æ] as in *mat,* and *Mary* the sound [ēy] as in *mate,* but in the merger all three of these words have converged on [e] as in *met.* Either of the earlier pronunciations for *marry* or *Mary* is worth special note because the merger has already spread through most of the United States, except in the South and on the East Coast. Other words to test for are *Larry, ferry,* and *fairy.* Note too that most speakers say [ðēy] with [ēy], but *they're* [ðer] with [e], so that *they're* sounds like *there.*

A widespread merger of two vowels has occurred before [r], in words such as *heard* (EME [e] or [e:]), and in words such as *sir* (EME [i]). These two in turn have begun to merge before [r] with the [ūw] of the sequence [yūw] (as in *cute*), so that some speakers rhyme *heard:cured* and *sir:sure.* In fact, in Los Angeles we got far more self-reports of a *heard:cured* rhyme than of one for *sir:sure.*

Various American communities have merged vowels before [l]. These include "short i" [i] *(mit)* and "long e" [īy] *(meat):* Before [l], these two vowels have become the same for many speakers, so that *pill:peel* are homophones. The same has happened with "short e" [e] *(met)* and "long a" [ēy] *(mate),* so that *fell:fail* have become homophones for some speakers. Last, the "short u" [u] of *put* and the "long u" [ūw] of *boot* have merged before [l], making homophones of *pull:pool.*

Various Southern and Southwestern dialects, and Black vernacular speech in urban areas of the United States, have merged "short i" [i] and "short e" [e] *(met)* before nasals so that, for example, *pin* and *pen* sound identical; and "short e" and "long a" [ēy] *(mate)* before [g], creating the rhyme *egg:vague,* with *egg* pronounced [ēyg], and a similar effect on other words like *egg—leg, beg,* etc. We cannot always say what a merged vowel sounds like, because pronunciations vary even among people in the same speech community. In the *pull:pool* merger, the resulting vowel sound has tended to be between the original [u] of *pull* and the original [ūw] of *pool,* sometimes sounding more like one, sometimes more like the other. What matters for our research is not the phonetic quality, but whether or not speakers judge potentially merged pairs of vowels to sound the same in what they regard as their normal pronunciation.

3.3 The Los Angeles Questionnaire for Homonyms and Rhymes

We studied the mergers just described through the self-reports of Angelenos. We found that reports of these mergers—or of their absence—correlated with patterns of stratification of social groups, ethnic origin, and age. The vowel mergers were studied with a questionnaire consisting of several tasks that revealed whether speakers judged historically distinct vowels to be identical in their speech.

In all cases, we assured subjects that there were no right or wrong answers, that they were only providing information about the everyday pronunciation of L.A. speakers so that we could discover what pairs of words might be giving L.A. children problems in reading and spelling. In administering the questionnaire, researchers used their judgment in deciding whether to let the respondent read through it and fill it out or whether to administer it orally, spelling out the words. We kept both methods available since some people resent questionnaires of any kind, associating them with tests and other unpleasant situations (such as filling out income tax forms). Tact was required in eliciting information about ethnic identification. Because this can be a sensitive matter, a researcher of the same ethnic background as the person being interviewed has an advantage.

The first part of the questionnaire asked about words that historically have been *minimal pairs,* pairs of words that differ in only one sound. Where vowels have merged, the words have become homonyms. Respondents were asked whether pairs of words sounded the same or different when they pronounced them in their normal way.

The minimal pairs included:

fell:fail	merry:marry
pill:peel	merry:Mary
collar:caller	Mary:marry
pin:pen	hock:hawk
cot:caught	since:sense
Don:dawn	

The second part of the questionnaire dealt with potential *rhymes*. Where minimal pairs are not available, potential rhymes can get a speaker to concentrate on stressed vowels. Respondents were presented with pairs of words and asked whether they rhymed words when they pronounced them normally. If the speakers reported rhymes, we assumed the stressed vowels were identical. In reality, the pattern of responses suggested that speakers sometimes report rhyme when vowel sounds are only similar. We used pairs of words that included the following:

sorry:starry	egg:vague
sorry:story	law:Ma
root:foot	limb:hem
heard:cured	sir:sure

3.4 Results

Los Angeles speakers responded to our inquiry with great variability. When we stratify the respondents by ethnic group we reduce the variability considerably, though not completely. The results indicate some features to be quite widespread in L.A., and others to vary by ethnic groups. Figure 7.1 shows vowel mergers correlated with ethnic groups. We compare responses from members of five ethnic groups on all items; we include data from a sixth ethnic group, Native Americans, for three items only because this is all the information we gathered on that group. The rhyme pairs *sorry:starry* and *sorry:story* are not further discussed. All respondents rhymed the first pair and none the second (*sorry:story* are rhymes in the Northwest of the United States and the Southwest of Canada). The pair *law:Ma* are presented as a separate item, our one instance of [ɔ̄] vs. [ā] in word-final position. All other instances involving these two vowels in potential merger *(caller:collar, caught:cot, hawk:hock)* are averaged together. For *marry:merry:Mary* we have displayed the percentage of respondents who treat all three as homophones, as opposed to those who do not.

Consider Figure 7.1. There is hardly a merger on which all groups agree. There is a tendency towards agreement among Japanese Americans (from the Gardena area), Jewish Americans (from the Los Angeles Basin and the San Fernando Valley), and Anglos (those who are white, of northern European descent, but not Jewish). Jewish Americans are worth considering separately from Anglos because their parents, more than parents of any other group, tend to come from Eastern urban areas, especially New York City. They distinguish themselves from the Anglos and Japanese Americans by their infrequent report of an *egg:vague* rhyme.

The merger of [i] and [e] before a nasal *(pin:pen)* is interesting because there we have the largest difference between white and nonwhite groups. The whites—Anglos and Jewish Americans—together with Japanese Americans, display a low frequency of merger in this case, while Blacks, Native Americans and Mexican Americans are considerably higher. Although the Black speakers report the highest degree of merger, the merger is less a marker of Black speech in L.A. than of speakers of southern origin. Figure 7.2 shows that the under-twenty generation of whites from the South display this merger to the same extent as Black speakers.

A wide separation on a number of features distinguishes the Black group from other groups. This reflects another speech community made up of most of the Blacks in Los Angeles. One could argue that the true dimensions of this speech community includes Black congregations in other parts of the country, since several mergers occur with great frequency among Black people in all geographical locations. Members of the Black community are very conscious of speech as a mark of their identity, using speech to identify insiders and outsiders. They have self-stereotypes and stereotypes of speech outside their community. In Black communities around the country the most frequent mergers include:

[i] and [e] before a nasal, e.g., *pin:pen, since:sense*

[e] and [ēy] before [l], e.g., *fell:fail*

[i] and [īy] before [l], e.g., *pill:peel*

The last two can be expressed as the merger of front lax and tense vowels of equivalent heights before laterals. The sample is drawn from Compton and South Los Angeles, largely Black communities. The pattern of segregation that insures the integrity of the Black community is as secure in L.A. as in eastern American centers. Although

Figure 7.1. (opposite) ***Ethnic Stratification of Vowel Mergers in Los Angeles***

Percentage of
Reported Merger

100
90
80
70
60
50
40
30
20
10
00

law:Ma
other
[ɔ̄]:[ā]
marry
merry
Mary
egg:vague
heard
cured
pin:pen
since:sense
pill
peel
fell
fail

Ethnic Groups (N = number interviewed)

○ Black (N=92)
□ Anglo (N=82)
△ Mexican American (N=30)
● Jewish American (N=21)
■ Japanese American (N=16)
▲ Native American (N=19)

the Black population is quite distinct from other ethnic groups in their relatively infrequent report of most common L.A. mergers (most of the [ɔ̄] vs. [ā] mergers and *marry:merry:Mary*), we can see evidence for the beginnings of cohesion with the larger L.A. community in *law:Ma*. This rhyme involves [ɔ̄] vs. [ā] at the end of the word, the most prominent place to test for vowel merger by rhyme (the rhyme depends just on the vowels). Rhymes were reported by 80 percent of the L.A. Black speakers interviewed. This is not a feature of Black communities elsewhere.

The *heard:cured* rhyme is interesting in two respects. First, with the exception of Mexican-Americans, all groups report the merger rather randomly (within the 45 to 55 percent range). Most likely the reason for this is that the pronunciations are quite close but not truly merged. The *y*-glide of the "u" of *cured* may distract the reporters from appreciating the closeness of these two vowel sounds. Secondly, the merger is of fairly limited distribution among American English speech communities (although it has been observed in certain parts of the Midwest). Therefore, it is likely that L.A. Black speakers have acquired it from adjacent groups in L.A. Considering that the major source of the Black community in L.A. is East Texas and the Southern Gulf states, the "*r*-lessness" (nonconsonantal pronunciation of syllable-final [r]) of Black communities in those areas affects words like *heard* and *cured*. Very few L.A. Black speakers reported that *father:farther* sounded the same, although they do in most *r*-less dialects of English. The indications are that the acquisition of *r* by speakers in the L.A. Black community has as a consequence the merger (or near merger) of *heard:cured,* at least as an outwardly directed norm.

3.5 Replication of the Results and the Generation Jump Pattern

Figure 7.2 shows part of the results of a *replication* of the original survey with a totally new sample population, this time controlled for the *age* of the respondents. The display in Figure 7.1 was for a sample population largely between the ages of twenty and thirty-five, the same age group as the researchers themselves. The replicated study took a sample equally divided between speakers under twenty and speakers over forty. In Figure 7.2 we see the results for speakers all of whom are under twenty. Here we do not have data on Japanese Americans or Native Americans, but we have added the category of Southern Whites.

Figure 7.2. (opposite) ***Ethnic Stratification of Selected Vowel Mergers for Speakers Under Twenty in Los Angeles***

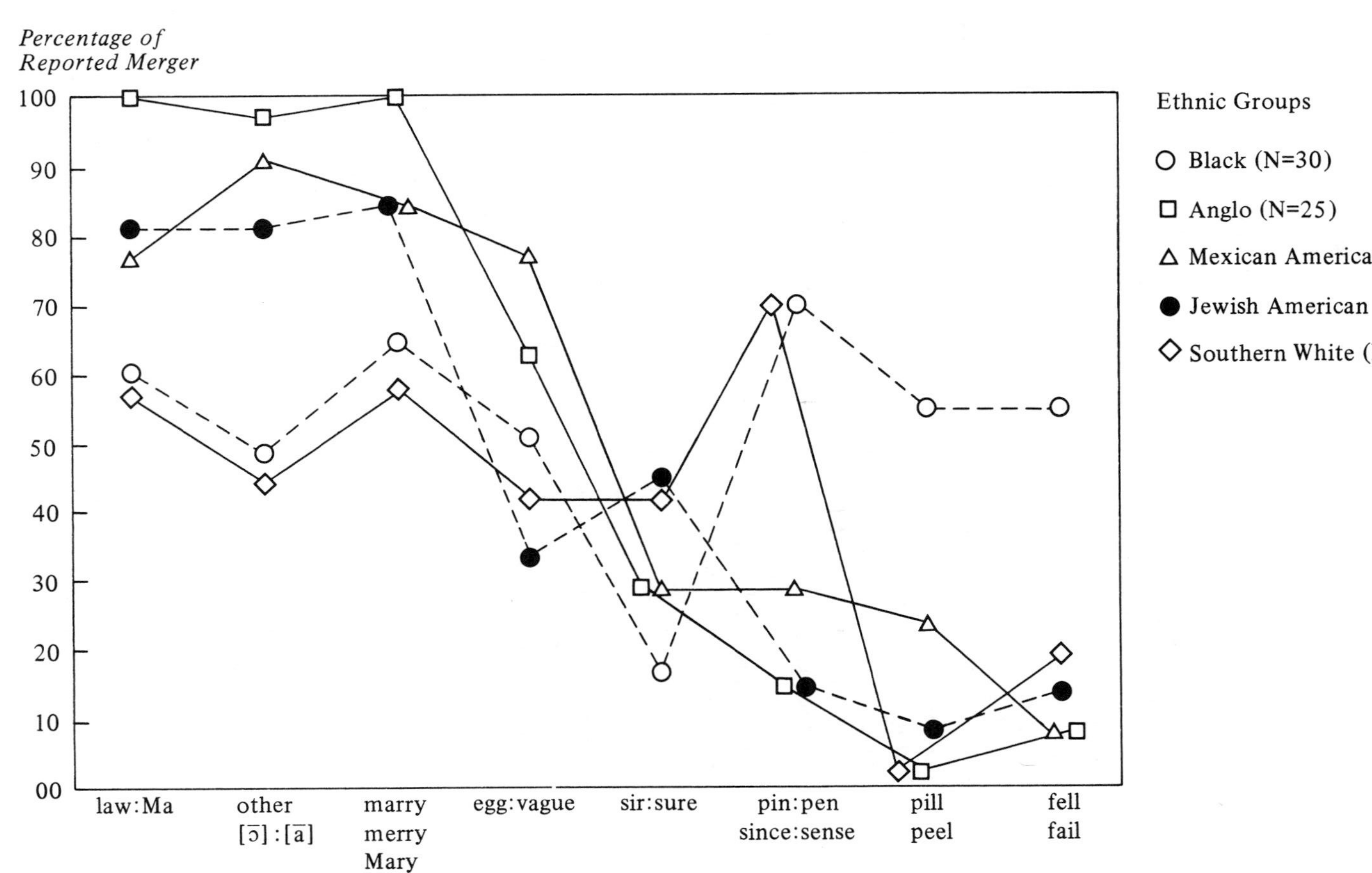
Percentage of
Reported Merger
100
90
80
70
60
50
40
30
20
10
00
law:Ma
other
[ɔ̄]:[ā]
marry
merry
Mary
egg:vague
sir:sure
pin:pen
since:sense
pill
peel
fell
fail
Ethnic Groups
○ Black (N=30)
□ Anglo (N=25)
△ Mexican American (N=30)
● Jewish American (N=68)
◇ Southern White (N=12)

In the replicated study we tested the rhyme *sir:sure* instead of *heard:cured,* and the frequency of merger for *sir:sure* was lower than that for *heard:cured.* The other items tested were the same, and the frequencies were notably similar. This gives us confidence that our sample populations are a reliable index to the L.A. population as a whole. When the patterns of ethnic stratification are as uniform as they appear here, extremely large samples are not necessary for an accurate study. Replication of studies is an excellent way to check reliability of results in any sociolinguistic investigation.

The speakers of southern white origin show a pattern similar to that of Black speakers, except in mergers before [l] *(pill:peel, fell:fail),* where they have a lower frequency of reported mergers than Black speakers. Those mergers before [l] remain a distinctive characteristic of the Black speech community in L.A.

When we compare the under-twenty sample population with the over-forty one, we discover a pattern we can refer to as *generation jump,* a pattern that jumps over, or leaves out the middle generation of twenty-to-thirty-five-year-olds represented in Figure 7.1.

Figure 7.3 compares two generations in L.A., those under twenty and those over forty. In each instance, the over-forty group is represented to the left of the under-twenty. The increase in merger for the younger generation is revealed in the lines that slope *upward to the right.* The predominant pattern is for the younger generation to merge more vowels than the older one and to come closer to the mean for all speakers interviewed. Statistics give some support to the conclusion that there is an *overall pattern* of growing homogeneity of the sort "everyone is getting more like everyone else."[4] The decisive evidence is for a different kind of growing homogeneity, one of everyone getting more like one particular ethnic group. That is, the growing homogeneity is developing not so much in the direction of some undifferentiated statistical mean, but in the direction of a socially identifiable

4. The statistical test involving binomial distribution is a useful guide here, subject to the qualification that each response by informants is being treated as an *independent* event. In 31 out of 37 changes (with three 'no change'), there is movement toward merger. Equating growing merger with growing homogeneity, we can say that the hypothesis that there is growing homogeneity has statistical significance. This measure we believe to have some validity, but it is open to the objection that mergers have a tendency to complete themselves regardless of social relationships. In 22 out of the 37 changes the younger speakers come closer than the older ones to the mean for all speakers interviewed: this is suggestive, but not significant statistically. Binomial distribution is especially useful in a research project of this sort where data has been collected on a number of variables but where the samples are too small for most of the individual comparisons to have statistical reliability.

Figure 7.3. (opposite) ***Ethnic Stratification and Generational Jump Patterns for Speakers in Los Angeles on Selected Mergers***
(comparison of speakers over forty and under twenty)

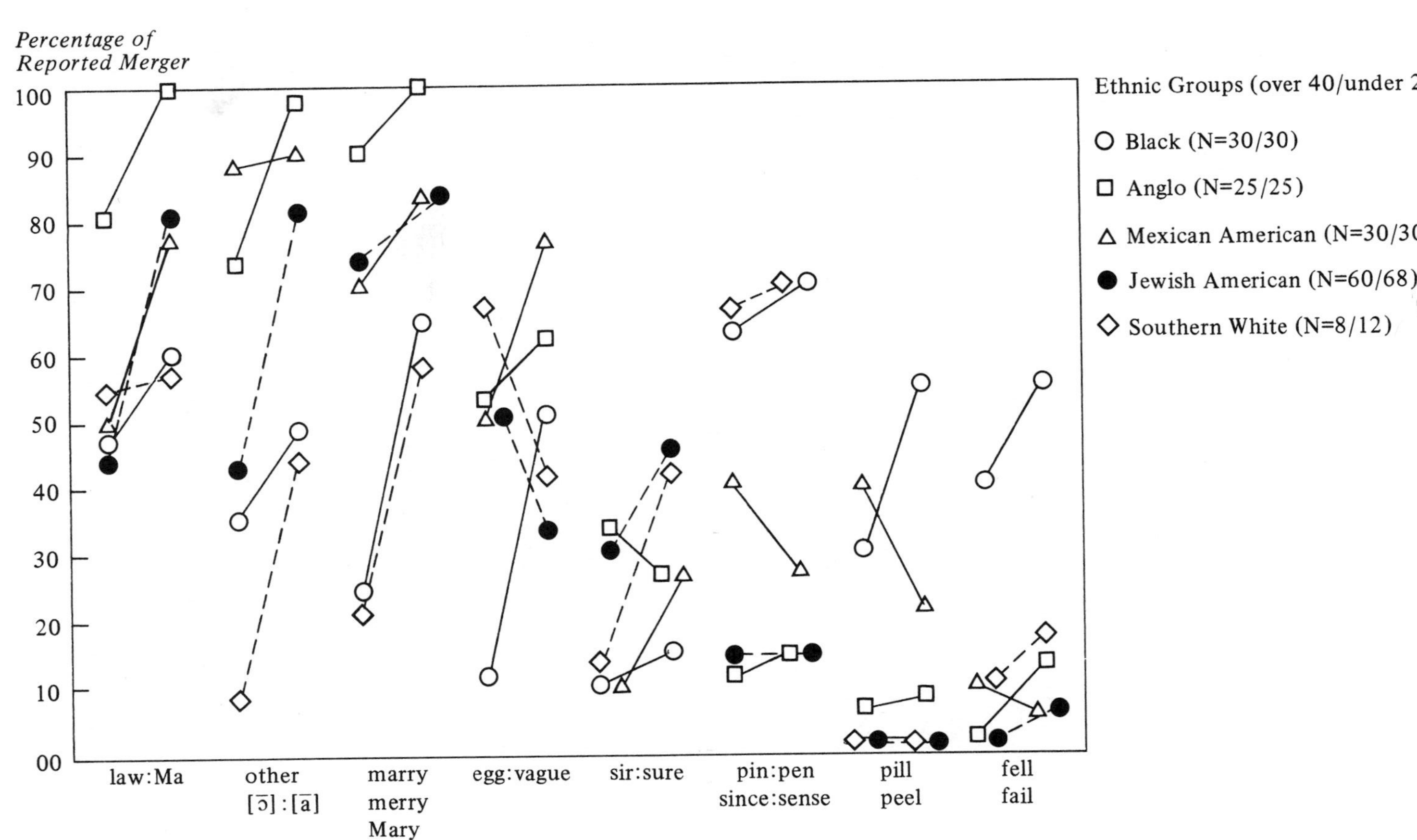
Percentage of Reported Merger
100
90
80
70
60
50
40
30
20
10
00
law:Ma
other [ɔ̄]:[ā]
marry merry Mary
egg:vague
sir:sure
pin:pen since:sense
pill peel
fell fail
Ethnic Groups (over 40/under 20)
Black (N=30/30)
Anglo (N=25/25)
Mexican American (N=30/30)
Jewish American (N=60/68)
Southern White (N=8/12)

target, and that target is the group which presumably has the most prestige in the city, the Anglos.

The Anglos are the longest established residents of the city. In the sample population over forty, only the Anglos were predominantly native to L.A., a reflection of the population structure of the city in general. In Figure 7.3 we can see that the non-Anglo groups tend to move toward the Anglos: non-Anglo younger speakers—but not the older ones—tend in the increases and decreases of reported merger to move toward the standard of the Anglos. No other ethnic group attracts a "movement toward" pattern of any significance.

This is true to a striking degree if we look at just those instances where the mean of a given ethnic group on a potential merger constitutes a clear *characteristic*—let us say below 15 percent or above 85 percent.[5] It is difficult to conceive of how variation much nearer 50 percent in *standards* could be transmitted to other ethnic groups. More evenly divided variation of that sort must be unstable, likely to resolve itself soon towards either 0 percent or 100 percent. This is a wholly different state of affairs from the one with speech behavior itself where variation can indeed be stable and spread across social groups (cf. the preceding chapter). We assume for Los Angeles that speakers of all ages constitute potential models and so examine the mean for the ethnic group as a whole in each case to see if it constitutes a clear characteristic; in only those cases do we look for 'movement towards.'

In six of the mergers (all except *egg:vague* and *sir:sure*), the Anglos present a characteristic, far more than any other group (Jewish-Americans three, Mexican-American and Southern Whites two, and Blacks one). They are the most unified group in their standards and thus the most prominent potential model. In fifteen out of the twenty-one relevant non-Anglo generation jump changes (three 'no change'), there is movement towards the Anglos. Using binomial distribution we see 15/21 to be a reliable ratio. In the hypothesis that there is 'movement towards' the Anglos by other ethnic groups, the chance for error is 0.025. The comparable figures for other ethnic groups are 4/11 for Jewish-Americans (one 'no change'), 5/8 for Mexican-Americans, 3/7 for Southern Whites (one 'no change'), and 1/4 for Blacks.

In the twenty-four non-Anglo generation jump patterns where the Anglos display a characteristic, there are only four changes where the non-Anglos move decisively *away* from the Anglo standard, and these all involve growing merger: the Blacks and Southern Whites in

5. In each of the events described by connected symbols in Figure 7.3, one can see the mean for the ethnic group as a point on the connecting line midway between the two symbols. For example, for *law:Ma* 25 older Anglo speakers are at 81 percent and 25 younger ones are at 100 percent. The mean for all Anglo speakers is then at 91.5 percent.

pin:pen, and the Blacks again in *pill:peel* and *fell:fail.* While in other parts of the vowel system the Blacks are moving towards the Angeleno prestige standard, the standard of the Anglos, in the last three columns they are differentiating themselves from the rest of the community. They are a community within the larger developing community, showing themselves to be Angelenos in the first three columns of Figure 7.3, but not Angelenos in the last three.

Of particular interest are the lines in Figure 7.3 that slope down sharply to the right, showing a marked decrease in merger. Some theories of phonological change argue that merger is irreversible, that once two pronunciations have merged, succeeding generations have no way of recovering the earlier pronunciations because they never hear anyone use them. But this is the case only when mergers are complete. We, however, are focusing on mergers that are incomplete. People who reported that they did not pronounce *hock:hawk* the same or did not rhyme *egg:vague* might sometimes produce the merger in their speech, but they still must be in contact with speakers who use the distinct nonmerged pronunciations. In no other way could they be aware of those pronunciations. We can also be sure there are speakers who do use the merged pronunciations.

Younger Angelenos have models in the older generation for both kinds of pronunciation; they can adopt either as their standard. As long as some speakers persist in using the earlier nonmerged pronunciation at least some of the time, the sound can change in either direction. The merger can move on to completion, or it can reverse itself. Just as a merger can start out in the speech of a small part of a population and spread, so too can it work the other way around, with a small number of people retaining the earlier pronunciation and then transmitting it back into the larger population. When merged and nonmerged pronunciations vary, the lines sloping upward to the right (increasing merger) are no more 'natural' than the ones sloping downward to the right (decreasing merger). From this point of view, the growing homogeneity of L.A. is all the more revealing.

It may be just an accident in the sample that Anglos have a slight downward slope in *sir:sure* and Mexican Americans in *fell:fail.* Two of the marked decreases occur with the *egg:vague* merger: among Jewish Americans and southern whites, both of whom in this instance move away from the overall pattern of growing homogeneity, and also away from the Anglos. It is likely that the *egg:vague* merger has been stigmatized within those two ethnic groups. The two remaining cases of sharp decreases are by Mexican Americans in the *pin:pen* and *pill:peel* mergers; in so doing, they are moving toward the standard of the Anglo and Jewish American populations, who report a notably low level of these mergers.

Here then is L.A. as a developing speech community. Across generations, the city is moving toward a distinctive standard for speech, with Anglos setting the standards. If the social impulse is there, Angelenos will have standards to refer to in taking on the full character of a speech community, standards they can employ in identifying insiders and outsiders and in creating stereotypes of the outsiders and self-stereotypes of themselves. If that happens, the outsiders may stereotype the Angelenos and put on imitations of them as well.

Suggestions for Further Reading

The development of a *new* speech community has not yet been the subject of any extensive research effort. Theoretical definitions of the concept *speech community* are developed in:

Gumperz, John J. *Language in Social Groups,* selected and introduced by Anwar S. Dil. Stanford, Calif.: Stanford University Press, 1971.

Hymes, Dell. "Speech and Language: On the Origins and Foundations of Inequality Among Speakers." In *Language As a Human Problem,* edited by Einar Haugen and Morton Bloomfield. New York: W.W. Norton, 1973.

See also:

Kurath, Hans. *Studies in Area Linguistics.* Bloomington: Indiana University Press, 1972.

This is a good introduction to the history of dialect studies and its issues. The book pays special attention to the development of American English dialectology and the contributions to it by the author and his coworkers. To complement this work see:

Wakelin, Martyn F. *English Dialects: An Introduction.* London: Athlone Press, 1972.

This is a good digest of the history of dialect studies in Great Britain, and its reports on the results of the dialect survey of England.

For those wishing to do background reading on the history of English phonology, the best source for the reconstruction of EME phonemes is Chapter 8 in:

Moore, Samuel. *Historical Outlines of English Sounds and Inflections.* Ann Arbor, Mich.: George Wahr Publishing Co., 1966.

The following two works can be combined to trace English sounds from their origins to early twentieth-century British variants:

Jespersen, Otto. "Sounds and Spellings." In *A Modern English Grammar,* vol. I. London: George Allen & Unwin Ltd., 1961. Copenhagen: Ejnar Munksgaard (this volume first published in 1909).

Wright, Joseph. *The English Dialect Grammar.* Oxford: Henry Frowde, 1905.

For details on the current situation with British dialects, see Wakelin, *English Dialects: An Introduction,* cited just above. For a useful reference work on American English dialects to complement Kurath, *Studies in Area Linguistics,* see:

Kurath, Hans. *A Phonology and Prosody of Modern English.* Ann Arbor, Mich.: The University of Michigan Press, 1971.

Appendix I

Questions for Speech Community Searching

1. Dialect Stereotypes

- **a.** Do people in X (name place, social group, etc.) talk differently from people around here?
- **b.** Can you think of any examples of how they speak? Can you think of any of the differences? Can you imitate them?
- **c.** Do you speak differently from the people in X? Can you think of any examples?

2. Mergers

We're doing a survey of everyday pronunciation in X (name place). We're interested in how people around here pronounce words so that we can figure out what kinds of problems children in this area might have in learning to read or spell. Educators have found that each area has its own set of problems because of local differences in pronunciation. There are no right or wrong answers to these questions, just differences from one area to another. In your *normal* pronunciation:

- **a.** *Minimal Pairs:* Do these words sound the same to you or different?
- **b.** *Rhymes:* Do these words rhyme for you?

(See Appendix II for some useful raw material for minimal pairs and rhymes.)

3. Alternate Pronunciations for Words

(Here is a research technique we have used to good effect as a part of larger interviews. It is contingent on finding words that have competing pronunciations in an area. In Los Angeles we used this approach with *roof,* [rūwf] vs. [ruf]; *room,* [rūwm] vs. [rum]; and *egg,* [ēyg] vs. [eg]. One asks people for their subjective evaluation of the competing pronunciations.)

We've noticed two different pronunciations of the following words. (Give the words in their variant pronunciations, one at a time.)

a. *Awareness:* Have you heard both pronunciations?
b. *Self-report:* Which is your *normal* pronunciation?
c. *Correct:* Which pronunciation would you advise a teenager to use if he had to give a speech at school?
d. *Local:* Which pronunciation do you think is most common around here?

Because you will want to correlate answers with social categories, you will have to ask additional questions to identify the social categories of your respondents. Sex needs no questions; age can be guessed but identified more accurately through a question. Other categories may be harder to identify—ethnic background and especially socioeconomic class. Birthplace, places one has lived, education, occupation, and income are the kinds of information one may try to elicit. Education, occupation, and income are the usual determinants for socioeconomic class.

Appendix II

Word Classes with Vowels Before [r] and [l]

The vowels most subject to change across English-speaking communities are those before [r] and [l]. Here are some words that can help you test for homonymy and rhyme. We organize the word classes with reference to a group of EME vowels. The reconstruction of EME vowels is tentative. The word classes are appropriate for most varieties of English. In dealing with local dialects of the British Isles, however, it may be necessary to go further back into the history of English. Early Modern English (1550–1750) is a standard dialect which had mergers that did not occur in other dialects of the same period. For the English of Ireland, Scotland, and the North of England, an earlier standard may be necessary. For example, EME [ōw] represents an earlier merger of [ōw] and [ō:]. In the present-day dialect of Norwich, there is an [ōw] class that includes *tow, know,* and *roll,* and a distinct [o:] class that includes *toe, no,* and *role*. Similarly, in some dialects, [ēy] may be

EME Vowel	Example	Before [r] Closed Syllables	Before [r] Open Syllables	Before [l] Closed Syllables	Before [l] Open Syllables
[i]	sit	bird	mirror	fill	filler
[e]	set	heard	merry	fell	cellar
[æ]	sat	—	marry	pal	salad
[o]	got	for	forest	doll	polish
[ə]	gut	fur	worry	dull	gully
[u]	foot	word	—	pull	fuller
[īy]	bee	fear	weary	feel	feeling
[ēy]	bay	fair	Mary	fail	failing
[āy]	buy	fire	wiry	file	filing
[ōy]	boy	(lawyer)	—	boil	boiler
[ūw]	too	poor	boorish	fool	foolish
[ōw]	tow	pour	story	foal	holy
[āw]	cow	(power)	cowrie	foul	howler
[yūw]	cue	pure	fury	fuel	mulish
[ɔ̄]	law	war	warring	call	caller
[ā]	Ma	far	starry	—	—

distinct from [ē:]; e.g., *ail:ale, made:maid* may be minimal pairs rather than homonyms.

The "broad a" class is not represented above. Dialects which have the "broad a" class exhibit "broad a" vs. [æ:] pairs which differ, such as the following: *aunt:ant, dance:pants, class:mass.*

The *r*-class dialects, such as those of urban Britain and the Eastern U.S., may have a separate set of vowel classes for their *r*-less syllables, syllables that used to be closed by [r] but are no longer.

Procedure

The words given in the table are tokens of word classes. In some cases syllables have been opened by putting suffixes on morphemes that end in closed syllables when they stand by themselves, e.g., *feel/feeling.*

In preparing a list of minimal pairs of rhymes from this list, first examine the list and determine for which sets of words you have the same vowel. If you are interested in a community other than your own, you will need the help of a community member. Search for other words of the same class—for example, *short* is in the same class as *for,* for all varieties of English, where we have EME [o] before [r] in closed syllables. But in some varieties, this class is not identical to words with EME [ōw] before [r]. Thus, *pour:for* is a rhyme in some dialects but not in others. The word *sport* rhymes with *short* only if there has been this merger before [r] of EME [ōw] *(sport)* and EME [o] *(short)*.

When you inquire about words on the list, transcribe phonetically how members of the community pronounce each word. Then get the judgments of a community member as to whether these words sound the same, rhyme, have the same vowel sound, etc.

You can identify historical mergers in your own language by searching any of the columns for vowels that sound identical. Thus, in the column for vowels closed by [r], most speakers should find the vowels of *bird, heard, fur,* and *word* to be identical, representing the merger of EME [i], [e], [ə], and [u] in this environment. In the column of open syllables before [r], Angelenos will find *forest* and *story* to have the same vowel, a result of the merger of EME [o] and [ōw] in that environment. New Yorkers, on the other hand, preserve the EME contrast for such words but identify the vowels of *forest* and *starry* as the same, showing that for them there has been a merger of [o] and [ā] in that environment. Most Bostonians preserve a contrast for all three word sets.

This procedure cannot anticipate new word classes arising through morphophonemic change; for example, London "cockney" English distinguishes *board:bored* as [bo^{u}d]:[bɔ̄:d] respectively. Here EME monomorphemic [o(w)r] in syllables closed by still another consonant is pronounced [o^{u}] (the vowel [o] with a slight upglide). In morphemes that *end* with the EME sequence [o(w)r], the pronunciation is [ɔ̄:], for example, *bore* = [bɔ̄:], and *bored* is analyzed as the morpheme *bore* plus the past-tense ending. Be on the lookout for anything and everything. No single mechanical procedure can uncover the significant phonological variation in English or any other language.